Al Davis

Behind the Raiders Shield

Al Davis

Behind the Raiders Shield

Untold Stories from Longtime Davis Confidants

by

Bruce Kebric *and* Jon Kingdon

with

Steve Corkran

RATHER
BE
FEARED

Dedication

To Liz, Angie and Kelsey — the triad that made my pro football journey a serene one. Thanks also to Al Davis, Sid Gillman, and Joe Madro for their guidance.   *Bruce Kebric*

To Karen, Kelly, and Stephen, for their love and support and for always keeping it interesting. Also, thanks to Mark, Ken, Carole, and Uncle Marty for their inspiration and unwavering support.
                                                        Jon Kingdon

To my wonderful wife, Diana, and our beautiful children, Alexander, Zachary and Sara, for their steadfast support, love, patience and understanding throughout this process.   *Steve Corkran*

Acknowledgements

The production of this book was made seamless as a result of the guidance, expertise and unconditional cooperation of Gary Peterson, Brad Mangin, Bob Larson, and Ron Riesterer, in particular.

We owe a huge thanks to Greg Papa, Peter King, and John Clayton for their kind words and high praise.

We also wish to recognize the contributions made by Alan Sparer, Jan Sprague, Natalie Lane, Bettyann Heppler and Doug Pensinger, Jerry Soifer, Russ Reed, Norm Fisher, and the Los Angeles Chargers.

TABLE OF CONTENTS

Preface

After leaving the Oakland Raiders some six months following the death of Al Davis, Jon Kingdon and Bruce Kebric decided that it might be interesting to write a book about their nearly 65 years of combined experience with the Raiders, in general, and Al Davis, specifically. There have been a number of books published about the Raiders, some highlighting the players, some delving into the team's outlaw image, and others searching to decipher the mind of Al Davis. This book, however, differs in that it is written by two player personnel department leaders who were closely involved with Davis in the decision-making process of selecting both players and coaches, as well as determining team rosters.

Frequently, when scouts are on the road evaluating prospects, they share stories of what has transpired in their particular team's draft preparation process. When telling their stories about the Raiders' draft room and how the players ultimately were selected, Kingdon and Kebric would often get stares of amazement while their NFL colleagues waited for a punchline that was not forthcoming. They had to reassure the audience that they were not making up the stories and certainly not telling jokes.

Former Raiders beat writer Steve Corkran expressed his interest about the idea of writing a book from the player personnel angle. He related to Kingdon and Kebric that he had been approached on several occasions about authoring a book on the Raiders, but was waiting for the right opportunity to arise. He issued one caveat: "It has to be warts and all."

There were some great draft picks and some truly outlandish selections. There was a "Commitment to Excellence" and, at times, a stubbornness which threw that commitment out the window. As Calvin Branch, a former Raiders player and later a member of the team's scouting staff, remarked after Davis' death: "Al Davis was the captain of the pirate ship and the rest of us were deckhands."

As Kingdon and Kebric tell it, working for Al Davis was exciting at its best, frustrating at its worst, but it was always challenging.

The Authors

Jon Kingdon

Jon was hired as an intern in 1978 and worked in various capacities. After spending 1979 as head coach Tom Flores' administrative assistant, Kingdon moved full time to the Raiders personnel department, beginning in an administrative role and then as a college scout. He eventually became the team's Director of College Scouting in 1993. Al Davis valued Kingdon's opinion and would ask for his feedback on myriad subjects. It was not uncommon for Davis to call Kingdon at home at all hours with any number of questions about the upcoming NFL draft and issues ranging from who he should hire as his head coach, the move-

ment of the franchise, how he should handle various player issues, who would be the first player taken in the WNBA draft and alerting him to the upcoming Jewish holidays.

Kingdon earned a bachelor's degree in English from Oberlin College, where he played tight end for the football team and was sports editor of the college newspaper. He later attended the University of Massachusetts, from which he earned a master's degree in Sports Administration.

Bruce Kebric

During his more than four decades in professional football, Bruce worked as an assistant general manager, director of player personnel, director of college and pro scouting, assistant director of player personnel and national scout. His player selections and recommendations played an integral role in the teams he worked for appearing in three Super Bowls and seven American Football Conference championship games.

Kebric's final NFL position was with the Oakland Raiders, where he spent 31 years assisting Pro Football Hall of Famer Al Davis not only in the player personnel realm but with coaching hires. He also worked closely with another NFL Hall of Fame selection, Sid Gillman, at the San Diego Chargers, Houston Oilers and the Oklahoma Outlaws of the United States Football League. Gillman is considered the architect of the modern passing game, and he also was the person who gave Davis his first professional football coaching job.

Prior to his NFL entry, Kebric was the assistant sports information director at Stanford University, where he had the opportunity to work with and learn from future NFL head coaches Bill Walsh, Dick Vermeil, John Ralston, Mike White and Rod Rust.

In 1969, Kebric was selected as a research fellow at the NASA-Manned Spacecraft Center in Houston, Texas, where he witnessed NASA's first moon landing at the Mission Control Center. His NASA research culminated in a publication entitled "Continuing Engineering Education at the NASA Manned Space Center."

Kebric additionally has written extensively for newspapers and magazines and has covered sporting events such as the Super Bowl, the Rose Bowl, the World Series, the NCAA basketball championships and the second Sonny Liston-Floyd Patterson heavyweight championship fight.

He received a bachelor's degree in Political Science from Stanford University, where he was a member of the basketball team, and a master's degree in Public Administration from San Diego State University.

Steve Corkran

From 1997-2010, Steve covered the Raiders on a year-round basis for the *Contra Costa Times*, *Oakland Tribune* and *San Jose Mercury News*. He also covered the Raiders on an occasional basis before and after he became the beat writer. During that time, he gleaned insight into how owner Al Davis presided over the Raiders and what made the iconic sports figure revered by some and reviled by others.

At one point, Corkran approached Davis about an interview for a season preview. Davis politely declined, saying that, "I don't think people care what I have to say." He ended the conversation by saying he might tell his story one day, and asked Corkran if he would be interested in writing that book. Both knew each other well enough to realize that Davis had no intention of participating in an all-encompassing book. From that point, Corkran worked toward finding a way to tell Davis' story in as complete a manner as possible. Teaming with Jon Kingdon and Bruce Kebric made that a reality.

Corkran's first enduring memory of Al Davis and the Raiders came in 1972, when Terry Bradshaw and Franco Harris teamed up for an improbable throw, catch-and-run play that resulted in a 60-yard, game-deciding touchdown in an AFC Playoff Game against the Raiders that kick-started the Steelers dynastic run of four Super Bowl wins in six seasons. Davis and the Raiders became must-see TV.

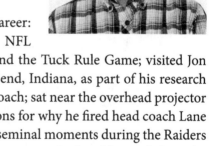

Six years later, he attended the game where Raiders safety Jack Tatum delivered a hit on Patriots wide receiver Darryl Stingley that resulted in Stingley being paralyzed from the neck down.

During his professional career: Corkran covered more than 400 NFL games, including four Super Bowls and the Tuck Rule Game; visited Jon Gruden's childhood home in South Bend, Indiana, as part of his research for a profile on the Raiders dynamic coach; sat near the overhead projector that Al Davis used to outline the reasons for why he fired head coach Lane Kiffin; and witnessed countless other seminal moments during the Raiders second stint in Oakland. Much of what was watched and learned along the way is reflected in the reporting, detail and writing featured in this book.

Foreword

A l Davis and I entered professional football at about the same time, both employed by newly-minted franchises led by future Hall of Fame inductees. Al was selected by coaching legend Sid Gillman to handle the wide receivers for the Los Angeles Chargers of the nascent American Football League in 1960. I was hired by Tex Schramm, perhaps the most influential general manager in National Football League history, as the personnel director of the expansion Dallas Cowboys team.

The two of us thus began a relationship, both personal and competitive, that existed until Al's death in 2011. For most of the decade of the 1960s, our two leagues competed against each other for both players and national attention. I had the opportunity to watch Al develop into one of the AFL's coaching and administrative leaders and a major figure, along with Schramm, in facilitating a merger between the AFL and NFL, which has led to five decades of unparalleled NFL success.

Our two organizations became so successful that the Cowboys were referred to as "America's Team," while the Raiders were named "The Team of the Decades." In the midst of such a competitive environment, both organizations had great respect for each other and closely monitored the success that saw either the Cowboys or Raiders as participants in nine of the first 18 Super Bowl games. Sadly, however, we never had the opportunity to face each other in one of these championship contests.

The authors of this book experienced long and illustrious NFL careers, handling both administrative and scouting roles. During their more than 60 years of combined work for Al Davis and the Raiders, Jon Kingdon and Bruce Kebric were privy to the majority of coaching, player acquisition and draft day decisions made by Davis. Numerous books and articles have attempted to convey the many facets of Al Davis, but this one is the first that actually transports the reader behind the Davis "Silver and Black Shield." It is packed with inside information never published from not only from the two principals but also from scouts, coaches and players. Readers of this book will learn about Davis' penchant for coaching hires, player signings, talent evaluation and, most important, the football mentality of a man who former NFL Commissioner Pete Rozelle once referred to as "a charming rogue."

I have known both of the authors for decades. Their scouting acumen, organizational skills and loyalty to Al Davis and the Raiders were beyond reproach. I initially met Bruce Kebric when he was working at Stanford University in the 1960s. We became re-acquainted when he joined the San Diego Chargers and l had the opportunity to follow his professional development with the Houston Oilers and Raiders. My first encounter with Jon Kingdon came in the 1980s when the Cowboys and Raiders held joint training camp scrimmages in Oxnard, California, and Thousand Oaks, California. I always looked forward to visiting with Jon at the Indianapolis scouting combine each year and in recent years, Jon has provided assistance in my current job at NFL.com.

As a close friend of Al Davis for more than 50 years, I found this book to be a fascinating read about Al's passion for football and his "Commitment to Excellence." I cannot think of two more appropriate individuals than Jon Kingdon and Bruce Kebric to share with the readers what transpired behind the scenes with Al Davis and the Raiders. As you will discover, it was never dull.

— Gil Brandt

Authors' note about Gil Brandt:

During his more than 30 years as personnel chief of the Dallas Cowboys, Gil Brandt guided the Cowboys from a National Football League expansion franchise to recognition as "America's Team." With his deft player personnel moves, Dallas appeared in five Super Bowls, winning two, captured 13 division titles, compiling a record 20 consecutive winning seasons from 1966 to 1985. Shortly after Brandt left the Cowboys in 1989, the team won three additional Super Bowl titles with players whom he had drafted.

Along the way, Brandt created numerous player evaluation practices that still are prominent in today's NFL. He took much of the conjecture out of scouting by developing and using technological and analytical procedures. Among these: The gauge that the 40-yard dash was the proper measurement of a football player's speed, that mental and psychological testing were important in determining the future development of a prospect, and that a computer program was the most rational device to analyze the abundance of information gathered on the various prospects. Brandt also went beyond just football and required his scouts to evaluate basketball, track and field and soccer players. He found a number of athletes from these sports, including Cornell Green, Bob Hayes and Toni Fritsch, all of whom developed into NFL All-Pro players for the Cowboys.

To many who have worked in the NFL scouting realm, Brandt is considered "The Godfather of Modern Scouting."

Introduction

From his arrival in 1963 until he died in 2011, Al Davis and the Raiders never were far from the headlines. Davis received immediate national attention when, in his first season as the Raiders head coach, he orchestrated the biggest turnaround in professional football history by taking the 1-13 team he inherited and guiding it to 10 wins. Two of those wins came against the American Football League champion San Diego Chargers, for whom Davis had worked as an assistant coach prior to accepting the Oakland job.

During Davis' first 23 seasons, the Raiders compiled a 229-91-11 regular-season record, won their division 12 times and finished second seven times. It was a record that any organization would envy and backed up the catchphrases that Davis so often employed to describe his Raiders: "Commitment to Excellence," "Pride and Poise," "Just Win, Baby" and "The Team of the Decades." Unfortunately, when an organization uses such hubris to describe itself and the on-field performance fails to live up to the hype, it becomes a major target for abuse, which many football observers enjoyed heaping upon Davis and the Raiders during his last twenty seasons.

There was no one who was indifferent to Al Davis and the Raiders. Like the New York Yankees, you either loved them or hated them with an equal passion. Davis did his part to fuel such emotions.

"When you hear Al Davis' name mentioned, people want to take sides," former Pittsburgh Steelers and Hall of Fame quarterback Terry Bradshaw told sports writer Steve Corkran at a Raiders training camp, long before Davis' passing. "Right or wrong, good or bad, if you look at the history of the league and you look at how the league has changed, when you look at who the personalities are involved in that change, you're going to find Al Davis."

Though Davis' persona created an array of contrasting emotional

40

responses that transcended the game of football, he never wavered in his belief that he was only a small part of the National Football League, even though he appeared to be in nearly constant conflict with his contemporaries by virtue of his multitude of lawsuits and conspiracy theories.

Outside of his commitment to his wife, Carol, if there was one consistency in his life, it was his love of football. Former Tennessee Titans general manager Floyd Reese, who also was a longtime NFL assistant coach, recalled one of his first NFL meetings, at which time Davis spoke:

"Al got up three or four times during the meeting, and I was always impressed because the first things out of his mouth always was, 'Keep in mind, gentlemen, this is the finest sport in the history of sports and it is our duty to keep it that way. Football takes precedence over everything.' The whole time, it was like, 'Here we are, caretakers of this entity and make sure we don't do anything to mess it up' kind of thing … He (was) very strong in his belief and how he (thought) things should get done, and it is hard to argue with success."

All-Pro cornerback Albert Lewis considered Davis "a man's man," someone who blazed trails that others eventually followed.

"I like a man that does his own things and doesn't follow along with the group," said Lewis, who played for the Raiders from 1994-98. "I don't like a malcontent, but that's not what he was. He was a man with his own mind and his own ideas. Sometimes those ideas got ahead of other people but sooner or later, you see them walking up the same street that he was walking up a year ago. He was quick to evolve. Now, if he had just evolved more from a strategic standpoint. But, from a business standpoint, Mr. Davis was great for the league."

As a fan of the Brooklyn Dodgers, Davis came to appreciate how important speed was for a team to be successful, though he would occasionally carry that belief to extremes, sacrificing football-specific skills for the extra tenth of a second in the 40-yard dash.

His admiration for the Dodgers also had roots in that organization being at the forefront in the integration of Major League Baseball. Upon Davis' death in the fall of 2011, there was no shortage of football luminaries who were willing to weigh in on the Davis legacy. At the top of the list of the unique qualities his peers mentioned was his "color blindness."

Davis had the distinction of being the first NFL owner to draft an

African-American quarterback in the first round (Eldridge Dickey, 1968), the first to hire a Latino head coach (Tom Flores, 1979) and the first to hire an African-American head coach in the modern era of the NFL (Art Shell, 1989). As Davis once so appropriately stated, "The Raiders have never been interested in a man's color, only his ability." Davis also was the first owner from one of the four major professional sports to hire a woman, Amy Trask, as his chief executive.

Many owners didn't care for Davis, but they respected him for his role in the AFL becoming a viable entity and ultimately forcing a merger with the once-dominant NFL, as well as for his foresight. As a result, owners oftentimes looked toward Davis for advice and sought his help in finding a resolution to a difficult issue.

Davis didn't shy away from taking credit for the power he wielded. At the same time, that wasn't a driving force in his grand scheme. He treated such entreaties as his duty, his obligation to the game that had given him so much over the years.

To that end, Davis poured all his energy and time into being the most insightful football person the game has ever seen. Sid Gillman, who gave Davis his first professional football job with the Los Angeles Chargers, once said about Davis: "Al thinks he is the smartest guy in football. He isn't. But he is going to be." Gillman told Bruce Kebric, when the pair worked together in San Diego, that he had recommended Davis for the position of AFL commissioner in 1966 because "if anyone could bring the NFL to his knees, it was Al Davis. And I wanted him out of Oakland."

Blessed with a combination of intellect, tenacity and extreme confidence, Davis generally found a large audience willing to listen to what he had to say.

"Whenever Al walked into a room, he took over," said Raiders senior executive John Herrera, who was hired by Davis in 1963 and still worked for the Raiders when Davis died. "Without exception. I never saw an instance where, no matter who was there, that Al didn't become the focal point when he entered the room. He was aware of that. And he relished that, too. He was confident in every situation."

At most events Davis was the "star of the show" and impressed those in attendance with his wide-range of knowledge on a variety of topics. As expected, most conversations would commence with football topics or references but could quickly diverge into discussions about history, politics, the stock market, the Middle East, or a host of other relevant subjects.

Davis was a bit of a Renaissance man. Though football was the dominant concern in his life, he might call Kingdon and ask how the election went.

"The one in Iran?" was Kingdon's response on one occasion.

"Of course, what else would I be talking about?" Davis replied.

A subject that Davis indicated that he was not fond of talking about was his legacy. In 2000, Corkran asked Davis what he thought his legacy would be, and Davis responded: "I don't know what my legacy is. That's not for me to say. You'll have to ask others about that. I care more about winning than my legacy." Though he denied it to others, Davis was keenly aware of his legacy. He was crestfallen when the Tampa Bay Buccaneers defeated his Raiders in Super Bowl XXXVII, depriving him of a fourth Super Bowl trophy.

"He took that loss to his grave," Kebric said.

There were owners who very much respected Davis' love for the game and the mindset he brought to the meetings, including Jerry Jones of the Dallas Cowboys, whom Davis greatly admired for both his business acumen and his willingness to speak out against the status quo.

"Al was a blessing to me," Jones said in 2013. "Of all the people I've met in the NFL, he was among the most special in guiding me. Our relationship was unique."

Then there were others, such as Houston Texans owner Robert McNair. When the league awarded the Rams and denied the Raiders the rights to move to Los Angeles in 2016, he said, "Oakland gets nothing. Al used to sue us all the time." Former San Francisco 49ers president Carmen Policy once proclaimed, "He's sued us how many times? He's ignored our efforts to be unanimous how many times? He doesn't vote on issues 90 percent of the time, but it's just his way of doing things."

As might be expected, the "Us" vs. "Them" mentality espoused by Davis and his organization did not endear him to many of his colleagues. They may have respected his football knowledge but in time became annoyed with his constant feuding and lawsuits against anyone who stood in the way of what he thought was best for both himself and the Raiders. This mentality was exhibited during one of his legal battles, when Davis commented, "I'm trying to think if I've ever lost a fight ... I did, maybe once ... in the sixth grade." Being told "no," despite the source, was never a barrier to his way of thinking.

When the NFL said "no" to Davis' proposed move from Oakland to Los Angeles in 1980, he sued and won a decade-long court battle. When the United States Football League (USFL) brought an anti-trust suit against the NFL, Davis, to the consternation of his fellow NFL team owners, agreed with the new league and testified that the NFL had indeed tried to destroy the USFL's Oakland franchise. When the NFL claimed that Davis had abdicated his rights to the Los Angeles market after the Raiders returned to Oakland in 1995, Davis sued for the rights he claimed he had purchased as part of the settlement in the original case. When a dispute with the Oakland-Alameda Coliseum Commission arose over its failure to deliver on a promise of sold-out games once the Raiders relocated to Oakland, Davis was back in court fighting for what he believed he had been guaranteed.

He seemed to relish these legal skirmishes as much as he did the on field battles, though he did admit that they took a toll on him physically.

"You're in court until four (o'clock), then after dinner you're back with the attorney until midnight or one o'clock," he related to Kebric. "You get a few hours sleep and then you start all over again at nine. Then, one slip up, one wrong word and you lose."

From 1986 through Davis' final season, the Raiders, though still colorful and endowed with very loyal fans, became somewhat of a parody around the sports world in general and the NFL specifically. The Raiders record during that time was 188-227, finishing in third, fourth or fifth in their division 20 of those 26 years. There were two second-place finishes and four first-place finishes, all but one of the latter coming during the Jon Gruden/Bill Callahan era from 1998-2002.

Yet, despite the downturn in the Raiders fortune, Davis never permitted himself to doubt his philosophy on how to win or how to run an organization. The total confidence that he could conquer all his opponents, except one — death — may be his greatest legacy.

Despite the lack of success in the later years, Davis' commitment to football and the effort he had invested in the game was not lost on people who had coached for him. "Well, there is always a respect level," said Mike Shanahan, who was fired by Davis four games into the 1989 season and who won two Super Bowls in the late 1990s as the Denver Broncos head coach. "He gave me an opportunity, even though it didn't work out. I have learned a lot from him. There is a respect level for what he has accomplished and done."

Mike Holmgren, who took three teams to the Super Bowl as the head coach of the Green Bay Packers and Seattle Seahawks, had this to say about Davis while still coaching: "As a young head coach in this league, and as a young assistant coach, he's always had time for me, been very helpful in conversation. I've got a lot of respect for him. Davis' time as a towering figure in the NFL has made football a better game, too. If you ask anybody, he's had a tremendous influence on the game. He is a brilliant football man, and that's acknowledged."

Why did it work? Why did it stop working?

Most evaluations of the Oakland Raiders and the environment fostered by Al Davis have been submitted by those outside the organization. This internal assessment, as described by people who worked closely with Davis, unveils what actually happened behind the "Silver and Black Shield."

Ron Riesterer

Al Davis had a distinctive look that made him recognizable everywhere. As seen here, when Davis arrived in Oakland ahead of his team's relocation from Los Angeles in 1995, Davis always traveled with a black bag with the words "Al Davis – Raiders," while wearing a diamond bracelet with "Al" in the center, and peering from behind dark glasses. Davis' wife, Carol, walks behind him as they are escorted from the Oakland Airport by a cadre of police.

Crafting an Image

A l Davis acted as if he didn't care what others thought about him, his appearance and his actions. In reality, Davis cared very much. He had a carefully crafted image and persona that he worked hard to cultivate and protect.

Jon Kingdon's first in-depth encounter with Davis came in 1978, when Kingdon was assigned to pick up Davis at Oakland International Airport.

When Al Davis stepped off the plane, there was no doubt who he was. He wore a black mesh sweater, carried a black bag with 'Al Davis — Oakland Raiders' stamped on it, wore a diamond bracelet with 'Al' on it and he had on his ever-present dark glasses.

Davis wanted to be met at the gate upon his arrival at the airport and to have his transportation readily available.

Prior to September 11, 2001, whoever picked up Davis was able to leave his big, black Lincoln at the curb in front of the terminal.

Everyone knew Davis' car, and it wouldn't be ticketed.

"At every request or suggestion, Al Davis expected, and usually demanded, an immediate result," Kingdon said.

Davis took a great deal of pride in his hair. His handlers knew to keep a supply of hairbrushes nearby at all times. Davis also made liberal use of a specialized hair spray that kept his well-coiffed hair in place and protected his distinctive ducktail.

When the Raiders played the Washington Redskins in the 1984 Super Bowl, Mike Ornstein was assigned the role of seeing to whatever Davis needed during the game. Ornstein handed over the role to Kingdon late in the game, so that Ornstein could tend to postgame matters.

Kingdon immediately approached Davis and made himself available.

"I knew not to congratulate him, even though there were only a few minutes left in the game and the Raiders led 38–9," Kingdon said.

Davis told Kingdon that he had an important task that he needed Kingdon to perform.

"What do you need?" Kingdon asked.

Davis said he wanted Kingdon to go down to the locker room and make sure there was a hairbrush available for Davis to use.

"I took no offense to the request," Kingdon said. "After all, he was going to be on national television in front of millions of people."

After Kingdon agreed to the request, he started to leave for the locker room.

Davis stopped Kingdon, called him back and outlined the plan.

"When I walk into the locker room, you are going to ask me if I would like a hairbrush," Davis said. "I will then say, 'Do I need one?' And you will say, 'If you like.' Okay, now do you have it?"

"Yes," Kingdon said, as he repeated Davis' instructions. "Would you like a hairbrush?" "Do I need one?" "If you like." "I got it."

At that point, Kingdon suddenly realized the folly of what he was being asked to orchestrate.

"I'm now feeling more than a little foolish," Kingdon said, "but, again, understanding who I was dealing with and respecting the fact that he was going to be on national television."

Kingdon prepared to depart for the locker room, as instructed, this time with a sense of urgency.

"Not yet," Davis said.

Davis wanted Kingdon to wait until the two-minute warning before he exited the press box.

When the time came, Kingdon dashed to the locker room and located Bobby Romanski, who handled the Raiders equipment. Romanski was working at a fevered pitch in anticipation of the onslaught of players and media about to descend upon the Raiders locker room.

"I called to him, and he gave me a look like, 'I am not going to stop for anything for you. Don't bother me,'" Kingdon said. "I said, 'Bobby, I need a hairbrush for Al.'"

Romanski expected such a request, walked over to where he had the brush stashed and handed it to Kingdon. From there, Kingdon worked on his lines as he waited for Davis to enter the locker room.

"Would you like a hairbrush? 'Do I need one?' 'If you like.'" Over and over.

Eventually, Davis walked into the locker room, with an entourage in tow. He made eye contact with Kingdon, as planned.

"Before I could get my line out, Al shouted for all to hear, 'Kingdon, where's my fucking hairbrush?' That ruined the first two lines of the script, so I ad-libbed and walked over to him, handed him the brush, and saved the last line: 'If you like.'"

Davis created an image that he wanted the public to see. He seldom wavered from his favored way of dressing, eating or acting. Yet Davis displayed only so much to the general public.

"People on the outside knew little about Al because he wasn't about to expose himself," Bruce Kebric stated. "He always enjoyed the 'charming rogue' label given to him by NFL commissioner Pete Rozelle, an archenemy of Davis.

"He tried to convey an image as a blue-collar, street-smart kind of a thug. He wore his hair back like Elvis, with the ducktail, and dressed in either all-black or all-white. That's the mystique that he wanted to portray."

One day, Davis painted a picture for Hall of Fame defensive tackle Warren Sapp about what his childhood was like. He talked at length about the area in Brooklyn, New York, that he called home during his formative years.

"That was my neighborhood," Davis said.

"That's where Mike Tyson's from," Sapp replied.

"Mike Tyson would have peed down his leg coming down my block," Davis said, without hesitation.

"Mr. Davis, it was that rough?" Sapp inquired.

"Young man, I'm telling you, my neighborhood was rough," Davis assured Sapp.

What Davis failed to describe to Sapp was how his Brooklyn neighborhood had changed over the years. The Crown Heights/Lincoln Terrace Park area of the 1940s had changed from a comfortable Jewish-Italian enclave to what some called a "gangster's paradise" 30 years later.

Davis and Kingdon dined together quite often when the Raiders were located in Southern California. Davis favored Carmine's, Matteo's and La Famiglia restaurants, with Carmine's being a particular favorite. He had a private table set up whenever he went to Carmine's, and the staff paid close attention to Davis and even hooked up a phone for his use at a time before cell phones were prevalent.

One night, Davis and Kingdon went to Matteo's in Beverly Hills. Davis phoned the restaurant in advance of their arrival. The maître d' assured Davis that a table would be ready when he showed up.

When Davis and Kingdon arrived, they learned that their table wasn't available. The maître d' apologized and said the delay was due to actor Dean Martin and the president of Universal Studios taking longer than expected. Davis and Kingdon waited at the bar — Davis, who was not a drinker, satisfied himself with non-alcoholic drinks during the wait. The maître d' came by and reiterated that the wait wouldn't be much longer.

"After two more minutes, Al said, 'We have to go,'" Kingdon said.

The maître d' pleaded with Davis to reconsider. Davis graciously declined and continued to the parking lot.

When they reached the car, Davis explained to Kingdon, "I just can't let people see me waiting."

Davis enjoyed fine restaurants, and it was common for him to dine with a few select guests the night before a Raiders road game.

"Some of my fondest memories of road trips are from those night-before-game dinners," senior executive John Herrera said, "because that was when Al was at his most charming and relaxed."

The group generally consisted of close friends Bob Albo and Sam Bercovich, former players such as Jim Otto, George Blanda and Ted Hendricks, Davis' brother, Jerry, Bill King, and all the wives.

"Dinner discussion was always lively and wildly entertaining," Herrera said, "and Al particularly enjoyed the give and take from this group of strong-willed, opinionated people unafraid to speak their minds."

Davis also had an affinity for fast food.

Davis' lunch generally came from Foster's Freeze, and it seldom varied — a double hamburger, without a middle bun, mustard and relish only, and French fries.

One day, Davis shared with Kingdon news that Kentucky Fried Chicken planned to open a restaurant near Davis' Marina del Rey residence.

"He said that with great enthusiasm," Kingdon said. "He seemed a little embarrassed to have such plebeian culinary tastes."

Maybe so, but Davis didn't care. He simply couldn't resist the urge. Lest there be any doubt, it was removed one night when Kingdon picked up Davis at the airport. As Kingdon headed toward Davis' home at the Marina City Club, Davis said he was hungry and asked Kingdon if he knew of a burger place near Davis' home.

Kingdon mentioned that there was a Fatburger just down the street.

"Let's try it," Davis said.

Kingdon and Davis walked in to Fatburger around 10 p.m. The fast-food restaurant was devoid of customers. Davis and Kingdon approached the counter, when the man taking orders perked up.

"Mr. Davis, back again," the clerk said. "You must really love this place. What is this, the third time this week?"

Kingdon turned and looked at Davis.

"He seemed embarrassed," Kingdon said.

"I really love this place," Davis conceded.

If it wasn't Kentucky Fried Chicken or Fatburger, it might be Mc-Donald's or Nathan's Hot Dogs. His drink of choice was Diet Pepsi. The only other option was water, which Davis drank a great deal of every day because he once got kidney stones. Davis also had a penchant for eating chocolate cake during the draft each year. Clubhouse assistant George "Run Run" Jones was the one who usually brought Davis the cake. Oftentimes, other Raiders employees would hide the cake from Jones so that they could watch him panic for fear of not pleasing Davis.

Davis purchased a car phone in the early 1980s, long before cell phones existed and at a time when few people indulged in such a luxury. It marked one of the few times that Davis was ahead of the curve in terms of technology. He used Betamax VCRs long after everyone else had moved on to VHS, and memorably used an overhead projector during the Lane Kiffin firing news conference in 2008.

Once Davis got the car phone, he was even less inclined to drive. Hence, he enlisted Kingdon to drive every Thursday night when they went to dinner. Davis enjoyed Kingdon's company, and he enjoyed the freedom to use his new toy.

"He would just start dialing people," Kingdon said. "He loved to chat and find out what was going on."

Davis phoned New York Giants coach Bill Parcells on one such outing. Davis and Parcells were close friends, and they talked quite often. At the time, Giants star outside linebacker Lawrence Taylor seemed to have a handle on the drug problems that hampered him early in his career. Taylor once again had been playing at a dominant level.

Davis asked Parcells how he managed to keep Taylor from getting suspended.

Parcells asked Davis if he was alone. Davis said, "Yes," and then he nodded at Kingdon.

Parcells then answered Davis' question, saying he made Taylor provide a urine sample every day for testing.

"Is that legal?" Davis asked Parcells.

"I don't give a fuck whether it's legal or not," Parcells said. "He knows he's going to be tested and that's how we are able to keep him clean."

The frequency with which Davis and Kingdon met fostered the kind of close relationship that Davis enjoyed with a precious few. Davis had an ability to make people feel as if they were part of his inner circle, one of his confidants, when, in fact, he trusted only a handful of people. As a result, people who had an audience with Davis routinely spouted information in hopes of ingratiating themselves with a man of such mystique and power.

"Al was adept at gathering a lot of information from people without giving out much information, if any, of substance," senior executive John Herrera said. "In fact, he was well-versed in doling out only the information he wanted to disseminate."

Kingdon was one of the few who succeeded at gaining Davis' trust. He did so over time, and their relationship grew naturally. It reached the point where not only did the two frequently dine together, but Davis also called Kingdon at home on a regular basis.

Kingdon had no idea when Davis might call, or what Davis might inquire about. All he knew was, he needed to be ready.

"He might call and ask, 'How many quarterbacks are coming out? And how would you rank them?' So, I always had the information at hand," Kingdon said.

Other times, Kingdon would meet with Davis at his apartment at the Marina City Club in Marina del Rey. Kingdon would arrive with film of that day's game or practice so that he and Davis could watch it together. Carol Davis, Al's wife, was always the perfect hostess. Once, she served white chocolate macadamia cookies.

"These are really nice," Kingdon told her reflexively. "Thank you."

From there on, every week Mrs. Davis would come into the room announcing: "Jon, I got your cookies," as she handed over a plate of the white chocolate macadamia cookies.

Another time, Kingdon had a New York Seltzer at the Davis' house.

"That's really nice," Kingdon said.

What came next didn't surprise Kingdon.

"I got your New York Seltzer," Mrs. Davis would proclaim during her weekly presentation of Kingdon's new favored drink.

Davis had become so reliant upon Kingdon that one night he phoned Kebric after receiving a wedding invitation from Kingdon.

"Did you know about Jon?" Davis said.

"What are you talking about?" Kebric responded.

"Did you know that Jon's getting married?" Davis asked.

"Yeah," Kebric replied.

"How come you didn't tell me?" Davis inquired.

"Well, because it's not my business," Kebric said.

"He's going to leave," Davis told Kebric.

Even though Kebric assured Davis that Kingdon's upcoming marriage would not interfere with his work, Davis was still not pleased with the announcement.

"Jon's getting married and things are going to change around here," Davis said. "I'm not going to have Jon anymore. He's going to get married and then he's going to have a family."

Kebric wasn't sure what to think.

"He went on and on like that," Kebric said. "I began to think that the guy was nuts. So, I said to him, 'Talk to Jon about it, don't talk to me.' From our conversation, I got the indication that Al felt that Jon's sole allegiance should be to him."

Davis generally wasn't one to get overly sentimental, and he certainly wasn't fond of showing his softer side. In fact, at his 70th and 75th birthday gatherings in Las Vegas, whenever someone spoke too glowingly about Davis, he cut them off.

However, Davis had a great deal of love for his players, even those with whom he had issues. This was driven home to Kingdon at training camp in 1985 when the Raiders traded wide receiver Malcolm Barnwell to the Washington Redskins.

Barnwell, typical of Raiders receivers, was very fast. He proved to be an able, complementary receiver to Cliff Branch and started the 1983 Super Bowl, though he didn't catch any passes in that game.

"Malcolm did have his demons and off-field concerns," Kingdon said, "and he was becoming more of a distraction than he was worth."

The Raiders netted a second-round pick for Barnwell, a seventh-round draft pick of the Raiders in 1980. The compensation was much more than anyone had anticipated.

"When I went by Al's room at training camp that afternoon," Kingdon said, "I was ready to congratulate him on getting so much for Barnwell in the trade."

Instead, he found Davis was incredibly maudlin and depressed. Davis started talking about Barnwell and how the Raiders had drafted him in the seventh round and how well he had developed and had started in the Super Bowl. Davis took great pride in using late-round picks on players from small schools — Barnwell attended Virginia Union — and developing them into productive NFL players.

"The more he talked about Barnwell, the more upset that he became," Kingdon said. "In fact, he began crying and, in a choked voice, he told me to leave."

Kingdon was taken aback that Davis would be so upset at losing someone like Barnwell and would be so hard on so many other more productive and less distracting players.

Davis seldom cried, by all accounts. It was even more rare to hear Davis tell a joke. Though Davis in the last few decades of his life seldom made public appearances, prior to that, it was not a rare thing for Davis to get up from the dais at some testimonial to speak. Kingdon came to know what to expect.

"He always told 'The Dog Food Story,' which only he seemed to enjoy. It had to do with the owner of a dog food company speaking to the employees about how they had the best dog food around, they had the best advertisers around and they had the best salesmen around. He then asks why they aren't selling more dog food, when someone yelled out, 'It's the damn dogs — they don't like it.'"

One December afternoon, Davis walked into the room where the Raiders scouts were meeting and started talking about a program he had seen on TV the previous evening.

"He not only surprised us with his appearance at that time but we were stunned to hear that he had actually watched anything other than game tape or a game on TV," Kingdon said.

Davis had watched a TV show that was the modern equivalent of *Candid Camera.* Davis related how on the episode he watched, someone would visit a house that was for sale. When the person returned for a second look, the house had been removed and all that remained was an empty lot.

"As he kept talking about the show, he laughed harder and harder," Kingdon said. "We looked at each other; it was an entertaining story, but all of us were more taken aback to listen to Al speak about a *Candid Camera*-like episode."

Occasionally, Davis would engage in banter that precious few ever witnessed. In 1994, standout cornerback Albert Lewis bolted from the Kansas City Chiefs after 11 superb seasons and signed with the rival Raiders.

For Lewis, it was like coming home to the place he always felt he belonged. In 1983, he had dreamed of following in cornerback Willie Brown's footsteps from Grambling to a pro career with the Raiders.

"I was just so sure that I was going to be a Raider that that never really left me, because of Willie Brown and all that," Lewis recalled. "Willie and I actually were on the phone when the Chiefs drafted me. He said that they were having some kind of argument about whether to take me or not. He wanted me to be there, and they wanted somebody else because they had a bad time on me in the 40."

The Raiders passing on Lewis fueled him during a stellar career.

The slight lingers to this day.

"I still have that 4.60 that the Raiders said I ran at the combine on my safe to this day," Lewis said in reference to a magnet that features the Raiders breakdown of his pre-draft workout.

Lewis got his wish of playing for the Raiders in 1994, when he joined a team that featured a load of talented players.

"When I got there, I said, 'Mr. Davis, you told me I was going to be starting,'" Lewis remembered.

Davis ran his tongue over his teeth and looked at Lewis.

"Ah, hell. Shut up," Davis said. "You should just be happy that I got you out of those ugly-ass socks."

Lewis burst into laughter.

"We went on for a couple of minutes, talking about those socks the Chiefs used to wear," Lewis said, with a chuckle. "I said, 'Yeah, they look like Ronald McDonald, don't they? Red, white, yellow stripes and all this stuff. I guess I should thank you for that.'"

Davis was a creature of habit in many respects. He also had his share of bad habits, as Kebric learned soon after being hired by Davis.

"He put his hands down, and I had never seen anything like it," Kebric said. "It was gross. There were practically no nails left on either hand. His thumbs were OK. But his fingers were bloodied. I wondered how he did it but I never asked him."

Kingdon spent more time around Davis on a daily basis. Therefore, he got to see for himself how Davis wore down his fingernails.

"He attacked his fingernails," Kingdon said. "He was an inveterate nail-biter."

This manifested itself most when things didn't go Davis' way, particularly in the draft. The more nervous he got, the more he bit his nails.

Kingdon recalled a time when Davis had reduced his fingertips to a bloody pulp.

Kingdon finally worked up the courage to broach the topic with Davis at training camp one year. They were in Davis' room, when Kingdon asked Davis if he could ask him a personal question.

"Go ahead," Davis said.

"How were you able to stop biting your nails?" Kingdon asked.

Davis looked at Kingdon and said he simply willed himself to stop. He then asked Kingdon if he had a nail-biting problem.

"Not for a while," Kingdon said.

"Which nail gave you the most problems?" Davis wanted to know.

"The ring finger on my left hand," Kingdon said, though he didn't have a particular problem with any finger.

Davis lifted his left hand to his mouth and pretended to bite on the ring finger.

"Yeah, that was a tough finger for me, as well," Davis said.

Soon after the Raiders beat the Washington Redskins in the Super Bowl, Davis summoned future Hall of Fame linebacker Ted Hendricks to his office.

Davis asked former Raiders linebacker Dan Conners, a team scout at the time, to sit in on the meeting, perhaps as a buffer against the ever-unpredictable Hendricks, who stood 6-foot-7 and weighed 220 pounds.

Davis confronted Hendricks about his alcohol consumption, which was not a secret to anyone who knew Hendricks, and told him that he wanted to keep paying him, but only if Hendricks addressed his problem by enrolling in a substance-abuse program.

Hendricks leaned toward Davis, and grabbed Davis by the wrist.

"Oh, yeah, look at your nails!" Hendricks shouted. "Look at your nails!"

How dare Davis question Hendricks' bad habit when Davis could not even control his own?

Despite his drinking, Hendricks had started every game during his final eight seasons and played at an All-Pro level for most of that time. He appeared to know when to turn it on, and when to have fun.

Davis, on later occasions, would talk about his giving Hendricks the ultimatum and then adding that "he should have just let Hendricks drink," Kebric said.

Davis also was quite superstitious, though he scoffed at the suggestion. His actions painted a different portrait.

He and Kingdon ate at Nate and Al's Deli in Beverly Hills one Thursday night. The Raiders won their game three days later. Naturally, Davis insisted that he and Kingdon eat at Nate and Al's Deli the following Thursday. Sure enough, the Raiders won again the subsequent Sunday. This went on for five straight weeks.

"I'm really getting tired of this food, but we have to keep coming here since we keep winning," Davis told Kingdon as they convened at Nate and Al's for the sixth straight Thursday. They ate there every week until the Raiders lost again.

Davis acted in a similar fashion when it came to hotels. If the Raiders won a game in Denver, say, Davis wanted his team to stay at the same hotel the next year, too. Conversely, Davis oftentimes demanded that the Raiders change hotels in a particular city if the Raiders lost there.

The Raiders lost to the Kansas City Chiefs 11 straight times, including one playoff game, at Arrowhead Stadium from 1989-98. That kept the person in charge of booking hotels for the Raiders in constant search of a new location. It also prompted long-time *Contra Costa Times* columnist Gary Peterson to say, "At this rate, the Raiders are going to be forced to stay in Kansas."

Davis' superstitious ways manifested themselves in other ways. For instance, Kingdon learned not to point at a player that Davis inquired about, but not before being snapped at by Davis.

"Don't point!" Davis would say. "Ah, fuck, now he knows we're talking about him."

Loyalty and respect were two areas that were very important to Davis.

"If Davis felt he was being disrespected, his demeanor could flip 180 degrees immediately," Kingdon said.

In particular, if someone who worked for the Raiders was critical of Davis to someone outside the Raiders organization, that was grounds for termination.

Personnel executive Mike Lombardi discovered this in 2007, when he violated this rule. When Davis received information from long-time scout and advisor George Karras about critical comments Lombardi had made about Davis and the Raiders, he summoned Lombardi into his office and informed him that he was going to be let go.

Lombardi had, in effect, been fired. He returned to his office, packed up his belongings and exited the team's facility soon after he met with Davis. Kingdon met with Davis later that day, and Davis detailed what had happened.

"Al told Mike that he was going to let him go and then asked him how he wanted it presented to the press," Kingdon said. "Did he want to say he left on his own? Did he want to say he was going to pursue something new?"

"Thank you, Mr. Davis," Lombardi replied. "I will contact my lawyer and get back to you."

Davis reacted in a familiar manner.

"You're going to check with your lawyer?" Davis snapped. "Get the fuck out of here! Clean out your fucking office and get the fuck out of the building!"

Disrespect manifested itself myriad ways in Davis' eyes. Entertaining the notion of working for another team also was viewed as a blatant show of disrespect.

"It was hard for Al to imagine that someone did not want to work for the Raiders," Kingdon said. "When people left, he took it personally."

In fact, Davis oftentimes didn't wait for someone to leave before he reacted. It was commonplace for Davis to phone an assistant coach after another team had called Davis to request permission to interview that coach.

"Al would tell them that they could go for the interview," Kingdon said, "but that they wouldn't have a job when they got back."

The day before the 1990 NFL draft, Davis called Kebric into his office. He wanted to know whether Kebric had any objections to Davis selecting linebacker Aaron Wallace in the second round.

"No," Kebric said to Davis, but he had been told that Wallace had a history of alcohol abuse.

Then-Texas A&M head coach R.C. Slocum told Kebric in 1990 that Wallace was the best pass rusher that he had ever coached. Davis, at the time, liked Wallace's potential as an impact player and felt that he could handle the problem. However, neither Raiders defensive coordinator Dave Adolph nor Raiders linebackers coach Sam Gruneisen wanted Wallace, at least in the second round.

Wallace was "not a football player," Adolph said, according to Kebric. The knock on Wallace by some was that he was a one-dimensional player, a pass rusher.

Right after Davis drafted Wallace, Gruneisen turned to Davis and said, "You can coach him."

Later that day, Kebric was working in the scouting room when Davis came by.

"Did you hear what Sam said about Wallace," Davis asked.

"Yes," Kebric responded.

"What do you think?" Davis said.

"About Wallace?" Kebric replied.

"No, about Sam," Davis clarified.

"I really like Sam," Kebric said, once he realized where Davis was headed.

"I like him, too, but I think I'm going to fire him," Davis said, as he walked away.

Sure enough, Davis fired Gruneisen soon thereafter, even though Davis had recruited and signed Gruneisen out of Villanova when Davis worked for the Chargers.

Just the same, "Gruneisen had challenged Davis in front of the group," Kebric said.

Davis occasionally would surprise even those who were close with his responses to various situations.

When the Raiders participated in the 1982 Quadra scouting combine at the Dallas Cowboys facility, Davis wanted to work out after one of the sessions. Kingdon and Cowboys equipment manager Thomas "Buck" Buchanan were the only other people who remained at the facility and Davis asked Buchanan if he could borrow some gear for his workout. Buchanan produced some Cowboys gear, which Davis put on.

"A picture of Al in that gear would have been priceless," Kingdon said.

Davis went through his workout, showered and changed into his clothes. Buchanan came by as Davis prepared to leave.

"Al thanked Buck effusively and then offered him $50," Kingdon said. "Buck turned him down very politely and said it was his pleasure to help him out."

Again, Davis offered Buchanan the money. Again, Buchanan insisted that it wasn't necessary.

"Al offered Buck the money a third time and said that it would upset him if he turned him down," Kingdon said.

"Thank you," Buchanan said, as he took the money from Davis. "I'll take my wife out to dinner with this."

Soon thereafter, Buchanan left.

Davis looked at Kingdon and said, "Do you believe he took the money?"

"I pointed out to him that Buck did turn him down two times."

In 1989, Raiders safety Stacey Toran died in an automobile accident. A short time later, a memorial service was held for Toran. He was a promising player, well-liked by his teammates and those within the organization.

Numerous people spoke at Toran's memorial service, which was attended by Toran's family and friends, as well as many people in the Raiders organization. The minister was the final speaker, and he thanked the Raiders for their support of Toran and for their efforts and involvement in the memorial service. He also thanked Aunt Kizzy's Back Porch for supplying the food.

On the way back to the office, Kingdon commented to Davis on how nice the service and catered affair had been. Davis glared at Kingdon.

"Who the fuck do you think paid for the food?" Davis said. "We paid for it. Where the hell does he get off saying that they paid for it? I'm not going to pay for it. To hell with them."

Davis, in most instances, had no problem taking care of the bill for those who had worked hard on his behalf or had displayed devout loyalty to him. But, at the same time, his largesse often was conditional.

A perfect example came in 1984, when the Raiders hosted the rival Pittsburgh Steelers in the teams' regular-season finale. A win would have given the Raiders a home game for the AFC Playoffs in the wild-card round. Instead, the Raiders lost 13-7 and were forced to play the Seattle Seahawks on the road six days later. The Seahawks ended the Raiders' season three days before Christmas with a 13-7 victory.

Davis handed out Christmas presents to everyone in the organization each year. Typically, Kingdon said, everyone received a black-and-white TV engraved with the recipient's name, "Raiders" and the year it was given. Word filtered down among the employees that 1984 was going to be the first year that Davis passed out color TVs.

"Fuck it," Davis said to the person in charge of placing the order for the color TVs after the Raiders lost to the Steelers. "Give 'em the black-and-white TVs."

Davis loved the recognition for his good deeds. He also loved simply being recognized.

"If there was one group that Al liked to be recognized by, it was other coaches," Kingdon said.

Kingdon, while wearing Raiders gear, ran into University of Iowa football coach Hayden Fry at the Hula Bowl one year. He introduced himself to Fry, who was very cordial. During their conversation, Fry asked Kingdon to say hello to Davis.

"He said that they had coached against each other in the military and that he had stolen much of Al's offense and used it for his team," Kingdon recalled.

Kingdon mentioned to Davis upon his return that he had met Fry. Davis perfunctorily asked how Fry was doing. Kingdon said that Fry looked fine and then told him what Hayden had said about stealing his offense.

"Really?" Davis said, immediately perking up. "He said that? That's great. He really said that? He's a good guy."

For all Davis' bluster, he was very empathetic to people when it came to illnesses or deaths in the family.

When Kingdon's father passed away, he called Davis to let him know that he wouldn't be at work for a few days. Davis had met Kingdon's father on more than one occasion and spoke very kindly about him, Kingdon recalled.

Davis' secretary, Karen "Fudgie" Otten, called Kingdon the next day and asked for his parents' address because Davis wanted to send a bouquet on behalf of the Raiders.

"Jews do not send bouquets to families after funerals," Kingdon informed Otten. "They send food. Fudgie said she knew, but Davis wanted to send a bouquet."

An enormous silver-and-black bouquet arrived the next day, with a note from Davis and the Raiders. The bouquet and gesture was well received from those in attendance.

"When I returned to Oakland, I went up to Al and thanked him for the flowers and told him how much it was appreciated," Kingdon said.

Davis wasn't one to take "thank you" very well.

"I then added how the young man who delivered the flowers was really impressed that the flowers had come from the Raiders," Kingdon said. "In fact, he said that this was better than delivering something from the President."

On that note, Davis perked up.

"Did he really say that?" Davis asked. "Really? That's great."

When Steve Corkran's father passed away in 2009, Davis had a floral arrangement sent to the service on behalf of the Raiders. Corkran, who was a longtime Raiders beat writer, arrived with the pastor who was to perform the service that day. Both were quite concerned about the fragile state of Corkran's mother, Janet, given she had lost her husband of 51 years. Janet Corkran rushed to greet her youngest son and Pastor Bill Barrett, eager to share with them a gesture that brought her to tears.

"My mom was blown away by how stunning the bouquet was that Mr. Davis and the Raiders had delivered," Steve Corkran said. "She ushered Pastor Bill and me inside so that we could see the arrangement for ourselves. Indeed, it was evident that Mr. Davis had spared no expense."

Mrs. Corkran also was impressed by the fact that the flowers were delivered by the floral shop's owner, at the insistence of Mr. Davis, as a means of making sure that they arrived in a timely manner and matched Davis' order.

Davis' empathy extended to players from other NFL teams, even hated rivals such as the Kansas City Chiefs. In 1988, he sought out Chiefs cornerback Albert Lewis before a game.

"We were on the field warming up, and Mr. Davis came over to me," Lewis recalled.

"Albert, I'm so sorry to hear about your father," Davis said.

"That meant a lot to me because we had never had a conversation to this point," Lewis said. "When he said that, it just gave me a whole new respect for him and the way he went about his business."

Davis took great delight in being selected as the presenter for inductees into the Pro Football Hall of Fame. In fact, the Raiders refer to that role as "perhaps his most singular honor" on the team's tribute page on its website.

He delivered a record nine presentation speeches for inductees into the Pro Football Hall of Fame in Canton, Ohio: Lance Alworth, Jim Otto, Willie Brown, George Blanda, Art Shell, Gene Upshaw, Fred Biletnikoff, Ted Hendricks and coach John Madden.

Cornerback Mike Haynes spent the first half of his 14-year NFL career with the New England Patriots. When he was inducted into the Hall of Fame in 1997, he had Howard Slusher, his agent, as his presenter.

Davis traded for Haynes in 1983 in one of the greatest deals in NFL history, as Haynes played a key role in the Raiders winning the Super Bowl that season. Haynes teamed with Lester Hayes to comprise one of the best cornerback duos ever. He played for the Raiders from 1983-89, at which time he retired. Naturally, Haynes invited Davis to attend Haynes' Hall of Fame induction ceremony — but not as his presenter.

"I'm not going," Davis told Haynes.

"He wasn't going to play second fiddle to anyone," Kingdon said.

Davis additionally achieved attention in ways that transcended football. That can be attested to by those who were on hand when Davis delivered eulogies for the likes of boxer Sugar Ray Robinson, jazz singers Sarah Vaughan and Billy Eckstine, and announcer Howard Cosell, among others. His name and one of his favorite phrases was prominent in the 2010 DJ Khaled rap video, "All I Do Is Win", with Snoop Dogg voicing the words,

"Al Davis said it best: 'Just Win, Baby, Win.'"

"He wrote everything himself," senior executive John Herrera said. "He would try out eulogies on me. He would try out Hall of Fame speeches on me, too."

All of Davis' speeches typically featured a common theme.

"When I walk into that great stadium up in the sky and I hear the crowd roar, I hear that … " was a favorite scene-setter used by Davis.

"It always had to do with stadiums, the crowd roaring and the guy coming out and being introduced this way or that way," Herrera recalled. "He had a thread that kind of weaved through every one of them but he wrote every word of every speech he ever made."

Davis didn't wait until the last minute, either. He worked hard on his speeches, labored over every word. He took pride in being asked to deliver eulogies or Hall of Fame presentations.

"There were countless times where he would say, 'I have to get back to working on my speech,'" Herrera said. "Or something would happen, and he would say, 'I can't worry about that right now because I'm working on a speech for John Madden, for Freddie Biletnikoff or whoever.' He was eloquent."

Davis often said he would rather be feared than respected. On one rare occasion, Davis was the one who feared for his own well-being.

In 1987, the tiny city of Irwindale attempted to lure the Raiders with the promise of a stadium to be built on the site of a quarry about 18 miles east of downtown Los Angeles and the Los Angeles Memorial Coliseum, where the Raiders were playing their home games at the time.

Davis had been using the Los Angeles Coliseum as a temporary home after moving the Raiders there in 1982. His desire to find a new stadium increased as the years passed, and Irwindale made an intriguing pitch.

Irwindale is situated in the San Gabriel Valley, adjacent to the 210 Freeway. Its population hovered just north of 1,000 residents in 1987, just as it did in 2016. Davis already had checked out places such as Carson and City of Industry before Irwindale emerged as a suitor. Irwindale backed up its pitch with a $10 million deposit to Davis.

"Where's Irwindale?" was Davis' initial reaction to the proposal.

Davis was so curious about the prospect of moving to Irwindale that he pulled Herrera off his assorted duties and assigned him to the project.

"I want you to work on this stadium thing," Davis told Herrera. "I've been getting calls from these different communities. I want you to check them out and visit with the people. Bring me into it if you find something you like."

Irwindale showed promise, but Davis had yet to see the proposed site, which was visible from the freeway. There actually were two possible sites for Davis to consider, one on each side of the freeway. The one on the north side of the 210 was far more dramatic.

Herrera inspected both sites at length and, once satisfied, commenced negotiations. Davis was very much involved in the negotiations. A couple of months into the process, Irwindale, led by chief negotiator Fred Lyte, and the Raiders agreed on the framework of a $20 million fee to be paid to the Raiders in exchange for the city's pledge to build a stadium.

"Well, I need to take a look at this site," Davis said.

"OK, do you want to drive out?" Herrera asked. "Or, Fred Lyte has offered to send a helicopter to pick us up and take us over there?"

Davis considered his options.

"How long of a drive is it?" Davis asked of the trek from where the Raiders practiced in El Segundo to Irwindale.

"It's about an hour," Herrera responded.

"Let's take the helicopter," Davis replied.

This was going to be Davis' first helicopter ride, as far as Herrera knew.

Lyte dispatched a helicopter to the Raiders' facility in El Segundo, on what used to be El Segundo Junior High School. The helicopter landed on the field, which was illegal and resulted in the local police awaiting their return to the facility.

The helicopter landed, with the pilot, Lyte and Xavier Hermosillo, the public relations consultant for Irwindale.

"Hermosillo was a massive man, weighing in the neighborhood of 400 pounds," Herrera recalled.

Davis, Lyte and Herrera boarded the helicopter, followed by Hermosillo.

"When Xavier got in, the helicopter sat down and just rocked," Herrera said. "Al was looking at Xavier, and he must have been thinking, 'Is this thing even going to get off the ground with this guy in here?'"

Once aboard, the helicopter pilot made an announcement:

"OK, strap in. We're going to be going over the Los Angeles [International] Airport on our way out to Irwindale."

"We're not 20 feet off the ground," Herrera said, "and Al is buried in the seat, white-knuckling it. Sweat started pouring down his face. Seconds into the flight, he was petrified."

As the helicopter traversed the Los Angeles International Airport, planes were visible landing and taking off.

"It kind of scared me a little bit," Herrera said.

Herrera's trepidation waned, but Davis' increased exponentially.

"Al was not happy with the helicopter ride," Herrera said.

No doubt as a coping mechanism, Davis fired off one-liner after one-liner the whole flight.

"Are we going to make it?" Davis quipped. "Are we going to die?"

Once the helicopter reached Irwindale, the pilot decided to land at the bottom of the enormous rock and gravel pit.

"The pit was really, really deep," Herrera said. "The helicopter didn't land on top, of course. We went down inside this big ol' pit, and as we descended below the rim of the pit, the helicopter sank like a rock. Words cannot describe the look on Al's face."

The helicopter finally landed, at which point Davis regained his equilibrium.

"We're driving back!" Davis exclaimed. "We're not taking the helicopter!"

Lyte arranged for a car for Davis and Herrera to take back to El Segundo. Davis confided in Herrera that he liked the site. The helicopter was another story.

"What the fuck was that?" Davis asked, referring to Herrera's decision to take a helicopter

"I got a little chuckle inside," Herrera admitted. "That's the only time I've ever seen him scared. He couldn't mask it on that one. He was terrified."

Bob Larson

Al Davis wasn't fond of having his picture taken, and he didn't hesitate to show his displeasure if a photographer got too close.

CHAPTER TWO

The Intimidator

Working for Al Davis posed a challenge even under the best of circumstances. He expected everyone to be just as consumed by football as he had been his whole life. Davis looked forward to the start of each football season the way others did Christmas. He had a philosophy that he employed from the outset, and it wasn't to be questioned.

In 1985, Jon Kingdon attended a free-agent tryout camp in Phoenix and later that day scouted a United States Football League game between the Arizona Outlaws and the New Jersey Generals, whose roster included Heisman Trophy winners Herschel Walker and Doug Flutie. While sitting in the press box, Kingdon was asked to do a halftime interview for a local radio station. He agreed to the request. Initially, he replied to general questions about the game. Then came the question, "How does the USFL's existence help the NFL?"

Kingdon responded that he didn't see how it helped the NFL at all and that it was actually making things much more expensive for the league and all its teams.

He added, "I'm sure Al Davis likes it because he's now able to watch football 12 months a year."

The Raiders were Davis' team, his passion, his life. He worked tirelessly to take the Raiders from a nondescript team to an elite team. Everything he did was designed to bolster and protect his realm.

Bruce Kebric compared the way Davis ran the Raiders to that of a pyramid structure.

"You have the king at the top and all the loyal subjects below," Kebric said. "Certain people were responsible for certain things. But Al controlled every area. Most businesses have a president, the vice-president(s), the chief financial officer and so on. There's a discernible structure and an upward communication process. The Raiders did have some specific department heads, but everyone in the organization reported directly to

Davis. He was involved in all the areas — football, business, public relations, etc."

Davis frequently ruled through intimidation. He kept people off balance, kept them guessing, always maintaining the upper hand. Just as was the case on the field, winning wasn't good enough for Davis. He wanted to dominate, be it football games, business, life, it didn't matter.

"Many of his employees worked in fear of him," Kebric said. "People, for the most part, don't like to be challenged, and Al always pressured you to think, improve and create. I quickly learned that if you knew the answer to his question, say it with conviction. If you did not know the answer, then be honest and skip the excuses."

Davis had an aura and enjoyed challenging people, Kebric said. Some responded well to it, but others quivered at his approach. He could be ruthless, too, especially if someone lacked conviction or wasn't as prepared and dedicated as Davis.

Davis got along well with those he trusted. He pounced on those who showed weakness.

"You just laid it right out there," Kingdon said. "If you're right, you're right. If you're wrong, you're wrong. But the key was that you did the work. I told the guys, 'You're permitted mistakes of commission but not omission.' Al looked for weaknesses. If he found the weakness, or if you hesitated, he would go right after you."

When a new coach or scout was hired, Davis would immediately challenge that individual to see how strong his convictions were and how confident he was in his work. No one in the organization was immune to Davis' attacks, even those who had served him for decades.

Mickey Marvin found out the hard way in 2008. Marvin had served Davis loyally for decades as a player on two Super Bowl-winning teams and as a scout. One of Davis's favorite mottos was "Once a Raider, Always a Raider." No one in the organization exemplified this sense of brotherhood more than Marvin.

Former Raiders head coach Lane Kiffin was being considered for the University of Tennessee head coaching vacancy. A few months earlier, Davis had fired Kiffin under acrimonious circumstances and was hellbent upon making life as difficult for Kiffin as possible.

Davis wanted Marvin, a University of Tennessee alumnus, to call

Volunteers athletic director Mike Hamilton and tell him not to hire Kiffin. Davis knew not only of Marvin's Tennessee ties but also that both Hamilton and Marvin hailed from the same region in North Carolina.

Kingdon made the call to Marvin to tell him what Davis wanted him to do. A short time later, Marvin called Davis and began the conversation by saying that he had discussed and prayed with his family about whether to make the call to Hamilton.

Davis roared: "Fuck the prayer! Are you going to make the call?" Marvin said he decided not to call Hamilton. That incensed Davis.

"Al wanted to fire Mickey," Kebric said.

Kebric intervened and told Davis that Marvin had called him when he received the request and asked Kebric what he should do.

"I told Mickey that he had to do what he felt was right," Kebric said.

Davis accepted Kebric's pleading on Marvin's behalf. However, he still felt that Marvin had to be punished. To that end, Davis agreed not to fire Marvin and instead prohibited him from scouting at Tennessee for the next two years. Kebric scouted Tennessee for the Raiders in 2009. Marvin was back scouting the Volunteers in 2010 without any issue.

Prior to the 2009 draft meetings with Davis, Marvin was advised by the scouts to avoid being caught by himself with Davis, knowing Davis' long memory on real or perceived disloyalty.

All went well until the end of meetings one day. Davis got up to leave the room. He was using his walker to get around. As he got near the door, Marvin jumped up and said, "I've got the door for you."

Davis glared at Mickey and said, "Mickey, I don't need you now. I needed you before."

In 2010, Davis was fascinated with Jacoby Ford, a wide receiver from Clemson University, who ran the fastest 40-yard dash at that year's scouting combine.

Davis, blinded by Ford's speed, wanted to know more about Ford. He inquired if anyone in the room knew Dabo Swinney, Clemson's head coach.

Marvin piped up, "Dabo is a really good friend of mine."

Davis coldly turned to Marvin and said, "You used to be a really good friend of mine, too."

Davis had backed down once on Marvin, but he let everyone know that he was not willing to forget or forgive a slight.

"Al had Italian Alzheimer's," Kingdon said. "He would forget everything but a grudge."

A story came out near the end of Davis' life about long-time Raiders senior assistant Bruce Allen's mother, Etty. She was raised Jewish but did not let her family know about her background. She said she had kept it secret from the family for decades, fearing they would suffer the same discrimination she had known in Nazi-occupied Tunisia. After disclosing her secret to her eldest son, George, a former Virginia governor and United States senator, in the summer of 2006, she made him promise never to disclose it, not even to his siblings.

Kingdon was in Davis' room at training camp in Napa discussing what had taken place at practice one day, when Davis suddenly changed the subject. Davis said that Jennifer Allen, Bruce and George's sister, wanted to interview him but that he would never talk with her again. He went on to explain how upset he was that the Allens had not shared with him the fact that Etty was Jewish.

"Since Al and I were both Jewish, he felt he could share his feelings with me on the subject," Kingdon said. "I told him that it was very possible that they were not aware of her background." Al closed the discussion. "Bullshit!" Davis said. "I told them that I was through with all of them."

Davis was proud of his Jewish heritage, Kingdon said, but he made it a point not to wear his religion on his sleeve.

For example, Davis met Dr. Robert Rosenfeld when he was at USC. An injury to USC quarterback Willie Wood brought together Davis and Dr. Rosenfeld. Wood, who would go on to be a Hall of Fame safety for the Green Bay Packers, had suffered a shoulder injury that most medical experts deemed serious enough to require season-ending surgery. Rosenfeld, an outstanding orthopedic surgeon, examined Wood and determined that he didn't need surgery and would be able to finish the season. Wood went on to have an excellent season. Davis never forgot Dr. Rosenfeld's role, and Dr. Rosenfeld became a lifelong friend and the long-time orthopedist for the Raiders. Players were constantly flying to Los Angeles to be examined by Dr. Rosenfeld.

Davis and Dr. Rosenfeld were both Jewish, though Davis one time tried to downplay it to Dr. Rosenfeld, as he did to others. Davis and Dr. Rosenfeld were having a private conversation one day when Dr. Rosenfeld used a Yiddish expression that every Jewish person should have been familiar with.

"What does that mean?" Davis asked Dr. Rosenfeld.

Rosenfeld confronted Davis, saying, "Cut the shit, Al. You're talking to Rosenfeld."

Al nodded, knowing that he had been caught.

Rosh Hashanah and Yom Kippur always fall during the NFL season. If Yom Kippur fell on a Monday and the league scheduled the Raiders to play on the holiest of Jewish holidays, Davis would take great offense because the league knew that Davis was Jewish.

A few days before Rosh Hashanah, the Jewish New Year, Davis asked Kingdon in a phone call, "Is this the big one? Is this the one you don't eat on?"

He was pulling the same line on Kingdon that he had previously tried to pull on Dr. Rosenfeld, though Kingdon didn't really challenge Davis.

"No," Kingdon replied. "That's Yom Kippur in a couple of weeks."

Senior executive John Herrera was on the receiving end of that side of Davis on occasion, as was most anyone who spent considerable time around Davis.

"Al was a master of keeping you off guard," Herrera said. "He could disarm you quickly. He was not afraid of embarrassing you in front of someone else, either. He wasn't the perfect guy in that respect.

"Some of the things that he would say were cringe-inducing. I had more than my share of times when I was around him when he said and did things to people where you just felt bad."

Herrera experienced similar veiled threats. Over time, he learned to take it in stride and realized that the threats were part of Davis' ruling philosophy.

Herrera was hired by Davis in 1963, when Herrera was 16 and Davis was in his first year with the Raiders. Not even such a strong relationship earned Herrera immunity from Davis' wrath.

Of course, Davis never fired Herrera. That would have been too clean, too easy. It was the prospect of being fired that achieved the desired effect.

"Maybe we should call it quits," Davis would tell Herrera. "You should look around. I'll look around for you, you look around."

At first, Herrera was terrified by the thought of losing the only job he had as an adult, the job he loved, working for the man he revered.

"It was never, 'You got two weeks,'" Herrera recalled. "It was always just left out there, so you never knew exactly where you stood. That's what made it tougher because you always felt like you were walking on quicksand. I'm sure I wasn't the only one."

Herrera also became adept at recognizing nuances that tipped him off about Davis' state of mind. It was unmistakable on phone calls.

"Hello, this is Al. Al Davis. You know, Al Davis," Davis would say at the beginning of some calls.

"Then I knew he was in a good mood," Herrera said.

Davis never hesitated to remind people that he was in charge. Occasionally, that entailed more than verbal lashings.

One time in the 1980s, Kingdon was speaking with Gary Huff, the head of the finance department. Huff told Kingdon how Davis would come up to him on Fridays and say, "I may fire you this weekend."

Davis never followed through on the threat, but it was not long after that Huff left on his own volition.

Mike Reinfeldt, a former Pro Bowl safety for the Houston Oilers, also served as the Raiders chief financial executive during the mid-1980s. He eventually left to take a similar position at the University of Southern California. The final straw, he told Kebric, came when Davis called on Christmas Day one year and told him to come to the office.

"Mike said he didn't mind working long hours, but he had had enough," when Davis expected him to work on Christmas.

Reinfeldt wasn't the exception. Kebric and Kingdon became accustomed to phone calls from Davis on Christmas and New Year's Day. They also worked on Easter.

"Al generally would call in the afternoon on Christmas to inquire about some player," Kebric said. "Or if a game was going on, he would ask if I was watching the game and who I liked. On New Year's Day, I would receive a call during the Rose Bowl game."

When Kingdon was scouting at USC, he visited with Reinfeldt, who related that, "The difference between working for the Raiders and USC was startling."

For instance, when Christmas break came, Reinfeldt said that he called USC's athletic director. Even though they were on a break, Reinfeldt started to tell the athletic director where he was going to be each day and how he would be able to reach him. The athletic director asked Reinfeldt why he was passing on this information.

Reinfeldt said that he was doing so in case the athletic director needed to call him for something.

"I'm not going to call you," the athletic director said, "and you better not be calling me as well."

Kebric said, "The job to Al was 24 hours a day, 365 days out of the year. He discouraged you from taking vacations and such."

Kingdon recalled Davis taking vacations before the NFL became a year-round job and Davis' health deteriorated.

"There was a general feeling of a break around the office," Kingdon said. "There was always a different feeling when Al was in the office and when he wasn't. Once, when Al was out of town, Raiders executive Mike Ornstein sprayed himself with Al's cologne and walked around the office. Everyone who assumed that Al was out of town really sprung to attention."

Since Davis enjoyed working on football-related activities every day, he didn't understand why everyone else didn't feel the same way.

Former Raiders defensive line coach Mike Waufle and his wife went to Hawaii one year during a break between offseason activities and training camp.

"Why in the heck does Mike Waufle want to go to Hawaii?" Davis asked Kebric. "That's a total waste of time. He could be here working."

Kebric offered a simple explanation.

"Maybe his family wants to go to Hawaii," Kebric said.

"Who cares about his family? Let his family go to Hawaii," Davis replied. "Why is Mike going? He could be here."

One day, Davis was poring over a resume of a former general manager in his office when Kingdon walked in with some information.

Davis asked Kingdon about the individual who had sent the resume and Kingdon gave him an evaluation. Davis then looked up at Kingdon and said, "You know, there are a lot of people out there that would like your job."

Kingdon didn't miss a beat.

"I bet there are a lot more people that would like your job," he said. Davis hesitated for a second, seeming to ponder whether he had been insulted, and then laughed.

"I guess you're right," Davis said. "I'll see ya."

It didn't matter who you were. Davis treated everyone the same. The common theme was that Davis was in charge.

He once ordered Oakland Mayor Jerry Brown to "get the fuck out of here" when Brown tried to enter Davis' suite at a game at the Oakland Coliseum. Davis had no respect for Brown because he felt as if Brown wasn't doing anything to improve the dilapidated Coliseum.

"Most people would have been surprised to see the mayor of Oakland dressed down so thoroughly by Al," senior executive John Herrera said, "but I had seen him do it so many times to so many people, it almost seemed natural."

Another time, in the midst of an exhibition game against the 49ers in the late 1970s, long-time ABC announcer Howard Cosell needed something to keep viewers tuned into a Raiders blowout.

As usual, Cosell had just the answer. He summoned Raiders executive Al LoCasale to the broadcast booth and said in his sonorous tone, "LoCasale, we're dying. Get me Al Davis for an interview."

LoCasale, in turn, dispatched a runner to pass along Cosell's bold request. It wasn't long before LoCasale had an answer for Cosell.

"Tell Howard, 'Fuck no,'" Davis said, through LoCasale.

At the same time, Davis instructed team employee Steve Ballard to dash to the locker room and fetch Davis' hair brush and hair spray.

This wasn't a coincidence, naturally.

Sure enough, Cosell pleaded with LoCasale once again to get Davis to consent to an interview. He was desperate to find a way to keep the attention of viewers.

LoCasale stalled long enough for Davis to get his hair in order, at which time Davis agreed to go on air with Cosell.

This was typical Davis. He had the leverage and used it to his advantage. By saying no to Cosell's first request, Davis asserted his control of the situation, forced Cosell to plead for the interview, then walked away with Cosell feeling as if he was indebted to Davis.

Davis hired Mike White in 1995 to be his head coach in large part because of a strong recommendation from former 49ers head coach and close friend Bill Walsh. Davis had hired Walsh to be on his coaching staff in 1966, and Walsh credited Davis with laying a foundation for his career as an offensive genius.

The Raiders jumped to an 8-2 start under White in 1995. However, they dropped their final six games that season and in 1996 posted a 7-9 mark. Davis fired White on Christmas Eve.

At an East-West Shrine Game practice at Stanford in early 1997, Davis spotted Walsh and teed off in a raised voice, so that those in attendance could hear his displeasure.

"Oh, the great Bill Walsh," Davis said. "You really gave me a great recommendation with Mike White."

"Bill just accepted it," Kebric said. "He apologized and said, 'I'm sorry that things didn't work out.' He was such a classy person."

Many of the other NFL coaches and scouts watching practice that day cringed at the sight of one legendary NFL figure berating another.

Like Kingdon, Kebric learned to stand his ground against Davis. Kebric said that Davis steamrollered those who failed to stand up to him. Davis advocated the Socratic Method of inquiry, whereby he would ask myriad questions as a means of fostering critical thinking.

"If you said player A was better than player B, and player B was better than player C, and then you said player C was better than A, he would jump on the contradiction," Kingdon said. "You knew not to B.S. him. Like a lawyer, almost always, when Al asked a question, he already knew the answer. He had great retention."

In many ways, Davis also was like a boxer. He spent time feeling out his opponent, searching for a weakness, probing, probing, probing. Then, when he spotted an opening, he delivered a strong jab, an opening strike to the face. He gained the upper hand from the outset, set the tone and dictated things the rest of the way. In fact, Davis was a big boxing fan. On a number of occasions when the Raiders were in Los Angeles, the scouts adjourned meetings so that Davis could watch closed-circuit boxing matches on TV in the video room. Some owners even referred to Davis as "Bummy," the nickname of a Brooklyn-based boxer from the late-1930s, early 1940s named Al "Bummy" Davis.

"He would always hit you where he thought you might not have an answer, where he thought he might know something that you didn't know or put you in a position of weakness," Herrera said. "I might be working on something and every day would be like studying for a final exam. You had to have all your facts straight, you had to have everything covered and you tried to have everything in order that he might ask.

"You wanted to make sure that you had, not just an answer, but the right answer. A well-thought-out, reasoned response to a question. Invariably, he would know what you were ready for and he would try to find the thing that he didn't think you weren't ready for. He had the knack to hit you where you weren't expecting it at all. You're on the defensive, back-pedaling from the outset."

Even so, Davis expected you to be on your game. It was acceptable to him if someone didn't know the answer to a question.

"As soon as you tried to bullshit Al, you were done," Herrera said. "It was all over. That would just take him to another level of anger. Then he's pissed. You're trying to B.S., and you don't bullshit a guy like Al. The second you start, he would say, 'This is bullshit, I don't want to hear it.' He didn't have time for that."

Yet, when Davis wanted to vent, he expected you to be all ears.

The Raiders, like all NFL teams, flew on private charters. The seating arrangement was for Davis, the coaches, Dr. Robert Albo, Jim Otto, and their spouses, to be in first class.

What essentially was business class would be reserved for the Raiders front office staff, followed by other guests and team sponsors. The players, separated by a curtain from the other sections, occupied the rest of the plane.

> "As soon as you tried to bullshit Al, you were done. It was all over. That would just take him to another level of anger."

Kingdon recalled the flights to road games as being fairly relaxed. The return flights, however, proved to be less than pleasant, especially after a Raiders loss. The worst aspect of such trips for Kingdon, on the heels of a loss, was having to meet with Davis at the front of the plane, going over what happened around the league and what had occurred in the Raiders game.

"What made it particularly unpleasant was how Al would, in a loud and clear voice, be critical of the coaches, either as a group or individually," Kingdon said.

It would put Kingdon in a rather uncomfortable position.

"You certainly did not want to agree with him and embarrass the coaches, which wouldn't be appreciated by the insulted individuals," Kingdon said. "At the same time, disagreeing with Al would be even worse, as he would make his point even louder."

Kingdon learned over time that the best solution proved to be showing Davis an expressionless face, neither agreeing nor disagreeing with him, just allowing him to blow off steam.

There was a fine line with Davis. Anyone who crossed that line incurred Davis' wrath and wasn't welcomed back in the Raiders family. Davis was the sole arbiter, fair or not.

"Once you crossed Al, you weren't getting back in," Herrera said. "He had brutal, exacting standards."

Longtime head athletic trainer George Anderson learned that lesson in the mid-1990s, when he got pushed out by Davis after 35 years with the Raiders. He joined the organization in 1960, its first year. Anderson's crime: He refused to go on national TV and criticize former Raiders team physician Dr. Robert Huizenga for his book *You're Okay, It's Just a Bruise*. Davis also wanted Anderson to defend then-Raiders orthopedist Robert Rosenfeld. Huizenga's book was critical of the Raiders, in particular Dr. Rosenfeld, for their handling of injured players. Huizenga had been treating Anderson's ailing wife, so Anderson said he didn't feel comfortable speaking out against Huizenga.

Davis didn't care. This was a test of Anderson's loyalty to Davis and the Raiders. If Davis didn't have that, Anderson didn't belong with the Raiders.

Davis was livid.

After a game in New England, Anderson approached Davis with the postgame injury report, as was customary.

"I'm through with you," Davis told Anderson. "If you can't defend a man you've worked with all these years, I want to have nothing to do with you."

Anderson said Davis fired him after that game. He actually worked the remainder of the season, without speaking to Davis again, and retired on his own accord.

Davis worked hard to control the flow and content of information that emanated from within the Raiders organization. He always remained vigilant.

In the mid-1980s, mini-camps weren't well publicized. Davis did everything he could to keep the Raiders offseason gatherings as private as possible.

One spring, Brigham Young University assistant coach Roger French learned that the Raiders were conducting a mini-camp (generally, three days of offseason team practices). Given that French was in Southern California on a recruiting trip, he phoned Raiders personnel director Ron Wolf and asked for permission to come and watch practice in El Segundo. Wolf agreed to the request.

Prior to practice, Kingdon received a phone call from Davis asking general questions about what time practice started and what was going on. Kingdon told Davis the practice time and, so that Davis would not be taken aback, informed him that Roger French, the offensive line coach at BYU, would be at practice

"How did he know about our camp?" Davis asked.

"It was in the papers," Kingdon replied.

"Who gave him permission?" Davis snapped.

"Ron," Kingdon said.

"If I see anyone talking to him and giving out any information, I may just fire them on the spot," Davis said.

At some point, Davis and French ended up near each other during the practice. Davis went over to French and engaged him in a conversation.

"Al could not have been more welcoming," Kingdon recalled.

"Roger, great to see you," Davis said. "Glad to have you here."

Davis proceeded to share with French whatever he could about his players.

"Roger, look at that guy, Vance Mueller. We drafted him this year. He runs a 4.4. Do you know Brad Cochran from Michigan? Did you play against him? He has great size and runs a 4.4."

Another time, Jon Kingdon's brother Ken was invited to attend a mini-camp. He was one of the few outsiders present. In the middle of practice, Davis called over Kingdon and pointed out a stranger on the practice field and asked who he was.

"It's my brother Ken," Jon Kingdon told Davis.

Davis started muttering.

"What the fuck?" Davis said. "A preacher. What the hell?"

Kingdon asked Davis if anything was wrong. Davis said, "No," and walked away.

Jon Kingdon learned later that day that John Herrera had been asked earlier who Kingdon's brother was, and Herrera told Davis that he thought it was the team preacher. Suddenly, it became clear to Kingdon what Al had been muttering about.

Few, if any, succeeded in crossing Davis and getting back in his good graces, even if the transgression seemingly was minor or unintentional. Chuck Pagano, who later became the Indianapolis Colts head coach, fell into this category in 2011, the year Davis died.

Davis had fired head coach Tom Cable and promoted offensive coordinator Hue Jackson to be his head coach. Naturally, anyone with ties to Davis got linked to vacancies on Jackson's staff.

So it was that Pagano, who was the Baltimore Ravens secondary coach, was asked by local writers if he had any interest in becoming the Raiders defensive coordinator.

"I had a great experience, or sentence … ," Pagano said, in reference to his stint with the Raiders as their defensive backs coach in 2005-06. "And congratulations to Hue Jackson, it's well deserved. And he will earn every cent that they pay him. It won't be much, but he will earn every nickel. But I had a great experience out there. And two years was plenty."

That's all Davis, who had contemplated offering Pagano the defensive coordinator's job, needed to hear.

Kingdon ran into Pagano at the Senior Bowl and asked him about his pointed remarks. Pagano was apologetic about what he had said.

"As I'm saying it, I can't believe the words are going out of my mouth," Pagano said.

Pagano then asked Kingdon if he should call Davis. Kingdon said he didn't think that Davis would take his call. Instead, he should write a personal letter to Davis explaining what happened. Davis read every letter that reached his desk.

Sure enough, Pagano wrote a very sincere and heartfelt letter to Davis, with a copy to Kingdon, explaining what happened. Davis never acknowledged the letter to Kingdon, "but I'm sure he appreciated the sentiment in Chuck's letter," Kingdon said.

Another example came in 2008, when head coach Lane Kiffin attacked Davis and, by extension, the Raiders on a daily basis. Their relationship soured soon after Davis hired Kiffin in January of 2007, but Kiffin at least kept private his displeasure with Davis for that first season.

Still, there were signs of a fissure in the relationship early on. Midway through the 2007 season, Kiffin wanted to fire offensive coordinator Greg Knapp, whom Kiffin called "a blackboard coach."

"You hired Knapp, not me," Davis said. "I'm not going to fire him."

The gloves came off in 2008. First, Kiffin attempted to fire defensive coordinator Rob Ryan. He also refused to wear Raiders gear at the Senior Bowl, expressed interest in a college coaching vacancy and criticized Davis for not bringing in enough players during training camp, among other things.

"Every day, Lane was firing a salvo at Al and the team," Herrera said. "It was unbelievable. I would say, 'Al, you got to see this.' He was ready to fire him before the season even started."

Instead, Davis waited until four games into the season before he fired Kiffin for cause, which meant Davis wasn't going to pay Kiffin the balance of his contract.

"Al didn't really care about the money," Kebric said. "He was going to have the last word. Al Davis not only fired Lane Kiffin, he was going to destroy Lane Kiffin. It wasn't good enough just to fire him."

Davis wasn't able to prevent Kiffin from getting hired at the University of Tennessee, but he did prevail in his case against Kiffin over unearned wages.

Sometimes, it wasn't enough for Davis just to fire coaches. It really bothered him to continue paying their contracts without getting anything in return. He wanted them gone on his terms.

After the 2006 season, Davis fired offensive coordinator Tom Walsh, quarterbacks coach Jim McElwain, assistant offensive line coach Irv Eatman and assistant defensive backs coach Lorenzo Ward. Davis offered the jettisoned coaches a much smaller percentage of their salary if they walked away from their contracts.

McElwain was hired soon after as the offensive coordinator at Fresno State University, so he took Davis' offer. Walsh, Eatman and Ward wanted full payment, which they were entitled to receive.

Instead, Davis came up with what Kingdon considered a rather odd suggestion. A month or so before the 2007 NFL draft, Davis told Kingdon that he wanted Walsh, Eatman and Ward assigned to go on difficult scouting trips. Davis hoped that the coaches would opt out of their contracts rather than beating the bushes.

"I told Al that their reports would be of little use in the draft," Kingdon said.

"I don't care," Davis said.

Kingdon suggested that Davis just have the coaches watch film at the Raiders facility in Alameda.

"I don't want them in the building," Davis responded.

Kingdon then pointed out that sending the coaches to the colleges, as Davis demanded, was going to be quite expensive.

"I don't care," Davis said. "I want them out there."

Kingdon tried another approach. He reasoned with Davis that the coaches likely would spend most of their time on the road looking for another job.

"Good, then we'll have cause to fire them," Davis said.

As instructed, Kingdon set up scouting plans for Walsh, Eatman and Ward. He assigned each coach eight colleges to visit. All three responded in a positive manner when informed of their new duty.

A few weeks later, Davis asked Kingdon how the coaches had performed. Kingdon told Davis that the coaches had fulfilled all of their assignments.

Then came a call from Davis a few weeks before training camp. Davis started by telling Kingdon that the bills for the scouting trips for the fired coaches had just come in and that they were really expensive.

"No kidding," Kingdon said.

Davis then queried, "Why did we send them out? Why didn't we just have them watch film in the office?"

"I reminded him that I had made that same suggestion when he first called me and that he said that he did not want them in the building," Kingdon said.

"That's right," Davis said, "Well, next time, we'll rent an office down the street."

The ill-fated strategy ended up costing Davis in the neighborhood of $20,000 for travel expenses.

There were a select few that Davis encountered during his nearly five decades with the Raiders who not only held their ground versus Davis, but were able at times to set Davis back on his heels.

Terry Robiskie was such an individual. Robiskie, 6-foot-1 and 210 pounds in his playing days, joined the Raiders as an eighth-round pick in the 1977 NFL draft. He had been a standout quarterback at Second Ward High School in Edgard, Louisiana, before he converted to running back at Louisiana State University. He was so dominant in high school — he turned quarterback sneaks into 97-, 84- and 80-yard touchdowns in one game — that he had offers from national powers such as Notre Dame, the University of Southern California, Nebraska, Oklahoma and UCLA. Robiskie's journey took him from a small school situated along the west bank of the Mississippi River, in the midst of cane fields, to the NFL. He oozed confidence and allowed nothing and no one to intimidate him.

Robiskie played for the Raiders from 1977-1979. On the day he was cut by the Raiders, Davis told Robiskie that he would make a good coach once his playing career ended. Robiskie played for the Miami Dolphins in 1980 and 1981 and then retired as a player due to a broken back.

True to his word, Davis hired Robiskie as an assistant coach in 1982 and during his 12 seasons with the Raiders he coached special teams, running backs, tight ends and served as the offensive coordinator.

In 1986, the Raiders signed running back Ethan Horton, who had been drafted in the first round by the Kansas City Chiefs in 1985 after a standout career at the University of North Carolina. Horton struggled his rookie season with the Chiefs, and he was cut before he received a second chance.

Davis pounced and signed Horton in one of his signature moves, taking another team's cast-off and developing that player into an integral performer for the Raiders.

"This was the perfect scenario for Al," Kingdon said. "Horton was a former first-round pick, he was big, athletic and a great person, and Al was going to convert him to tight end."

Robiskie, the tight ends coach, was charged with the task of teaching Horton the position.

Davis called Robiskie one morning to see if he had worked out Horton. Robiskie informed Davis that he had other things that had required his attention.

"What the fuck are you doing?" Davis said, as he exploded at Robiskie. "I can't believe you didn't find the time to work him out. I don't know what the fuck you're doing."

Davis then hung up the phone.

Later that day, Davis called Robiskie again and left a message for Robiskie to call back.

Robiskie received the message, but he didn't call back.

The next day, Davis reached Robiskie by phone.

"Terry, did you get the message that I wanted to talk to you yesterday?" Davis asked.

"Yes, I did," Robiskie said.

"Why didn't you call me back?" Davis wanted to know.

"Boss, I can only take being motherfucked by you once a day," Robiskie explained.

"OK," Davis said, and he then continued their conversation.

Even more important than his excellent coaching was Robiskie's ability to forge strong relationships with the players. This enabled him to serve as a buffer between Davis and the players.

By 1989, Davis and running back Marcus Allen had a strained relationship. Allen had gone from lead back to just another player on the sideline with the addition of Bo Jackson, a Davis favorite.

Robiskie, then the running backs coach, inserted Allen late into a 1989 game against the Phoenix Cardinals. The Raiders trailed 14-9, but had the ball at the Cardinals four-yard line. Allen had played sparingly to that point, running two times for six yards and catching one pass for nine yards.

Jackson had rushed 22 times for 114 yards and Steve Smith had carried eight times for 30 yards. Allen was an afterthought. But Robiskie called upon Allen, even though he knew it was against Davis' wishes.

"He wasn't supposed to be in," Robiskie said. "I put him in. I said, 'OK, we got to win the game. I'm going to either win it with him or lose it with him.'"

Allen converted a fourth-and-one play into a Raiders first down with a leap over the top of the pile for three yards. On the next play, he scored a game-deciding touchdown with 40 seconds left in the game.

After the game, Robiskie was on his way out of the locker room, just as Davis was on his way inside. Davis grabbed Robiskie.

"You took me on and won," Davis said, as he gently slapped Robiskie's face a couple of times, as if a mafia member doing so for effect.

Robiskie also recalled Davis saying, "Oh, man, I can't believe you put him back in the game. He wasn't supposed to be in. Why did you put him back in?"

Robiskie wanted to win the game just as badly as Davis. Enough said.

"I'm glad it worked," Davis added. "I'm glad you put him in. We won the game."

Allen said Davis gave him a dirty look after the game on his way to the locker room. He chalked it up to just another chapter in an already awkward relationship.

It was Robiskie who kept tense situations from boiling over by providing levity. He also spoke his mind, without fear.

In 1993, the Raiders signed wide receiver James Jett, who went undrafted out of West Virginia due to concerns about a knee injury. Jett, a member of the 1992 U.S. Olympics track team, ran the 40-yard dash in the low 4.3s, and caught every ball thrown to him in a mini-camp.

At the end of the camp, Davis met with the coaches to go over the players. When Jett's name came up, Davis asked some of the offensive coaches where, in retrospect, they would now draft Jett. The answers ranged from the first to the third round.

Davis then asked Robiskie the same question.

Robiskie said he wouldn't draft Jett.

Incredulously, Davis asked why he wouldn't draft Jett after what he had seen the prior three days.

"Why would I draft a player that I could sign as a free agent?" Robiskie said.

Davis knew that he had been topped and had no comeback and simply responded, "Let's go to the defense."

On very few occasions did someone have the temerity to challenge Davis in public. Senior executive John Herrera not only went toe-to-toe with Davis, he traded verbal blows and remained employed even after the high-profile encounter.

Herrera knew the showdown was coming for months, with no way to head it off.

The wheels were set in motion when the schedule came out in April one year. At that time, Herrera learned the dates of the Raiders 10 road games — eight regular-season and two exhibition. Once he got that information, he commenced securing things such as hotels, transportation vehicles, police escorts, practice fields and meals in every city the Raiders were scheduled to play that season.

As the Raiders advance man, Herrera faced a daunting task putting in place everything the team needed on its trips away from home. At the top of his list was finding top-notch hotels that featured the many things the Raiders desired: at least 100 rooms, concentrated on two or three floors; properly-sized meeting rooms; proximity to the stadium where the Raiders were going to play that week; and a tailored menu.

More times than not, NFL teams find a hotel to their liking with little difficulty. In this instance, Herrera encountered an insurmountable obstacle from the outset when he tried to book a hotel in Baltimore. A convention taking place the same week as the Raiders-Ravens game filled the hotels in downtown Baltimore before Herrera got a crack.

That left a hotel about 30 minutes away from downtown Baltimore as the next-best option. Redskins opponents that couldn't find a hotel in Washington, D.C., often stayed at the hotel Herrera booked.

"You want to be as close to the stadium as you can so that on game day you have the shortest ride," Herrera said. "You don't want the guys sitting on the bus any longer than they have to."

In addition to being the nicest hotel available outside of Baltimore, the people who worked there were accustomed to dealing with the needs of an NFL team.

"It was a nice facility," Herrera said. "They had everything we needed. It's a big production, a major deal."

Herrera typically wrapped up the roster of hotels within five or six weeks after the schedule was released. Once he reached that point, he distributed a spreadsheet to an array of people.

"The first thing I would do from there is put it on Al's desk," Herrera said, "so he couldn't say, 'What the fuck are you doing? I never saw a copy.'

"He claimed that he didn't know about it until we got there. But he always had that information. I was always braced for a question, but he liked to ignore it until the time came to make the trip. Then he was interested."

For months, Herrera feared this trip. It didn't matter how nice the hotel had turned out to be, Davis was bound to find fault with the distance from the stadium. It wouldn't have done any good to broach the topic in advance, either. Herrera just had to deal with the fallout on the spot.

"Oh, yeah, I knew it was coming," Herrera said. "I knew that he was not going to be happy with this place."

Herrera had an added worry. Davis no longer was riding on one of the six buses used by the team on road trips, so Herrera had to find a driver for Davis who could follow certain prompts.

"I tried to coach the drivers up so that they knew what to do whenever Al started to bitch about, 'How much further do we have to go?' which he would do every single time. 'How much further do we have to go? Where is it?' I said, 'Look, when he starts in with that, tell him that it's 10 minutes, at the most, and we'll be there soon,'" Herrera said. "All the other teams do it. It's a piece of cake. Just really downplay it.

"Every once in awhile, some yahoo driver would say something like, 'Oh, the Chiefs stayed at the Marriott, two blocks from the stadium. I'm surprised you guys didn't stay there.' Somebody would play that card. Al would get out of the car fuming. 'What the fuck! The Chiefs stayed there! Why are we 15 minutes away?' I got that a few times."

On the Baltimore trip, Herrera knew that it was imperative that Davis' driver keep Davis distracted and not preoccupied with the length of the drive. Herrera had made the drive a couple times before, and he sensed the potential for Davis to become irritated. As Herrera rode on one of the Raiders buses, he experienced a sinking feeling. The trip seemed to take forever. He could only imagine what was going on in Davis' car.

"I knew when we were driving, and we're driving more, I was thinking, 'Oh, shit, Al is going to be absolutely fucking pissed,'" Herrera said. "It seemed like it took a week and a half to get out there because I'm worrying about it."

When the buses arrived, Herrera went inside the hotel lobby and made sure that all the players, coaches, staff and guests received their room keys, itineraries and whatever else they requested.

Davis liked to hang outside and watch the proceedings, almost like a shepherd keeping tabs on his flock. He wanted to make sure that everyone made it off the bus and into the lobby.

Once Herrera finished, he waited in the lobby for Davis to make his way inside so that he could give Davis his room key and then ask Davis when he wanted to eat. No matter when the Raiders arrived somewhere, the first thing Davis wanted to do was eat a meal. Herrera would find out who Davis wanted to dine with, and then he would take care of the invitations.

Davis ultimately made his way into the lobby, and Herrera made his way over to a group that included Davis' brother Jerry, Dr. Bob Albo, George Blanda, Ted Hendricks and a few others.

"It was still pretty crowded in the lobby, too," Herrera said. "And Al just goes off."

"What the fuck are we doing out here?" Davis asked Herrera in a raised voice. "What the fuck were you thinking? What the hell? It took us 45 fucking minutes to get out here. What are we going to do? You're going to have the guys sitting on the buses for 45 minutes. They're going to be stiff by the time they get to the stadium."

Herrera was not surprised by Davis' outburst, though others were stunned.

"Everybody was looking, kind of like, Oh, shit. Now what? What's coming next?" Herrera said. "I tried to throw some soft shots in there like, 'Al, a lot of teams have stayed out here. It's a little further distance than we like, as you know. But the Inner Harbor was totally jammed. There were no available hotels when the schedule came out.'"

"Why didn't you call me?" Davis said.

"I couldn't say, 'Look, I gave you the list five months ago.' That wouldn't fly," Herrera said.

"Why didn't you tell me? Why didn't you call me? I could have called Barron Hilton," Davis persisted.

"Of course, there is no Hilton Hotel in the Inner Harbor," Herrera said. "I wanted to say, 'What's Barron going to do, Al, build a hotel in four months so we can stay there?'"

No answer was going to satisfy Davis. He was out for blood. Herrera had had enough, though.

"That's it," Herrera said. "I don't appreciate you taking me on like this in front of all these people in the lobby. I don't think it's fair. It's fucked up. You're wrong. It pisses me off. I always do what's best for the team, and you. You know that. This was the best I could do here."

Davis kept up his attack.

"I finally had enough," Herrera said. "That's it. Screw it."

There were 25-30 people watching this exchange.

"I just whipped around and left Al standing there," Herrera said. "Nobody does that to Al. You get dismissed. Nobody talks to him like that. Nobody. People were mortified. It was kind of like a scene in a movie where everybody is just dumbfounded. I didn't care at that point. He had crossed the line."

The exchange lasted about five minutes. Herrera retreated to his hotel room. He didn't have a lot of time to cool down, but it was enough to know that it wasn't over.

"I just knew that I was in trouble," Herrera said. "I knew that he wasn't going to let it go. And that there was going to be fallout."

About 30 minutes later, Herrera returned to the lobby. He then encountered Davis and his group as they prepared to dine. He tried to gauge Davis' mood and was told that he was not very happy with the location and the hotel. He chose to avoid Davis if possible.

When game day rolled around, Davis was still carping about every little thing. Davis fired off some of his comments toward senior assistant Bruce Allen, who tended to find such things funny, especially when he wasn't the one in Davis' crosshairs.

"I bet you really hope we win this game," Allen said to Herrera.

The Raiders lost. Soon after the Raiders returned to the Bay Area, Herrera was informed that he had been replaced as the team's advance man.

"Al never presented it to me like, 'Boy, you really screwed up,' it was just explained to me that it was something that had been under consideration for a while," Herrera said.

Davis did have the ability to tailor his demeanor to suit the situation.

"He had dual personalities," Kebric said. "He could be very, very charming in certain settings and strong and demanding in others. When he was in a good mood, he would quickly transition into his Southern accent."

Bay Area radio personality Bruce Macgowan, also a long-time member of the Raiders radio broadcast team, remembers some fascinating telephone conversations with Davis, where the pair would discuss a variety of subjects other than football.

"Two things that Al loved to talk about were politics and history," said Macgowan, who first met Davis in 1977. "I remember one particular conversation where he said he was an admirer of Vladimir Putin, not necessarily as a person but as a leader. Al said, 'That country is a mess. Like it or not, at least under the Communist regime, they had a system. People don't realize what a mess Russia is today, and that guy is holding it together. I give him some credit.'"

Macgowan went on to add that, "Al had an oddball sense of humor, along with an amazing memory."

Kingdon and Kebric accompanied Davis to dinners, parties, political events and funerals, where top corporate executives, Hollywood stars, famous athletes and national politicians were present. In those settings, Davis would exude charm and personality. He always became the center of attention, even in places filled with a variety of influential people.

"Those in attendance seemed to forget about the other famous names in the room and peppered us with questions about Al," Kebric said. "What is Al Davis actually like? What is it like to work for Al Davis? And, of course, are the Raiders going to the Super Bowl this year?"

Hall of Fame defensive tackle Warren Sapp loved talking to Davis and soaking up some of his vast knowledge. In particular, Sapp enjoyed hearing stories about the AFL, a league "where all the bad-asses came from." To that end, Sapp said he sought out Davis and relished their conversations.

Sapp was in the minority among the players when it came to making time for Davis. In his first year with the Raiders, in 2004, he was walking down the hall at the team's facility with cornerback Charles Woodson and a couple other players.

"Man, you should have seen these fools scramble," Sapp said. "I was like, 'What are you all doing?' They're like, 'You don't smell him?'"

Everyone in the Raiders organization was cognizant of Davis' distinctive cologne. The odor from his cologne arrived long before Davis, which afforded employees ample time to adjust their behavior or disappear.

Sapp, Woodson and the other players were in the doorway of the locker room when the warning was issued.

"Do I smell him? Man, what the hell you talking about?" Sapp asked Woodson, who already was on the move.

No answer was forthcoming. Instead, Sapp heard a booming voice from down the hallway.

"Warren?" Davis said.

"Hey, what's going on, Baby?" Sapp responded.

"It sounded like there was a bunch more around this corner just a second ago," Davis said.

"Well, they went to go to breakfast or to work out, or to the training room," Sapp said. "I was thinking, 'Holy shit, they just take off running like this when he's around?'"

Sapp later found out why players scrambled.

"Because Al would roll up on you and say whatever the hell was on his mind," Sapp said. "He caught Bobby Hamilton coming out of the shower one time."

"Hey, Bobby, it looked like they were running in the 'C' gap," Davis told Hamilton, who played defensive end for the Raiders in 2004-05.

"I swear to God, we get back to the film room, and they are running in the 'C' gap, right where Bobby is," Sapp said. "I swear to God. If that old man said something to you about your play on Sunday, that shit was so true. He didn't miss nothing. He didn't miss nothing.

"He might have missed on a couple pieces of advice from some people that he shouldn't have listened to but, hey, man, when you've done it your way, and you're a champion, and the team of the decade, and the winningest franchise, all the things that he was, what the hell? It's like Donald Trump. Donald Trump ain't turning no corner softly. When you're already successful, why change?"

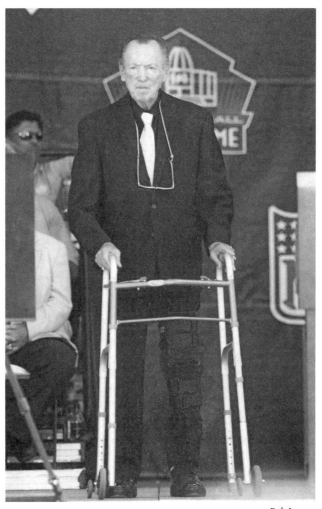

Bob Larson

Al Davis initially resisted using a walker in public because he wanted to project a strong, healthy image. Later, he decided it was more important to be seen (above, at the 2006 Pro Football Hall of Fame induction ceremony in Canton, Ohio) even with a walker.

CHAPTER THREE

The Fighter

Al Davis loved to fight. He fought the National Football League when the Raiders were members of the upstart American Football League and helped bring about a merger. He fought against segregation in the South when a hotel refused to accommodate his African-American players for an exhibition game in Mobile, Alabama. He fought NFL commissioner Pete Rozelle when the league tried to prevent the Raiders from moving from Oakland to Los Angeles. Davis battled running back Marcus Allen, coaches Mike Shanahan, Jon Gruden and Lane Kiffin, media, other owners, game officials, you name it. It's as if he needed an enemy, real or imagined. Anything. Anybody. Bring it on. And Davis usually won.

Yet he never found a way to defeat the one thing he fought against longer and harder than anything his entire life: death. Davis said numerous times that death was the one thing that he couldn't figure out a way to dominate and overcome. No amount of time breaking down video, diagramming defensive schemes or intimidating the opponent mattered when it came to fighting death, and that frustrated Davis to no end. Davis died in 2011 at the age of 82 as a result of heart failure.

Until the end, Davis was consumed by death and contemplated its meaning all the time.

Jon Kingdon once walked into Davis' office for three straight days and informed Davis of the death of someone Davis knew.

Walking by Davis' office on the fourth day, Kingdon approached Davis, who yelled, "Don't come in here. I don't want to hear who died."

It got so bad that, at one point, Davis complained that all he had been doing was presenting people to the Pro Football Hall of Fame and going to funerals.

It was a never-ending battle for Davis against an opponent that had no discernible weakness. Davis was encouraged by the fact that his mother, Rose, lived a long, healthy life. However, it became apparent several years in advance of Al Davis' death that he wasn't going to live as long as his mother, who passed away in 2001.

"My mother, you know, she lived a long time, 103," Davis said in 2008. "I hope nothing happens (to me), because disease is the one thing, boy, I tell you, it's tough to lick. It's tough to lick those goddamn diseases. I don't know why they can't."

Davis went to great lengths to help friends, family and those who worked for him to combat illnesses and medical conditions. His outspoken desire to beat death didn't go unnoticed.

Kingdon recalled a letter Davis received one day from a woman, in which she said, in part:

"Mr. Davis: I read recently about your inability to dominate death. If you are looking for eternal life, you should consider accepting Jesus as your Lord and Savior."

The letter went on to outline for Davis the benefits of becoming a born-again Christian. "In that Al was Jewish, I'm sure he did not see this as a real option," Kingdon said.

Davis was very self-conscious about his diminishing capacities. He first allowed the public to see his increasing physical limitations in 2005, when he arrived at training camp in Napa, California, using a walker. He had been using the walker for some time, but this marked the first time Davis allowed media and whomever else might be in attendance at the typically closed practice to see him needing an aid to get around.

"The thing that Al really fought was conceding that he needed to use a walker," Kingdon said. "He resisted this as long as he could."

At the behest of the Raiders team physician, Robert Albo, Davis yielded to this need after falling down a couple of times. On one such incident, Davis fell backward and cracked open his head.

Bruce Kebric said it was quite difficult for Davis to allow people to see him using a walker, particularly those outside the Raiders organization.

"He wanted to project a healthy, strong image," Kebric said. "He was using the walker long before, just not in public. He reached a point where he wanted to go to practice and the only way he could go to practice was to use the walker. He was determined that, 'I don't care what people say about me, I'm going to go out and see these players.'"

Yet Davis did not capitulate easily. He worked hard on keeping his body in shape. He had daily workouts with Chris Pearson, one of the Raiders' assistant strength and conditioning coaches. Still, using a walker showed that, no matter how much time and effort he spent on his health, Davis was mortal. His most-feared opponent had built a sizable lead and was running out the clock.

Steadily, Davis lost ground as his health deteriorated. Yet, he remained steadfast that one day he would prevail, just as he had in most things he encountered his whole life.

Evidence to the contrary mounted. In 2006, Davis stopped attending the annual NFL scouting combine in Indianapolis, as his mobility became more limited. Chief executive Amy Trask told the media that Davis had a good excuse for why he didn't attend that first year.

"The rumors about his health are false. Al is as healthy and as vital as ever," Trask said, when asked at the time about Davis' absence. "He had no reason to attend the combine when we had people in place there and he could watch the workouts on the NFL Network."

Kingdon offered a different perspective:

"He opted not to go because he lost the ability to walk up the six steps from the field to his usual spot in the first row. His legs would not allow him to do that. He certainly did not want to have people see him being carried up the steps."

Perhaps coincidentally, Colts general manager Bill Polian brought it to Kebric's attention that private suites were available during the combine, for $10,000 for the week.

"If you want one, give me a call," Polian told Kebric.

More and more teams were going that route so they could have all their personnel in one private area. Kebric passed along the information to Kingdon and asked him to check into the prospect. Kingdon followed up with the Colts and relayed the information to one of Davis' secretaries.

"She said that when Mr. Davis saw it, he angrily asked who got the information," Kingdon said.

The secretary informed Davis that Kingdon secured the information and that it was done just in case he was interested.

"He later called me and said that it wouldn't be necessary," Kingdon said.

That's also about the time that Davis stopped riding on one of the team buses on road trips. Senior executive John Herrera was working as the advance man for the Raiders at the time. He traveled ahead of the team and made sure that Davis and the Raiders had everything taken care of, which included a portable step for Davis to use in making his way on to the bus.

Things generally went off without a hitch on road trips. However, during a trip to Arizona for a preseason exhibition game against the Cardinals, the bus driver Herrera hired forgot to bring the portable step.

"I used this guy like 100 times," Herrera said. "This one time he forgot to bring his little step stool."

Davis processed the situation and decided to make a go of boarding the bus without the extra step.

"Al was standing there looking at the stairs," Herrera said. "He always had to kind of psych himself up to make that first step. He was standing there and everyone was waiting for him to make a move. Everyone was afraid to say anything."

Everyone knew better than to offer Davis help. He was going to figure out a way to overcome the obstacle, regardless how long it took or how difficult the challenge.

"He tried a couple of times and he couldn't do it," Herrera said.

Rather than asking for help, Davis turned to Herrera and vented his anger.

"What the fuck, you didn't get the step?" Davis said. "You didn't get it done."

Herrera kept his composure and defused the situation.

"Look, Al, I got a car right there," Herrera said. "Let's just get in the car, I'll put the car right in between the buses and you'll be right in the middle of everything. We'll be part of the escort."

That mollified Davis for a few minutes.

"All they could find was a car that you wouldn't want for Al," Herrera said. "He was just pissed. After that incident, we made sure there was always a black Lincoln Town Car there with the buses, and the car rode with the bus caravan."

In spite of his declining health, Davis never gave up. He always sought ways to combat his ailments, underwent numerous medical procedures and worked out as often as possible. It angered Davis when people quit fighting and seemingly accepted their fate. In particular, Davis struggled with the news that longtime friend and former San Francisco 49ers head coach Bill Walsh had opted against further treatment in his battle against leukemia. Walsh died in 2007 after a three-year fight.

"Al's biggest complaint was that Bill did not fight it to the end," Kebric said. "He never could understand why Bill or anyone would quit," no matter the circumstances.

Of course, Davis didn't go through strength- and morale-sapping chemotherapy treatments as Walsh had. Davis still held it against Walsh.

"Al was really upset with Bill because, Al said, 'Bill quit,'" Kebric said. "Al never quit. He fought it till the end."

> *It's clear that Davis suffered from something that robbed him of his mobility, strength and vitality for several years ... his body was essentially shutting down.*

Kingdon pointed out to Davis in a phone call that "the cure for Bill might have been worse than the disease."

"Bullshit!" Davis said, and slammed down the phone.

It's clear that Davis suffered from something that robbed him of his mobility, strength and vitality for several years. He never complained, though, according to Kingdon.

"His body was essentially shutting down," Kingdon said. "I assumed that it was some type of neurological problem, though he always blamed it on problems with his quadriceps."

In 2008, Davis said he received a battery of tests four times a year. He offered this assessment of his health.

"Other than the quadriceps and a little trouble with the walking, based on total balance, I'm fine," Davis said. "I'm healthy. You're going to have to have me around for a while."

Kingdon was around Davis every day at training camp in 2010, the last one that Davis attended. He would inform Davis about what transpired at training camp and around the league each day as Davis ate dinner. Even eating became a struggle.

"He could no longer make a fist and had to use two hands to do simple things like holding a glass of water," Kingdon said. "But he was adamant about not accepting help. He would battle with his food, having a fork in one hand and a knife in the other and battle to cut his food."

Davis' ability to swallow gradually diminished. It often seemed as if Davis was choking on his food. Hence, every meal was served with several tissues next to Davis' plate so that he could spit up the food that he wasn't able to swallow.

On one occasion, Kebric stopped by to speak with Davis. Kebric's arrival coincided with Davis again-having trouble swallowing his food. Kebric's instinct was to slap Davis on the back in an attempt to help.

"As he raised his hand, I immediately caught his eye and strongly shook my head," Kingdon said, cognizant of Davis' reluctance to seek help. "Bruce caught my signal and sat down."

Another time, talk show host Larry King and his wife Shawn Southwick, whose son Danny Southwick was a member of the Raiders coaching staff, joined Davis for lunch at training camp. It didn't take long for them to see that Davis wasn't at full strength.

"You could see how taken aback King was to see how much Al was having trouble with his motor skills, along with all of the spitting and choking," Kingdon said. "It was not a pretty sight to watch him suffer."

The muscles on the inside of Davis' wrists ceased functioning properly and the muscles on the back of Davis' hands pulled his fingers backward. This became evident at the handful of news conferences that Davis attended in his final years. Raising a glass to his mouth became a real chore, as he would trap the glass between the palms of his hands and bring it to his mouth in an awkward manner. Using a straw would have been easier, of course, but that also would have been tantamount to yielding ground to the enemy.

Heart failure was the official cause of death, but Davis' day-to-day symptoms bore the hallmarks of a disease called inclusion-body myositis, or IBM. The aforementioned slowly progressing disease attacks specific muscle groups, causing the affected muscles to atrophy as the immune system turns on the body. There is no cure, no known cause. Physical therapy is thought to help maintain and slow the loss of mobility for the chronic, progressive muscle inflammation and weakness. IBM primarily affects men, especially those at least 50 years old, and it isn't believed to be life-threatening. It's common for IBM to attack the muscles associated with the quadriceps and feet and the flexor muscles around the hands and wrists. It also interferes with swallowing in the latter stages, affects a person's grip and is the cause of frequent stumbles. Tripping and falls usually are the first signs of the disease.

Through it all, Davis remained involved with football activities until the day he died. He no longer attended practice every day. Rather, Davis kept abreast of his team by watching video taken from several cameras high above the football field.

As Davis' eyesight diminished, he leaned on others to help him identify players on the video that he watched.

Davis relied upon faxes a great deal, long after most people ceased to use that form of information sharing. As his vision deteriorated, the font size on the faxes for Davis increased.

"He would not concede that his vision was sorely diminished," Kingdon said.

Kingdon faxed stories each day. These were stories written by local, regional and national media about the Raiders and the league. Upon being provided the stories, Davis called Kingdon to discuss the subject matter.

"Not knowing how much he was reading now, I asked if he had gone through the stories," Kingdon said. "He ignored the question and said, just to go over what I had faxed. It was apparent that he was not able to read the stories, so I knew that I would from then on have to summarize the stories I was sending him. In spite of this, he still insisted on them being faxed each morning."

Davis did the best he could do every day, even though the tasks he once took for granted had become quite arduous.

"He probably was the most mentally tough person I've ever been around," Kebric said. "He would push himself, push himself. Despite his condition, he forced himself to do things."

Kebric frequently witnessed Davis in the weight room, catching medicine balls from aide Chris Pearson and lifting weights on three machines that Davis had designed.

"He wasn't going to give in," Kebric said. "He fought it until the end."

It, being death. Davis found a way to beat the Pittsburgh Steelers in the '70s despite season-ending defeats in 1972, '74 and '75. He found a way to beat the league in the courtroom. He discovered ways to beat opposing offensive and defensive schemes. But he went 0-1 against his most-feared opponent.

"Al said to us a number of times, 'There's only one thing in this world that I can't defeat, but I'm working on it,'" Kebric said.

Even with his health failing and his stamina lacking, Davis still enjoyed preparing for the draft each year. The process includes watching hundreds of hours of video on college all-star games and individual players. In his last couple of years, he restricted himself to watching video of one-on-one drills between offensive and defensive linemen from the Senior Bowl and East-West Shrine games, as well as profile tapes on the draft prospects.

The scouting and video departments put together the profile tapes which typically lasted about five minutes each and highlighted the positives and negatives of each player. Davis used these tapes to form his evaluation, Kingdon said.

Davis would then identify a couple of players he coveted in each round of the draft. In the last couple of years, lacking the endurance, Davis would come up with only one name per round.

"If that player was taken, he would have to go with whom the scouts suggested," Kingdon said.

During Davis' final draft in 2011, it was speculated that the player he most coveted was University of Nevada-Reno quarterback Colin Kaepernick, who was selected by the San Francisco 49ers in the second round at No. 36 overall. Then-head coach Hue Jackson said that he and Davis wanted Kaepernick and that both were angry when the 49ers traded up so that they could get the athletic signal-caller.

Davis, in fact, never even considered Kaepernick. Davis had traded for veteran quarterback Jason Campbell a year earlier, and, as his health was deteriorating, he didn't have the time to wait for a young quarterback to develop. The only player Davis targeted was University of Miami offensive tackle Orlando Franklin.

The question was, would Franklin last long enough for the Raiders to get him in the middle of the second round? Oakland didn't have a first-round pick as a result of a trade for New England Patriots defensive lineman Richard Seymour in 2009. Davis placed all his stock in Franklin making it to the Raiders at No. 48.

"Al was having a very difficult time physically at this point," Kingdon said. "It was very difficult for Al to sit for a long time. Somehow, he made it through the first day of the draft."

So did Franklin. Then, two picks ahead of the Raiders choice in the second round, the Denver Broncos selected Franklin. Davis had gambled that Franklin would fall to the Raiders, and he did not have a backup choice. Though reluctant, he agreed with the scouts and coaches to select offensive lineman Stefen Wisniewski, whose uncle Steve played for the Raiders from 1989-2001.

"We were all pleased to get Stefen," Kingdon said. "Al was incredibly frustrated at coming so close to selecting Franklin and was really steamed and aggravated. Thus, everyone knew to give him his space.

"The scouts were the only ones in the room with Davis after the Raiders picked Wisniewski. Recently hired offensive coach Bob Wylie hadn't been made aware of Davis demanding his space, especially on draft day. He also did not know that Davis wasn't fond of being touched in such a familiar manner. So, Wylie walked into the room and placed his arm on Davis' shoulder and happily said, "Nice pick, coach."

"Al turned ever so slowly and looked Bob right in the face and said, in a loud, clear voice, 'Get the fuck out of this room,'" Kingdon recalled.

Davis got one of the two players he wanted in the third round, University of Miami cornerback DeMarcus Van Dyke. That's the only selection Davis approved of during the first two days of the draft. To no one's surprise, Van Dyke posted the fastest 40-yard dash time at the scouting combine.

The Raiders then traded a 2011 seventh-round pick and a 2012 second-rounder to the New England Patriots for third- and fourth-round picks in 2011.

"He had taken a future-is-now philosophy," Kingdon said.

With the added third-rounder, Davis was hoping to select Curtis Marsh, a cornerback from Utah State.

Once again, the draft gods frowned upon Davis, as the Philadelphia Eagles selected Marsh two picks before the Raiders.

"The angst and anguish were very apparent on Al's face," Kingdon said.

With no one else in mind, Davis left it up to others. Jackson and assistant offensive line coach Steve Wisniewski pushed for Louisiana State University offensive tackle Joe Barksdale, a player Wisniewski worked out before the draft and felt strongly about. The Raiders selected Barksdale near the end of the third round.

"We could hear the coaches down the hall celebrating," Kingdon said.

"Do you believe the coaches are happy with this pick?" Davis asked Kingdon, with incredulity.

The way things unfolded was rather typical for a Raiders draft.

"The atmosphere pervading the Raiders drafts was unique to the organization, and not in a good way," Kingdon said. "What should be the most upbeat, optimistic and forward-looking day of the year for every team was generally a miserably depressing and angry day for the Raiders."

The Raiders are fond of the motto: "There are 31 teams in the NFL, and then there are the Raiders."

"This was particularly true in the Raiders draft room," Kingdon said. "If Al Davis did not get every player that he wanted, in every round, it was a cause for anger and frustration.

"Once, after Al stepped out of the draft room in the early 1990s, someone commented that 'there have to be happier people in Bosnia,' which at the time was suffering from genocidal violence. This bitingly perceptive comment at least broke the tension."

But only momentarily.

"During the draft, Al would agonize over every pick that was taken, expressing his frustration at his inability to get a particular pick," Kingdon said. "I even had a towel thrown at me when he didn't like my opinion on a certain player that he preferred."

Kebric didn't sense that 2011 was going to be Davis' final draft. He sat next to Davis in the draft room, which afforded him the opportunity to keep tabs on Davis at all times.

"I told him that I had watched him and that I had seen that his stamina was not good," Kebric said. "He continually denied any problems to me."

When it was mentioned that Davis might stay home during the first day of the 2011 draft since the Raiders were without a pick, Davis said, "Well, something might happen."

Despite the scouts' plea, Davis refused to miss the opening day of the draft. He feared that a situation might arise, perhaps a trade proposal that could get the Raiders a first-round pick that day, and that his presence was needed in case a quick decision had to be made.

At the end of the second day of the draft, unbeknownst to the scouts, Davis was so exhausted that he had to be transported to his apartment at the Oakland Hilton by an emergency medical technician team.

"He couldn't move," Kingdon was told the next day.

The third and final day of the draft kicked off early in the morning. The scouts were assembled in their meeting room when they received word that Davis wanted them to convene in the draft room.

"We went in there, and it was empty," Kingdon said. "We assumed Al had gone to the bathroom."

Kebric said, "Everybody is like, 'Where's Al? Where's Al?' Nobody knows where Al is."

Out of nowhere, "we heard Al's voice," Kingdon said.

Davis was calling from the Oakland Hilton. He was on the speakerphone.

"He didn't offer any explanation," Kingdon said, "but we put two and two together."

"We got Al on the phone, and he's not going to be able to come in today," one of Davis' assistants said.

The scouts could hear former Raiders safety Eddie Anderson, one of Davis' personal assistants, talking while inside Davis' apartment at the Hilton.

At one point, Kingdon said, "You could hear Al talking, and he asked Eddie to give him 'the blue book.' We all smiled because we took 'the blue book' to mean Mel Kiper, Jr.'s annual draft guide."

The Raiders made five picks that day — cornerback Chimdi Chekwa, running back Taiwan Jones, wide receiver Denarius Moore and tight ends Richard Gordon and David Ausberry.

Once the draft ended, Davis returned to the phone and said to those who remained in the draft room:

"This is the worst fucking draft in the history of the Raiders!"

"He wasn't there and he didn't get his picks," Kebric said. "Despite his ailments, he sounded like he was ready to fight someone."

Davis' health may have declined rapidly in the final decade of his life, but he never lost his desire to fight.

Hall of Fame defensive tackle Warren Sapp was in the locker room at the Oakland Coliseum on October 23, 2006, as he and his teammates celebrated a win over the Arizona Cardinals after five straight losses to begin the season. The festive atmosphere was overshadowed by Davis seizing upon an opportunity to address an issue with *San Francisco Chronicle* columnist Scott Ostler. Davis was upset with Ostler for a column he had written about Davis' recent invisibility portending health issues for Davis, who was 77 at the time.

"Oh, my god, Mr. Davis lit him up," Sapp said. "The locker room was almost empty. Al came out the back, from the training room, and stopped the walker."

"You son of a bitch," Davis said.

Oakland Tribune columnist Monte Poole and Sapp looked at each other in disbelief.

"Oh, shit," Sapp said.

Sapp and Poole "went quiet" and waited for Davis' next move.

"You son of a bitch," Davis continued. "You have all my friends in New York thinking I'm about to die. If I was 20 years younger, I would kick your motherfucking ass."

Sapp had heard Davis curse many times before, but he had only heard stories about Davis' combative side.

> *"You son of a bitch," Davis said. "You have all my friends in New York thinking I'm about to die. If I was 20 years younger, I would kick your motherfucking ass."*

"I almost died," Sapp said. "The funny part about it was, Ostler was backing up like he was really afraid of Al. This man's got a walker. Are you shitting me? I shit you not. Mr. Davis took two steps toward him when he was talking: 'If I was 20 years younger, I would kick your motherfucking ass.'

"I had never experienced it. I was like, 'Holy shit, I play for a gangster. I love it. Yes, sir.' Mr. Glazer (Tampa Bay Buccaneers owner Malcolm Glazer) would have never said that to anybody, and definitely not when somebody else could have heard it. Holy shit."

"Welcome to Oakland," Poole said to Sapp.

"Yeah, 'Holy shit, welcome to Oakland.' It blew my mind. I'm like, that is wonderful."

Davis accompanied the Raiders to Denver for the teams' 2011 regular-season opener, on a Monday night. He stayed behind when the Raiders flew to Buffalo four days later for a game against the Bills. That seemed understandable, given there wasn't much time between trips and it was a cross-country flight. It was a long season. Why push it right away?

Then again, Davis seldom missed games. It didn't matter where the game was played, the importance level — he attended every exhibition game — the weather, or the lack of time between trips. The Raiders were Davis' passion.

"If they played a game, preseason or otherwise, Davis was there, period," Herrera said.

Prior to missing the Bills game in 2011, Davis had missed only two other games that Herrera could recall. The first came in 1979, when Davis missed a game in Denver so he could be with his wife, Carol, who was hospitalized as she recovered from a heart attack and subsequent stroke.

As has been mentioned often, Davis never left his wife's side during her time in the hospital. Al told Kingdon that, when she awoke, her first question was how the Raiders did. He told her that the Raiders had won and she said to him, "That's nice."

The other game Davis missed came in the regular-season finale against the Tampa Bay Buccaneers in 2008.

Herrera said Davis missed the Buccaneers game because of residual swelling in his right knee and ankle as a result of a fall earlier that month. Davis' doctors cautioned Davis against making the trip, and he heeded their advice.

With the Raiders at 2-2 in 2011, they prepared for a game in Houston against the Texans. Nothing seemed out of the ordinary. Davis and Herrera spoke every day the week of the game. Kingdon and Davis spoke Friday, the day the Raiders departed Oakland International Airport for the game.

"In my last conversation with Al, I went over what was going on around the league," Kingdon said. "It was obvious that Al was not going to make any more road trips but, again, he would not allow himself to make this concession either to himself or anyone else."

Davis told Kingdon that he might fly to Houston on Saturday. He had flown separate from the team on occasion, but not very often.

"That would be great," Kingdon told Davis. "Suddenly his voice got incredibly hoarse, and he muttered 'thank you.'"

Those were Davis' final words to Kingdon, who had been told that Davis recently had undergone throat surgery to help him with his breathing.

Herrera wasn't as convinced that Davis wouldn't make this trip. In fact, he expected Davis to walk through the door as the plane boarded.

"I just assumed that he was going to be on the trip, on the plane, because he didn't say anything otherwise to me," Herrera said. "He never indicated to me that he wasn't going. I didn't know he wasn't going to go until they closed the door, and he wasn't on the airplane."

Herrera dismissed Davis' absence and rationalized that it might have been the result of Davis opting to pick his spots on road trips or, perhaps, the need to undergo a procedure that day.

"He would have stuff done all the time and he would never tell you," Herrera said. "He would just do it."

Herrera, Kingdon and the Raiders landed in Houston on Friday night. Neither spoke with Davis that night. Neither received any word about Davis' status.

Herrera's phone rang at 5 a.m. in a Houston hotel. It was Raiders chief financial officer Marc Badain.

"The phone wakes me up," Herrera said. "As soon as the phone rang, I went, 'Oh, no. I know what that is.' Absolutely. From being around Al all my life, it was just a sixth sense."

Herrera's mind raced to the day before. What seemed insignificant at the time now made perfect sense.

"And that he didn't get on the airplane. When they closed the door, and he wasn't there, I didn't take it any further than, hopefully, he's just having a bad day or he'll come tomorrow. Maybe he'll fly private and come down the next day, which he had done on occasion. Not normally but every once in a while, he would fly private to get somewhere. So, I just kind of pushed it out of my mind, but it was there. I tried to push it out, but it was there."

Then came the call.

"When the phone rang, I'm going, 'Oh, shit,'" Herrera said.

Herrera and Badain exchanged a quick greeting. Nothing else needed to be said.

"I just went, 'Oh, no.' He goes, 'Yeah.' He didn't even tell me who it was who died," Herrera said. "I just knew. The conversation was fairly brief."

Davis had passed away at the Oakland Airport Hilton, where he rented three rooms in the back of the property. The three rooms had been converted into what Davis called "my apartment." Toward the end of his life, Davis moved to the Hilton on Hegenberger Road, a short drive from the team's year-round facility in Alameda and much closer than his home in Piedmont, located in the Oakland Hills.

Davis always portrayed strength and allayed concerns about his health. When he hired coach Lane Kiffin in 2007, Davis showed Kiffin a picture on a table in his office. One by one, Davis pointed out coaches from the 1959 University of Southern California team that he worked alongside that season. Davis punctuated the identification of each coach by telling Kiffin that the coach was "gone."

"There was one coach left, and Lane looked at me," Davis said. "I said, 'But I'm not going anywhere, Lane. Don't worry about it.'"

In retrospect, Kebric said, Davis first entertained the notion that he might not live forever in 1996. That year, Davis disappeared for a spell, without letting anyone know where he went. Dr. Albo told Kebric that Davis went to the Cleveland Clinic to get checked out.

That same year, on a walk back to the hotel at the NFL scouting combine in Indianapolis, Davis invited Kebric to dinner.

Davis insisted on an 8 o'clock seating.

"Al always ate late, and he didn't seem to have a problem," said Kebric, who had already eaten by the time he sat down with Davis. Davis got right to what was on his mind.

"I want you to promise me that if anything happens to me, that you will be loyal to Carol," Davis said of his wife, whom he oftentimes called Ca-ro-lee.

"I kind of just stared at him," Kebric said.

Davis grabbed Kebric's hand at that point.

"I want you to promise me that if something happens to me, that you'll be loyal to Carol," Davis said again.

"Sure, sure," Kebric said.

"No, I'm serious," Davis said. "I want that promise."

"Al, I promise you," Kebric said. "If something should happen to you, I will be loyal to Carol. If she needs anything from me, all she has to do is ask."

Up until the end, Davis wanted people to think that he was fine. He had two rooms set aside for himself at the 2011 training camp in Napa, though he didn't spend the night there at any time during the month-long camp. Sure, death might beat Davis, but he was going to make the most of every second on the metaphorical clock.

"Al Davis never for a second considered stepping away from football and going quietly into the night," Kebric said.

To that end, Davis didn't make provisions for someone else taking over. One of the few people to bring up the idea of a succession plan was Al Michaels, who filled in for *Sports Illustrated's* Peter King on his "Monday Morning Quarterback" column in 2011:

"For 20 years, I've asked dozens of insiders, including commissioners, owners and those I felt had accurate inside information: "What is the Raiders' succession plan? Who will own and run the team when (or maybe, if) Al Davis dies? No one has the answer. Even people who like to brag that they're wired on the inside can't give me the answer. Vegas would take this bet off the board."

The 1960 Los Angeles Chargers coaching staff, one of the best in pro football history, included Al Davis (seated, right), head coach Sid Gillman (seated, left), Joe Madro (left), Chuck Noll (second from left) and Jack Faulkner. Davis, Gillman and Noll are members of the Pro Football Hall of Fame.

♟ CHAPTER FOUR ♟

Joe Madro: The Friend for Life

In 1960, after being let go by the University of Southern California, Al Davis was looking for work. That was when Joe Madro paved the way for Davis' career in pro football, which spanned more than five decades.

Davis spent most of the 1950s coaching in the collegiate ranks, while doing what he could to become known to those in the NFL of his desired destination.

Davis' coaching career began in 1950 after he graduated from Syracuse University with a degree in English. He coached the offensive line at Adelphi University for two years, followed by a year as head coach of the U.S. Army team at Fort Belvoir, Virginia. He then spent two years at The Citadel as its offensive line coach, and served at USC from 1957 through 1959, also as an offensive line coach.

Madro was regarded as one of the great offensive line coaches in NFL history. He spent most of his career working as an assistant coach for Pro Football Hall of Fame coach Sid Gillman, from college to the NFL to the AFL.

He was highly respected by other offensive line coaches in both college and the pros, as he always was available to share his knowledge and techniques to all who were interested.

Madro was blessed with great foresight and relished the opportunity to work with players that others disregarded as legitimate prospects. His greatest project might have been Russ Washington, a defensive lineman out of the University of Missouri who was taken by the San Diego Chargers as the fourth overall pick in the first round of the 1968 draft.

Washington stood 6-foot-6 and weighed 290 pounds, exceptionally large for anyone at that time, and was a dominant college player. However, his play with the Chargers frustrated defensive line coach Bum Phillips, who went on to great success as the head coach of the Houston Oilers.

Before Washington's second season, Gillman asked Phillips at training camp how Washington was progressing. Phillips responded negatively, but very cleverly: "The grass he don't kill standing on, his shadow kills." Phillips felt strongly that Washington wasn't going to amount to much as an NFL defensive lineman. Madro, the Chargers' offensive line coach, seized upon the opportunity, saying, "I'll take him if you don't want him."

Under Madro's tutelage, Washington went on to play in five Pro Bowls and ultimately was elected into the Chargers Hall of Fame.

Madro entered the NFL in 1955 as the offensive line coach for the Los Angeles Rams, under Gillman. As part of Madro's duties with the Rams, he scouted players at USC and had become acquainted with Davis.

"Joe liked what he saw in Al," Bruce Kebric said. "He always talked about Al's brilliant football mind."

Davis was saddled with a dubious reputation. When he left The Citadel after the 1956 season, he did so amidst allegations of breaking NCAA rules. As it turned out, he went from one messy situation to another. Davis arrived at USC in 1957 at a time when that institution was on NCAA probation.

The NCAA sanctioned USC again in 1959 after it was discovered that the school had played a role in getting recruits signed by other colleges to ignore their original commitments. Head coach Don Clark resigned at the end of that season. Davis was turned down for the head coaching vacancy, and subsequently was fired by new head coach John McKay.

Davis had had enough with the restrictions of college football.

When asked about his college coaching experience, Davis facetiously told Kebric, "I really enjoyed it, but it cost me almost as much as I made."

Davis' checkered track record didn't deter Madro. He recognized that Davis was a valued part of Clark's staff and that Davis' role in USC's success transcended his coaching skills. In particular, Madro was impressed by Davis' recruiting ability. Six players on the USC football team in 1959 had roots on the East Coast, which for years had been fertile recruiting ground for Davis. One of Davis' earliest coups was convincing standout running back and track star Angelo Coia into transferring from The Citadel to USC. Coia was one of three Trojan players from Pennsylvania who enjoyed NFL careers. The others were Mike Bundra, drafted by Detroit, and Dan Ficca, who was drafted by San Diego when Davis served as an assistant coach with the Chargers. Another Davis recruit, Willie Wood, from Washington, D.C., was the first African-American quarterback in Pacific Coast

Conference history and later starred as a defensive back for the Green Bay Packers teams of the 1960s. Wood was inducted into the Professional Football Hall of Fame in 1989.

Davis, at the time unemployed, first approached Madro about a position with the Los Angeles Chargers at a 1960 coaches convention in New York City. Madro, who had just joined the team, was immediately intrigued with the moxie and competitiveness that Davis would bring to both the team and the nascent American Football League and lobbied Gillman, the head coach, on Davis' behalf.

"Joe told me that Sid originally said no, but that Joe persisted," Kebric said. Gillman told Madro that, "I can't hire the guy for two reasons. Every place he has been, he has burned bridges. He has burned every bridge that he has crossed. And he's Jewish. I'm Jewish, and people are going to think I'm doing it just for that reason."

Madro, who was highly respected by Gillman, finally prevailed, and Davis became part of a Chargers staff that included Gillman, Madro, Chuck Noll and Jack Faulkner. Gillman, Davis and Noll later were inducted into the Pro Football Hall of Fame, and some regard that group as one of the best coaching staffs in pro football history.

Davis coached with the Chargers for three seasons before he was hired by the Raiders in 1963. According to Madro, Davis had developed a reputation not only for his coaching accomplishments but also for recruiting a number of future Hall of Famers to the Chargers.

Davis was always looking for an edge to help his team. He signed University of Arkansas wide receiver Lance Alworth underneath the goal post after Alworth's final collegiate game, while San Francisco 49ers head coach Red Hickey sat in the stands.

> *"I can't hire the guy for two reasons. Every place he has been, he has burned bridges. He has burned every bridge that he has crossed. And he's Jewish ... people are going to think I'm doing it just for that reason."*

Alworth had been a first-round pick of the 49ers in the 1962 NFL draft, and a second-round selection of the Oakland Raiders in the AFL draft. The Chargers, in turn, compensated the Raiders for the rights to sign Alworth.

Two years earlier, Davis had signed offensive tackle Ron Mix, whom Davis had coached at USC and was a first-round pick of the Baltimore Colts. Alworth and Mix eventually were inducted into the Pro Football Hall of Fame. Madro, in fact, presented Mix to the Hall of Fame. Alworth was presented by Davis. Madro felt that Davis' work played an integral role in the Chargers appearing in the first two AFL Championship games and winning the AFL title in 1963.

While with the Chargers, Davis learned the passing game from Gillman, who has been called the "Father" of the modern passing game.

"Sid's passing offense was predicated upon five-step and seven-step drops and emphasized the vertical routes," Kebric said. "Al always lived by this offense and never varied despite the fact passing styles changed over the years. Daryle Lamonica was his prototype quarterback, and he was always searching for someone with Lamonica's size and arm strength."

The Chargers beat the Raiders all six times they played from 1960-62. In Davis' first season with the Raiders, however, he led his team to two wins over the 11-3 Chargers, who went on to win the AFL Championship, beating the Boston Patriots 51-10 in the title game.

Madro also had great respect for Davis' work ethic. Whenever the Chargers prepared to play the Raiders and the coaches finished work for the day, Madro frequently said to the staff, "That guy up in Oakland is still working on the game plan."

Along the way, Madro gleaned more and more about what made Davis tick, the things that proved critical to Davis' success.

It didn't take long to see that Davis' drive to be the best was, perhaps, the single greatest determining factor in helping him achieve so much, so soon and to stay on top for so long.

Many times, Madro told Kebric: "The difference between Al and the rest of the coaches was, when we were in training camp, as soon as the meetings ended, most of the other coaches would head to the bars to drink and relax. Al Davis was back in his room watching film, making phone calls and watching more film."

Davis constantly looked for ways to gain an edge on the opposition.

During the Chargers training camp in 1969, Kebric was assigned phone duty one night. Before long, the phone rang and Kebric answered.

"Who's this?" the caller asked.

"Bruce Kebric," Kebric replied.

"What do you do?" Davis inquired.

Kebric explained his duties with the Chargers.

"This is Al Davis," the caller responded.

"With the Oakland Raiders?" Kebric asked.

"Yes," Davis confirmed.

Kebric asked Davis if he wanted to speak with Gillman.

"Maybe later," Davis said.

Davis then proceeded to ask Kebric how he liked the Chargers training camp, which was at the University of California-Irvine for the first time that year. He then wanted to know which players were doing well in practice and which players Kebric liked.

After Kebric finished with his rundown, Davis said "thank you" and hung up. When Kebric saw Gillman later that evening, he told Gillman that Al Davis had called and asked about the Chargers camp and players.

"Did you give him any information?" Gillman wanted to know.

"No," Kebric assured Gillman. Davis also called during the 1970 Chargers camp. Again, Kebric was on phone duty. That time, Kebric told Davis that he was too busy to talk. Davis left a number for Gillman to call him back.

Two years later, Kebric, as a member of the Houston Oilers scouting staff, was at the Lubbock, Texas, airport awaiting a flight to Dallas. Davis, who was in the west Texas city as well for the Coaches All-America Game practices, approached Kebric.

"I was surprised he knew my name since I had never met him previously," Kebric said.

"Where's Pete?" Davis asked of Bill Peterson, who was the Oilers head coach.

Kebric informed Davis that Peterson was in the restroom, so Davis and Peterson didn't get a chance to converse.

Kebric and Peterson sat in coach on the one-hour flight to Dallas, while Davis was in first class.

"Al came back to our seats and stood in the aisle, trying to convince Peterson to trade Ken Burrough, who at the time was one of the fastest receivers in the NFL, to Oakland," Kebric said. "Finally, the flight attendant told Al that he had to return to his first-class seat."

Davis called a couple more times about Burrough, but "When Cliff Branch developed, we never heard from Al again," Kebric said.

Davis also had a penchant for working the sidelines before games, where he had unbridled access to opposing players.

"The week after we played Oakland, Elvin Bethea generally would come by my office and say he wanted to be traded to Oakland," Kebric said of the standout Oilers defensive end whose 16-year career culminated with his induction into the Pro Football Hall of Fame.

Madro and Davis were roommates when they were with the Chargers and in the 1961 team photo, below, they can be seen standing next to each other. During that time, they forged a lifelong relationship. Madro remained with Gillman and the Chargers through the 1971 season. He coached with the Houston Oilers from 1972 through 1974, was the Oilers player personnel director from 1975 through 1977 and then at Davis' invite joined the Raiders, where he worked as an assistant coach, and then moved into both the pro and college personnel departments, and even handled special projects, until his death in 1994 at the age of 81.

When Gillman was inducted into the Pro Football Hall of Fame in 1983, it was Madro whom Gillman selected as his presenter. Madro became just as fond of Davis.

"Joe loved Al, and Al never forgot what Joe did for him," Kebric said. The extent of Davis' respect for Madro as a coach was revealed when

Los Angeles Chargers

Joe Madro (far left, second row) helped Al Davis (next to Madro) land his first coaching job in pro football in 1960. Davis never forgot the role Madro played in his career, and he remained loyal to Madro until his passing in 1994.

Davis sought a replacement for John Rauch in 1969. Rauch spent three seasons as an assistant to Davis from 1963 through 1965, and then replaced Davis as the head coach in 1966 when Davis was named commissioner of the AFL. Rauch guided the Raiders to a 33-8-1 record from 1966 through 1968 and presided over the team's first Super Bowl appearance. However, he tired of Davis' meddling after Davis returned to the Raiders in 1967, and accepted a job with the Buffalo Bills.

Davis wanted to interview Madro for the head coaching job. He asked Gillman for permission, but Gillman denied Davis' request.

"Joe didn't know about it until much later," Kebric said. "He was upset at Sid because Joe said he would have liked to have been a head coach and work with Al."

Gillman and Madro had been together for 25 years or so by the time Davis requested the Madro interview. That included stops at Miami of Ohio, Cincinnati, the Rams and the Chargers.

"I don't know if he would have gotten the job ahead of John Madden, but he certainly was much more qualified at that time," Kebric said.

Kingdon also considered Madro and his wife, Pat, a second family. The Madroes went to great lengths to help Kingdon acclimate to the Bay Area, often having him over for dinner when he joined the Raiders in 1978.

"At this point, Joe was working in pro personnel and he allowed me to watch film with him, often pointing out things that I would not have noticed had he not highlighted them for me," Kingdon said.

Though Madro worked less and less for the Raiders as the years passed, Kingdon remained in constant contact, even though the Raiders had moved to Los Angeles and Madro lived in Alameda.

"Al knew I would regularly call Joe, and he would always ask how Joe was doing," Kingdon said. "He would have me to fly up to Oakland and take Joe out to lunch and make sure that he was not in need of anything."

Another shining example of Davis' loyalty to those who served him faithfully came in 2011 when serious health issues forced Coia, a collegiate recruit of Davis' and later a longtime Raiders scout, to consider retirement. Davis originally had recruited the highly sought-after Coia to The Citadel and when Davis left to take a position at the University of Southern California, Coia followed him and became a Trojan star in both football and track and field.

Some years earlier, Coia had contracted hepatitis-C through a blood transfusion. As he moved into his 70s, Coia no longer was able to maintain his duties as a full-time scout. Yet Davis continued to pay Coia a salary commensurate to that of a full-time employee as well as to provide his medical insurance.

At one point, Davis told Kingdon that he was thinking about cutting Coia's salary but, before doing so, wanted Kingdon to check with Coia to make sure the move would not create an unnecessary burden on his finances. The implication was, if Coia didn't want to take the pay cut, then Davis would not make such a move.

"I went to Angie with the reduced salary figure, and he laughed," Kingdon said. "He said, 'That's really generous of Al' and what he offered was a lot more than Angie expected." Coia added that his primary concern was being kept on the Raiders insurance plan because Medicare didn't cover his hepatitis-C treatment.

Kingdon returned to Davis with Coia's response.

"Angie's concerned that I would cut him off insurance?" Davis said. "I would sooner sell the team then cut him off insurance."

Madro had been in ill health before his death, so when the calls came to inform people that he passed away, it was not a surprise. Kebric was in Provo, Utah, at the time, when he received a phone call from Claudia Madro, Joe's daughter, informing him of Joe's passing.

"When is the funeral?" Kebric asked.

"Monday," Claudia Madro said.

"I'll be there," Kebric said. "I'm in Provo right now, but I'll be there, no matter what happens."

That caught Claudia off guard.

"Well, Mom was going to ask you if you would be a pallbearer, but we didn't think you could come," she said.

Joe's son Thom, along with his other siblings, appreciated how much affection his parents had for Kingdon and Kebric.

According to Kingdon, "When we walked into a luncheon Al had set up for the out-of-towners after the funeral, Bruce and I walked in together, Thom announced for all to hear, 'Here are my parents' adopted sons.'"

The Raiders had a game in Los Angeles the day after Madro died. Kingdon and Davis flew to the Bay Area after the game.

Davis arrived by limousine at the church for Madro's service. He spotted Kebric as soon as he exited the limo. Kebric walked over to greet him.

Davis still hadn't moved past the Raiders' 26-24 loss to the San Diego Chargers the day before the funeral.

"Al started talking about the game," Kebric said. "Right in front of everybody."

Kebric was aghast.

"Al, please, don't talk about the game today," Kebric asked Davis. "This is Joe's day. Joe was special."

"Yeah, you're right," Davis said.

Toward the end of the service, it was time for communion. Everyone stood and prepared to go to the front of the Catholic church and receive communion. Kebric, Kingdon, Davis and his wife Carol were seated in the same row.

Kebric stood up, then he noticed Davis getting up, too.

"I didn't think anything of it," Kebric said. "I looked back and they were not following me."

Kingdon, who's also Jewish, forcefully grabbed Davis.

"I saw that Al unwittingly was getting in line to receive communion," Kingdon said. "I grabbed his arm and pulled him back, telling him that they were giving communion. He gave me a nod and a look of real appreciation for saving him from what could have been a really embarrassing situation."

An awkward situation had been averted. Another one loomed.

Kebric, Kingdon, Gillman, Davis and Walt Sweeney were the pallbearers. Sweeney was another former Chargers player who achieved allstar status after Madro converted him from tight end to offensive guard. Soon after the service, they were carrying Madro's casket toward the grave. Kingdon and Kebric were in front, on either side of the casket. Davis was in the back, on one side.

"All of a sudden, there was this commotion," Kebric said. "We looked back and Carol was grabbing on to Al."

With good reason.

"Oh, my, God!" Carol Davis shouted, as she grabbed Al, just as one of his feet gave way.

This wasn't an ordinary misstep, either.

"Al almost fell in the grave," Kebric said. "Everybody that was there saw him. It didn't seem to bother him."

"Al maintained his composure," Kingdon said. "But he was in the right crowd wherein no one was going to make an issue about it."

Madro coached Ron Mix for the first 10 seasons of what turned into a Hall of Fame career. In addition, Madro had given Mix one of the great nicknames of all time: "The Intellectual Assassin." Mix, an attorney at the time, was unable to attend Madro's funeral, but he penned a eulogy that was delivered by Kingdon:

Joe Madro was my coach. There is no fonder description one person can give of one another. When I think of him, I am reminded of the scene from that wonderful play, "A Man For All Seasons," when Saint Thomas More, then a college professor, is visited by a student who is in trouble because he does not know what to do with his life. "Continue your studies towards becoming a teacher," counseled More. The student replied with some disdain: "A teacher, but who would know?" "Well," said More, "you would know. Your students would certainly know. And God would know. A fine audience that."

And that is what a coach is, a teacher. Teaching a skill while at the same time teaching the value of respect, discipline, hard work, loyalty, and playing by the rules. You know, Joe never taught his offensive linemen to hold. If one did and cost his team a 15-yard penalty, Joe would yell, "You lost your team 15 yards; you could play 10 years and you'll never gain us 15 yards."

He had a sharp, caustic wit and was quick to criticize but like all great teachers was quicker to praise.

Ninety percent of the time an offensive tackle blocks the man in front of him which means the entire playbook can be learned in minutes. Most of the time we take two steps and hit. We never touch the football. I have heard it is somewhat cylinder shaped. With work conditions like those, the potential for boredom was great. But Joe always kept it interesting. How many times our line meetings rang with so much laughter that the other players would ask what the heck was going on in there. He told stories, talked about current events, hammered the Republicans, prodded and railed ... but mostly he taught. And at that he may have had equals but no one was better.

When Joe was my presenter into the Hall of Fame, I said I shared the honor with my college coaches, Mel Hein and Al Davis, and my profes-

sional coaches, Sid Gillman and Joe Madro. I meant it. For 10 years, I spent most of my waking hours with Joe. He enriched my life. Pat, Thom, Robert, Martin, Claudia, and Cynthia, you had so much more time with him. How fortunate you are.

Norm Fisher

Raiders personnel executive Ron Wolf posed for a photo with running back Kenny King (33) and nose tackle Reggie Kinlaw (62), all three of whom attended the University of Oklahoma, during the week of the Super Bowl in the 1980 season. In 2015, Wolf was inducted into the Pro Football Hall of Fame.

CHAPTER FIVE

Ron Wolf: The Valued Associate

During their first three years of existence, the Raiders won a total of nine games and were fresh from a 1-13 season when Al Davis was hired to be the head coach in 1963. One of his first moves was to bring aboard Ron Wolf as his personnel advisor.

The turnaround, with Davis and Wolf overseeing the football operation, was immediate and remarkable. The Raiders won 10 games in 1963, and in 1967 played in the first of their five Super Bowls.

Wolf played an integral role in building the Raiders into a perennial contender and one of the league's best franchises.

Wolf's stamp was all over the 1976 Raiders team that crushed the Minnesota Vikings in the Super Bowl for the first of three titles in an eight-year span, even though Wolf had left the organization in 1975 for an opportunity to lead the Tampa Bay Buccaneers expansion franchise.

Wolf returned to Oakland in 1979. During his second stint with the Raiders, the team collected its second and third Super Bowl titles. They were positioning themselves to make a run at another Super Bowl when Wolf abruptly departed once again. This time, he wasn't coming back.

In the early part of 1990, Wolf's final year with the Raiders — he worked through the draft and into June before he accepted a job with the New York Jets — he was searching for the players the Raiders needed to take the next step toward becoming an annual playoff contender. The Raiders posted an 8-8 record in 1989, but were a team on the rise, especially with the recent additions through the draft of wide receiver Tim Brown and running back Bo Jackson.

Wolf was in Indianapolis for a follow-up to the NFL scouting combine. The later session was conducted for players who weren't able to work out or take physical exams at the original February date and the event took place outdoors, at the Colts practice facility. Even though it was now April, it still was very cold and windy in the Hoosier State's capital city.

When Wolf returned to Los Angeles, where the Raiders were located at that point, he was not feeling well. Later that night, he called Raiders staffer John Otten and told him that he thought he was having a heart attack. It was a stroke of good fortune that Otten was available, given that Wolf's wife Edie and his two sons were out of town visiting relatives in Massachusetts.

Otten drove Wolf to Cedars-Sinai Medical Center, where Wolf's self-diagnosis was verified by the hospital's medical personnel.

Wolf was hospitalized just when the Raiders were preparing for the draft. That's one of the most critical times of the year for NFL teams, and the Raiders were without their point person.

"We had to meet without Ron," Bruce Kebric said. "Every morning, Al would come in and ask, 'How's Ron? Get John Otten in here. Get Rod Martin in here.'"

Davis would then ask Rod Martin, the Raiders trainer, "Rod, does Ron need doctors? Tell me what Ron needs."

"Rod would say, 'No, he's being well taken care of,'" Kebric said. Not long after Wolf had been hospitalized, Kingdon and Kebric received word that they were allowed to visit Wolf. Once they had wrapped up their draft preparation for the day, they headed to Cedars-Sinai.

"Have Ron give me a call," Davis said to the pair as they were leaving the Raiders offices.

"I'm not going to do that," Kebric shouted back.

Having realized how "ridiculous and insensitive" his request sounded, Davis quickly added, "only if he feels up to it."

Kingdon and Kebric entered Wolf's hospital room and witnessed their boss hooked up to machines, numerous tubes protruding from his body.

Kingdon's first thought was, "This is not someone who is concerned about the upcoming draft, given his serious medical condition."

During their visit, Wolf called over Kebric and Kingdon and told them to "look at that piece of paper," which was on a table next to Wolf's bed.

There was a notepad with a list of names of people from around the league who had called to check in on Wolf and pass along their well-wishes.

The list included John Math (Rams, player personnel director), Jack Faulkner (Rams, pro personnel director) and retired Raiders scout Joe Madro, among others.

"Do you see who's missing?" Wolf asked.

A long pause ensued, as Kebric and Kingdon waited for the answer.

"Do you see Al Davis' name?" Wolf said.

Kingdon asked, with some surprise, "Al never called?"

"No," Wolf said.

Kebric assured Wolf that Davis cared.

"Ron, every morning Al asks about you," Kebric said. "We spend the first 15 to 20 minutes talking about you."

"Do you see Al Davis' name down there?" Wolf said.

"No," Kebric said.

"I want you to promise me, if you ever become a boss and your employee gets sick, that you'll give him a phone call," Wolf said to Kebric.

A few years later, Kingdon related the story to Art Shell, the Raiders head coach at the time. Upon hearing Kingdon's words, a look of enlightenment came over Shell's face.

"That explains it," Shell said.

Wolf had given Shell the same directive about checking up on sick employees. However, Shell thought Wolf was being critical of him and wondered what he had done wrong.

Kebric and Kingdon had one more thing to take care of before their visit with Wolf ended, as uncomfortable as it might be.

Davis had told them to "give Ron my best," Kebric said. "And ask Ron if he's going to be here for the draft."

Kebric passed along Davis' sentiment. Then he posed the question about whether Wolf would be present for the draft.

"Ron kind of got upset," Kebric said.

"Hey, you tell Al that I'll be there under two conditions," Wolf said. "One, there's no smoking in the room. And, two, Bill Urbanik keeps his mouth shut."

Kebric told Wolf, "You know what, I think we can control the first condition. But we might not be able to control the other."

As promised, Wolf made it back in time for the draft. His wish was granted about no smoking in the draft room. During the meetings, Urbanik, the defensive line coach, was "really vocal" about the Raiders selecting defensive end Anthony Smith, a talented but troubled player from the University of Arizona.

The Raiders had the 11th pick of the draft. Urbanik had been to

Smith's hometown in North Carolina to work out the prospective first-round selection. He had no doubt that this was the player the Raiders should select if he was still available.

Kebric had written a detailed report on Smith. In that report, he pointed out to Davis that Smith had a checkered background. Kebric liked Smith, but Smith came with a ton of baggage.

"I had documented all his problems in the report," Kebric said. "At 12 years old, he had no parents and he was running the streets of Brooklyn. He had all kinds of problems. Finally, he went down to North Carolina with his brother and he settled down a little bit. Then he was recruited by the University of Alabama.

"After being dismissed from the Crimson Tide program, Smith ended up at the University of Arizona because one of the Wildcat football coaches previously was on the Alabama staff."

Smith, who had played for three seasons at Alabama, enrolled in a Tucson, Arizona, junior college for a semester before he joined the University of Arizona team. He played well enough and stayed out of trouble long enough to get on the Raiders radar.

Smith told stories about being bounced from relative to relative after he had been orphaned at three years old. He claimed to have used an array of illegal drugs such as heroin, cocaine and PCP, but had gotten clean after a lengthy rehab stint. A younger brother supposedly overdosed on heroin. On it went.

Urbanik wasn't swayed by the numerous red flags. Smith's talent was too intoxicating to ignore. Besides, the Raiders All-Pro defensive linemen Howie Long and Greg Townsend were at the tail end of their prime. Davis felt it was time for the Raiders to groom a replacement, and who better to learn from than Long and Townsend?

After the Raiders drafted Smith, Davis received a phone call from Ray Perkins, who had recruited Smith to the University of Alabama, when Perkins was the head coach there. Perkins, at the time of the call to Davis, was the Tampa Bay Buccaneers head coach.

"Al's all excited because Ray Perkins calls," Kebric said.

"Hey, I don't know what happened after I left, but this guy was a special player," Perkins told Davis.

"Al loved that," Kebric said. "Calls like that meant a lot to Al."

Yet there were enough signs along the way that using such a valuable draft pick on Smith entailed a huge gamble.

The day after the Raiders selected Smith, a story in the *Los Angeles Times* outlined Smith's litany of problems, none of which surprised Kebric.

"Al was furious," Kebric said.

"Why in the fuck didn't you tell me about this?" Davis screamed at Wolf.

Kebric was greeted by those heated words when he arrived that morning. Davis and Wolf were together in one of the coaches' offices at the time Kebric heard Davis' raised voice.

"Al was just screaming at Ron, and Ron was just coming off a heart attack," Kebric said. "I opened up the door because I had an idea what was going on. I said, 'Al, everything that is in the *Los Angeles Times* today is in my report.'"

"Get the fuck out of here. I'm not talking to you," Davis said.

Kebric looked at Wolf, who "kind of gave me an it's-no-use look."

"I think when Al finally got through yelling at Ron that Ron may have just said to himself, 'I'm done here,'" Kebric said.

Smith played well for the Raiders, though he missed his entire rookie season after suffering a torn medial collateral ligament and a cartilage tear in his right knee during a late-August practice in 1990. He made his NFL debut in 1991, at which time he developed into a consistent pass-rush threat behind Long, Townsend and Scott Davis. Smith registered 10½ sacks his first season, second only to Townsend's 13. He amassed 57½ sacks in 98 games during his seven seasons, all with the

> "Al was just screaming at Ron, and Ron was just coming off a heart attack," Kebric said. "I opened up the door because I had an idea what was going on ..."

Raiders. He opted out of his contract after the 1997 season and never signed with another team.

The concerns about Smith were well-founded, to say the least. In November of 2015, Smith was convicted of the killings of Ricky and Kevin Nettles in 1999 and the 2001 death of Dennis Henderson. In addition, jurors found special circumstance allegations that Smith committed kidnapping, torture and multiple murders. He was sentenced to life without the possibility of parole in January of 2016.

In 1982, the Raiders moved from Oakland to Los Angeles. Five years later, the Green Bay Packers called Davis and asked for permission to interview Wolf.

Wolf informed the Packers that he wasn't interested in going to Green Bay, so it would be a waste of time for the Packers to fly him out for an interview. Davis prevailed upon Wolf to go.

When Wolf returned, Kingdon asked him how it went. "He said it went 'fine' and that he told the Packers he wasn't interested and informed Al what happened."

Davis called Kingdon later that day and expressed real concern about what it would mean if Wolf accepted a job with the Packers.

"I told Al that Ron had told me that he turned down the offer," Kingdon said, "and he said that he had informed you of his decision."

Then came an awkward period of silence, followed by Davis saying, "I'll see ya."

Davis' fear of losing Wolf was realized in 1990, soon after Wolf's heart attack and perhaps because Davis had slighted him one too many times.

Wolf reached his decision in June. He informed Davis, then he phoned Kebric.

"He called me one night and said, 'I'm leaving,'" Kebric recalled. "I said, 'What?'"

"I'm leaving and I've recommended you for my job," Wolf said.

"You can't leave, Ron," Kebric said.

"I have to," Wolf responded.

"What are you going to do?" Kebric asked

"I'm going to go to work for my brother-in-law in Massachusetts," Wolf said. "He's in the jewelry business. Al is going to be giving you a call tomorrow."

"I don't like this," Kebric said. "I really enjoy working with you."

"Well, this is the best thing for me to do," Wolf explained.

"Al called me the next day and said, 'Ron has recommended you for his job.' I said, 'That's great. Thank you.'"

"Al said, 'Do you want it?'"

Kebric said, "Yeah, I'll take it if I don't have to move to Los Angeles."

Kebric had worked for NFL teams in San Diego and Houston and USFL teams in Tulsa and Phoenix. His two daughters were young, and he had spent a year away from his family while working in Tulsa.

"We liked Arizona, and I didn't want to move again," Kebric said. "So, I told Al, 'I will take the job but I'm not going to move.'"

"Well, I'm not going to give you a title until you move," Davis said.

"I don't care about a title. I have been an assistant general manager, a director of player personnel and a director of college and pro scouting, and another title means nothing to me. But before you offer me the job, you need to talk to Kent McCloughan. He's been here longer than I have."

McCloughan called Kebric the next day and said, "Bruce, what are you trying to do, give me a heart attack, too?"

Kebric asked McCloughan, "What are you talking about?"

"Al just called me and told me that you recommended me for Ron's job," McCloughan said.

"Well, Kent, you're the senior guy here. I could work well with you," Kebric said.

Davis called Kebric later that day and informed him that McCloughan turned down the job.

"So, I said, 'OK, same deal. I will run things but I'm going to do it from here. I can just jump on a plane and be in Los Angeles in an hour.'"

Davis reiterated to Kebric that he wasn't going to give Kebric a title.

To end the conversation, Kebric remarked, "If we ever go back to the Bay Area, I would consider moving, since that is where I am from."

Kebric made that comment just to get Davis off his back. He had no intention of ever moving to the Bay Area, but once you told Davis something, he never forgot.

Sure enough, soon after the Raiders returned to Oakland in 1995, Davis called Kebric.

"When are you moving?" Davis inquired.

"What?" Kebric answered.

Davis then reminded Kebric of the statement he had made five years earlier.

"You said you would move up here if we ever came back to the Bay Area," Davis said.

Kebric was taken aback with Davis' memory, but he did manage to say, in a stammer, "My wife would divorce me," thinking that would remedy the situation.

"But, you'll always have me," Davis quickly replied.

Davis later told Kebric that New York Jets general manager Dick Steinberg had called Davis about another matter, when Davis informed Steinberg that Wolf had left the Raiders.

Steinberg said, "Do you mind if I talk to him? I need a player personnel director."

Shortly thereafter, Wolf was hired by the Jets and spent a year and a half with that organization before moving on to Green Bay.

Packers president Robert Parins hired Tom Braatz as general manager in 1987 after having interviewed Wolf and offering him the position. Parins' successor, Bob Harlan, fired Braatz in November of 1991, and immediately sought out Wolf to be the team's executive vice president and general manager.

Kebric initially was surprised by Wolf's attitude change about Green Bay, a place Wolf once refused to consider. Wolf had spent much of his life in cold-weather cities in Pennsylvania and then later in Germany while in the U.S. Army.

"Ron's change of heart surprised me since he had told me on a number of occasions that he didn't like cold weather," Kebric said.

A few years later, Kebric encountered Ron and his wife Edie at an all-star game and inquired as to how they had adapted to Green Bay.

Edie said, "It's so nice that the boys can leave their bicycles out on the front lawn at night and no one disturbs them."

Kebric recalled, "She did not appear amused when I replied, 'Yeah, because they're covered in six feet of snow and nobody can find them.'"

Losing Wolf was a blow to the Raiders. However, it wasn't as substantial as one might think, given he worked for Davis.

"After Ron Wolf left, it wasn't the same," Kebric said. "We really didn't have a center."

But the Raiders still had Davis, so there still existed the potential for him to draft players he coveted and ignore the advice of his scouts.

For instance, the Raiders had the sixth pick in the 1988 NFL draft. Wolf pushed for Oklahoma cornerback Rickey Dixon; Davis wanted Wisconsin offensive lineman Paul Gruber. When it came time for the Raiders

Matt Campbell
Getty Images

The Raiders are inextricably linked with many of the most memorable games in NFL history, games that were labeled with enduring nicknames such as "The Immaculate Reception," "The Ghost to the Post," "The Sea of Hands" and "The Holy Roller." None, perhaps, is as widely known as "The Tuck Game." In that game, Raiders cornerback Charles Woodson (24) knocks the ball from Patriots quarterback Tom Brady's hands in the fourth quarter of an AFC Divisional Playoff game January 19, 2002, at Foxboro Stadium. Raiders linebacker Greg Biekert (54) recovered the ball, but officials overturned the initial call while citing the little-known "Tuck Rule," and the Patriots rallied for an overtime victory.

First-year Raiders head coach Al Davis and his quarterback, Cotton Davidson, teamed to lead the Raiders to a 10-win season in 1963, a nine game improvement.

Ron Riesterer

Al Davis was a creature of habit. That included nail-biting, something he did more of when he became nervous, especially during the NFL draft.

Ron Riesterer

Al Davis spent considerable time, money and effort in an attempt to find a player comparable to Daryle "The Mad Bomber" Lamonica, whom Davis viewed as his prototypical quarterback, after Lamonica retired at the end of the 1974 season.

Ron Riesterer

Al Davis, seen here with quarterback Daryle Lamonica on the sideline before a game in 1971, spent an inordinate amount of time creating an image that he wanted to project at all times. In particular, Davis was fond of his hair, to the point where a brush and spray were always available.

Ron Riesterer

Ted Hendricks (83) was an All-Pro linebacker for three NFL teams, which included a nine-year stint with the Raiders. Hendricks' size and athleticism struck fear into opposing quarterbacks such as David Woodley (16) of the Miami Dolphins.

Ron Riesterer

Ron Riesterer

Marcus Allen (32) and Ronnie Lott (42), both USC products, eventually became teammates when Lott left the 49ers and signed with the Raiders in 1991.

Larger-than-life, 6-foot-8 defensive lineman John Matuszak, and quarterback Kenny Stabler, a future Hall of Famer, played prominent roles in the Raiders' first Super Bowl victory in the 1976 season.

Al Davis prided himself on watching his team practice as often as possible. He is captured in this 1985 photo observing a practice with scout Jon Kingdon during the Raiders training camp.

Tom Flores (left) coached the Raiders to their second and third Super Bowl titles in the early 1980s. He and senior executive John Herrera (center) were two of Al Davis' favorites from the Raiders owner's first year with the Raiders in 1963 until his passing in 2011. The three are pictured on the field in Canton, Ohio, before Flores' first-ever game as Raiders head coach in 1979.

Russ Reed

Mickey Marvin, right, who embodied Davis' motto "Once a Raider, always a Raider," played for 11 years on an offensive line that featured Gene Upshaw (left) and Art Shell, future Hall of Famers. Marvin was the starting right guard on two Raiders Super Bowl teams and also was a long-time scout.

Ron Riesterer

Offensive coordinator Terry Robiskie and quarterback Todd Marinovich played roles in the Raiders advancing to the 1991 AFC Playoffs.

Associated Press

Albert Lewis

Albert Lewis signed with the Raiders in 1994 after 11 years with the rival Kansas City Chiefs. When Lewis questioned the amount of his playing time, Raiders owner Al Davis told him, "You should just be happy that I got you out of those ugly-ass socks." The socks, which Lewis agreed looked like something Ronald McDonald would wear, are visible above as Lewis breaks up a pass while with the Chiefs.

Pictured above at the 1997 free-agent signing of quarterback Jeff George, the first selection of the 1990 draft, are (left to right): Leigh Steinberg, the "super-agent" who was the inspiration for the movie *Jerry Maguire*; Raiders senior assistant Bruce Allen, who Al Davis provided with his first NFL job and who later was hired as the general manager of the Tampa Bay Buccaneers and as president of the Washington Redskins; and George, who passed for an NFL-best 3,917 yards in his first season with the Raiders.

Jon Gruden's personality proved infectious, as he transformed the Raiders from a 4-12 team the year before he was hired as head coach in 1998 into a playoff team in his third season.

Al Davis traded head coach Jon Gruden to the Tampa Bay Buccaneers after Gruden's fourth season with the Raiders. The Buccaneers crushed the Raiders in the Super Bowl in Gruden's first year with Tampa Bay.

Warren Sapp, right, signed with the Raiders in 2004, Jerry Rice's final season in Oakland. Sapp played for the Buccaneers team that defeated Rice's Raiders in the Super Bowl two years earlier.

Warren Sapp displays the game face that struck fear into opposing quarterbacks during Sapp's Hall of Fame career, which concluded with the Raiders in 2007.

Dino Vournas /Associated Press

Al Davis (seated) engages in playful banter with Raiders beat writer Steve Corkran (far right) as several other writers and Raiders senior executive John Herrera (far left) look on during a news conference at training camp in Napa, August 1, 2007.

Raiders head coach Art Shell (right) and NFL Players Association Executive

Director Gene Upshaw converse during a 2006 Raiders training camp practice in Napa. The former teammates, both Hall of Fame members, manned the left side of the Raiders dominant offensive line from 1968-81, including Super Bowl victories over the Vikings and Eagles. The small-college resumes of both (Upshaw at Texas A&I and Shell at Maryland State) did not deter Al Davis from taking Upshaw, a guard, in the first round and Shell, a tackle, in the third.

Brad Mangin

Brad Mangin

Head coach Bill Callahan and All-Pro center Barret Robbins chat at practice in happier times. Callahan, who is one of only two first-year NFL head coaches to lead his team to the Super Bowl, made game plan changes two days prior to the Super Bowl clash with Tampa Bay in 2003. That prompted Robbins, who later was diagnosed with bipolar disorder, to go AWOL for nearly 24 hours prior to the game. Callahan, against Al Davis' wishes, suspended Robbins for the game and the Raiders were upset by the Buccaneers 48-21.

Bob Larson

Tim Brown (81) starred as both a receiver and a kick returner during a 16-year career with the Raiders. Brown, a nine-time Pro Bowl selection and a member of the NFL's All-Decade team of the 1990s, became another of Al Davis' draft selections who was inducted into the Pro Football Hall of Fame after totaling 1,094 receptions for 14,934 yards (both figures sixth in NFL history through the 2016 season) and 100 touchdowns (ninth in NFL annals).

Five years after he had retired as a player and joined the Raiders scouting staff, Calvin Branch (standing) was asked by Raiders owner Al Davis to return to the field. After one of the six games he played in 2005, Branch posed for a photo with the five current teammates that he had scouted as college players — (from left to right) quarterback Andrew Walter, cornerback Chris Carr, linebacker Kirk Morrison, linebacker Ryan Riddle and cornerback Stanford Routt.

Raiders scouts Bruce Kebric, Jon Kingdon and Calvin Branch (left to right, second row of stands) time the 40-yard dash at the 2012 NFL scouting combine in Indianapolis.

Memories of three Super Bowl wins were prominent as Davis and his guests celebrated his 75th birthday. "Loyalty, Passion, Friends" was the theme of the celebration, as can be seen on this dinner menu created for the occasion, above left. Above right, a floral replica of the Vince Lombardi Trophy. Attendees received a crystal football engraved with the Raiders logo and the party theme.

Bruce Kebric

Bruce Kebric (left), Elizabeth Kebric and Jon Kingdon were among the select guests in attendance for Al Davis' 75th birthday party on July 4, 2004.

LOYALTY PASSION FRIENDS

JULY 4, 2004

Al Davis loved staying in touch with his former players and coaches. Thirty-one, including 11 Hall of Famers, attended his 75th birthday party in Las Vegas in 2004.

"*Here's to great memories*"

Four *more years to* 80!

Hope you are well

...Al & Carol

Your view from Bellagio...

Only one year removed from his 75th birthday celebration, Al Davis was eagerly anticipating another Las Vegas gathering of his family and friends for number 80. The above card was sent to those who had attended the earlier event. Davis, due to health issues, was forced to cancel the 80th affair and then passed away two years later in 2011.

to make their selection, Gruber and Dixon were gone, taken by the Tampa Bay Buccaneers and the Cincinnati Bengals, respectively, with the fourth and fifth picks.

With both players gone, Wolf favored Miami wide receiver Michael Irvin, while Davis sought Notre Dame wingback Tim Brown because of his punt- and kick-return abilities. It can't be overlooked that Brown also won the Heisman Trophy, which carried added weight with Davis, and ran a 4.39-second 40-yard dash on AstroTurf at the scouting combine, while Irvin timed at 4.58 on grass at Miami.

"I hadn't seen Tim Brown," Kebric said, "but I had seen Michael Irvin. I liked Michael. Ron went to his workout, and Ron liked him, too. But Al went with Tim Brown because he could return punts and kick-offs, as well as play receiver. Of course, Tim also was much faster than Michael."

Davis' sights that year actually were set upon Nebraska defensive end Neil Smith. To that end, Davis inquired about a trade with the Detroit Lions for the No. 2 pick. The Lions ultimately traded with the Kansas City Chiefs, who moved up from No. 3 and drafted Smith at No. 2.

In the same draft, the Raiders traded veteran defensive end Sean Jones to the Houston Oilers for the No. 9 pick. Wolf wanted Oklahoma tight end Keith Jackson. Kebric fought hard for Arizona State guard Randall McDaniel. Kebric even went so far as to tell Davis that McDaniel's girlfriend told him after McDaniel's pre-draft workout at ASU, "Every night when we go to bed, we pray that we will be Raiders."

Davis wanted University of Tennessee cornerback Terry McDaniel. That's all that mattered.

Wolf worked extremely hard, was very well-organized and had a photographic memory of past and present players. Whenever Davis could not remember the name of a player, Wolf had the name on the tip of his tongue.

"He had as good a work ethic as I had ever been around and he was great to work for because he would just give you an assignment and he would let you do it," Kebric said. "His success at Green Bay and his later induction into the Pro Football Hall of Fame were no surprise to those of us who had the opportunity to work with him at the Raiders."

Ron Riesterer

Al Davis was enamored with speed from his youth, when he watched the Brooklyn Dodgers use speedy players to their advantage. He found an ideal player to terrorize defenses with his swiftness when he drafted wide receiver Cliff Branch in 1972. As former Raiders quarterback and head coach Tom Flores once said, "There is Fast, Really Fast, and Cliff."

🏈 CHAPTER SIX 🏈

The Need for Speed

From the outset, Al Davis' Raiders were synonymous with speed. The faster, the better, Davis believed. To him, it was paramount to success in the NFL. He never was satisfied when it came to speed.

"It got to the point where we used to joke, 'Some people collect stamps, some people collect coins, some people collect baseball cards, Al Davis collected fast players,'" Bruce Kebric said. "Al had to have the fastest guy at the combine, and he would get upset if somebody drafted him ahead of us."

Davis also valued size and strength, particularly with his offensive and defensive linemen, but it was speed that trumped all. How fast a player ran a 40-yard dash, one of many metrics used by other NFL teams in evaluating prospects, became the gold standard for Davis.

The Dallas Cowboys and Gil Brandt are credited with implementing the 40-yard dash as a standardized test in pre-draft workouts. It is Davis who latched on to the 40-yard dash as the all-important measuring stick for players.

"If a guy couldn't run, Al didn't care," Kebric said. "That's the one thing that former Raiders personnel director Ron Wolf pointed out in 1991, when he went to the Jets. He said, 'You guys don't realize how easy you have it at the Raiders because if a guy can't run, Al doesn't care. The guy can turn out to be an All-Pro, but Al doesn't care. But at our place, we have to watch and grade every player.'"

Davis' obsession with speed stemmed from his years watching the Brooklyn Dodgers at Ebbets Field during his youth. Yet it took a while for Davis to fully appreciate the value of speed.

Davis' first love was power. The way the mighty New York Yankees dominated games, series and seasons with a power-filled lineup resonated with Davis. He witnessed the Yankees rack up World Series titles and he loved how they did so in dominant fashion.

The Yankees had won only three World Series before Davis was born in 1929. They won five more by the time he was 10 years old and had 17 titles by the time he joined the Raiders. The reliance upon power from players as far back as Babe Ruth in the 1920s and on through Mickey Mantle and Roger Maris in the 1950s and '60s was not lost upon Davis.

When Davis joined the Raiders in 1963, he already had spent years mapping out how he wanted his team to look in uniform, how he wanted his players to perform and the attributes he felt were essential for a player to be dominant.

This was made clear one day in a conversation with Kebric.

"Al said the colors came from the black of Army, which in his youth was a dominant team," Kebric said. "He always liked the silver of the Detroit Lions. He emphasized that, even though he grew up in Brooklyn, his number one attribute was the power of the Yankees. He liked the speed of the Dodgers but, he said, power beats speed."

Eventually, Davis ended up fascinated by speed more than anything. He filed away what he gleaned from watching the Dodgers on the base paths and implemented it as soon as he joined the Raiders in 1963 as a first-time NFL head coach.

He signed fleet-footed wide receiver Art Powell and paired him with the likes of Irvin "Bo" Roberson, who had won a silver medal in the 1960 Olympics as a long-jumper. Powell caught 73 passes for 1,304 yards and 16 touchdowns in '63, as the Raiders posted a 10-4 record on the heels of a 1-13 mark in 1962.

Davis was just getting started. In 1964, he acquired running back Billy Cannon and converted him to tight end. Cannon, while with the Houston Oilers, had led the AFL in rushing in 1961. With the Raiders, Cannon became a receiving tight end, taking advantage of the 9.4-second 100-yard dash time that Cannon had recorded at Louisiana State University, as well as the strength that had enabled him to be a top shot-putter in college.

Davis' need for speed carried over to the defense, as well. In 1964, he watched a college game between Kansas and Nebraska during which Huskers safety Kent McCloughan ran down standout running back Gale Sayers, who was recognized as the fastest and most-talented player in college at the time.

Davis wasn't able to get Sayers — he went to the Chicago Bears — but he eventually acquired McCloughan in a trade with the Houston Oilers in 1965. He immediately moved McCloughan to cornerback so he could match up against standout San Diego Chargers wide receiver Lance Alworth.

Davis came to view speed as the difference maker in a sport where the talent level between players is oftentimes negligible.

To achieve this, Davis collected as many fast players as possible. He searched far and wide for anyone who could run at an elite level. The Raiders conducted a private workout for British decathlete Daley Thompson, who won gold medals at the 1980 and 1984 Summer Olympics.

Thompson ran a disappointing 4.55 seconds in the 40-yard dash, and it became readily evident he wasn't a natural pass-catcher and that he didn't have the potential to develop into a reliable receiver anytime soon.

Thompson warmed up for a bit, then lined up to run a 40-yard dash.

"There was great anticipation to see what he would run," Kingdon said.

Thompson surprised Kingdon by running a 4.55-second 40, which Kingdon termed "very average."

Yet the way Thompson lined up at the start of the 40 surprised Kingdon most of all.

Thompson placed his left hand on the ground, with his right foot well behind.

"When the workout was over, I went over to Thompson and said, 'Daley, I have nothing but respect for what you have done in track and I don't mean to be presumptuous, but when you put your left hand down to run the 40, wouldn't you put your left leg back rather than your right?'"

Kingdon awaited Thompson's response, fully expecting a revealing explanation as to why he chose such an unorthodox stance.

Instead, Thompson looked at Kingdon and with a thick British accent said, "You might have something there, mate."

It was obvious that Thompson probably never attempted to catch a football prior to this workout.

"And it showed," Kingdon said. "His hands weren't very soft, and he tried to trap every ball thrown to him."

Davis believed that coaches could not teach speed, though it was not for lack of effort. At one point the Raiders hired Jim Bush, who had been a well-respected track coach at UCLA, though there were no great transformations as a result of his efforts. If a player is fast but doesn't play football well, Davis felt it was the job of the coaches to teach him how to become an NFL-caliber player. The Raiders could make a decent football player out of a fast runner. No one, however, could make a marginal football player run on par with elite track stars.

In 1972, the Raiders drafted University of Colorado wide receiver

Cliff Branch in the fourth round. He was exceptionally fast. Former Raiders quarterback and head coach Tom Flores once said about speed, that "There is Fast, Really Fast, and Cliff." Yet Branch's hands were lacking coming out of college. Countless hours spent working with Flores, however, turned Branch turn into a star NFL receiver.

"From that point on, Al never ceased looking for another Cliff Branch," Kingdon said.

Davis' never-ending search for speedy wide receivers focused on John Ford in 1989. When Ford's name was brought up in the team's draft meetings, Davis asked scout Angie Coia what he thought about the tall, fast receiver from the University of Virginia.

"Angie, what about John Ford?" Davis said.

"Well, Al, he can't catch," Coia replied.

"Angie, does it bother you if a receiver doesn't have good hands?" Davis asked Coia, who had been an accomplished receiver in college and the NFL.

Coia wasn't sure what to make of Davis' query. He looked around the room for help, as if Davis had asked him a loaded question.

Everyone sort of shrugged their shoulders at Coia, not knowing where Davis was heading with such an obvious question.

"Yes, Al, it would bother me if he couldn't catch," Coia said.

"What if one out of the three balls he catches is for a touchdown?" Davis asked. "Would it still bother you?"

Coia reiterated that he felt it was important that a receiver be able to catch the ball on a regular basis.

"I'm not so sure," Davis said as the conversation ended.

The Detroit Lions drafted Ford in the second round. Two years later, Kebric was watching tape at Clemson. He related to fellow scouts in the dark film room how Davis had asked Coia if it mattered if a guy can catch and how Coia had responded. When Kebric mentioned Ford's name, Lions director of player personnel Ron Hughes blurted out from the back of the room, "Hey, Bruce, tell Angie that he was right."

Ford caught five passes for 56 yards and no touchdowns in seven games for the Lions in 1989, his lone season in the NFL.

Raiders scouts were compelled to check into every fast prospect. Davis wanted to know everything about a prospect, especially if that person had a track background.

This fascination with speed all too often dictated many of his draft picks.

In 2005, Davis used Oakland's first- and second-round draft picks on University of Nebraska cornerback Fabian Washington and University of Houston cornerback Stanford Routt, respectively. Washington and Routt clocked the two fastest times at the scouting combine, according to the times recorded by Raiders scouts. In the third round, Davis fancied a linebacker from Cal Poly-San Luis Obispo named Jordan Beck. Calvin Branch had scouted Beck, and he wasn't overly impressed. Davis queried Kingdon and Kebric, both of whom said they favored San Diego State's Kirk Morrison.

Defensive coordinator Rob Ryan and linebackers coach Don Martindale also preferred Morrison. In fact, they were very high on Morrison.

"Kirk was the best player at San Diego State, even better than Matt McCoy, who went in the second round to the Eagles," Kebric said. "But Kirk just didn't run well."

Kebric had timed Morrison on an indoor tartan surface in 4.74 seconds, which converted to 4.85 on grass. But Morrison more than made up for his lack of speed with great instincts.

A few days prior to the 2005 draft both Ryan and Martindale were dispatched to San Luis Obispo and clocked Beck in 4.50. If the Raiders were going to draft a linebacker, Beck was the guy because of his speed.

Kebric watched Beck on video and thought he would be an intriguing free agent.

"But Al wanted to draft Beck," Kebric said.

Usually, that was enough. End of story. In this case, however, Ryan and Martindale continued to lobby hard on Morrison's behalf. That gave Davis pause.

Davis then did what he typically did in such situations; he simply sought the opinion of others in the room in hopes of finding support for the player he wanted.

One by one, Davis polled those in the room and asked which player they favored. Morrison was the unanimous choice.

"I was upset at Al at the time he asked me," Kebric said, "because he bypassed Aaron Rodgers in the first round so that we could take our fastest-timed player in the combine. So, I supported Kirk Morrison, though I felt like he was more like a fourth- or fifth-rounder."

"Fine, then take Morrison," Davis snapped.

"Al was mad," Kebric said. "He went into a tantrum."

"This son of a bitch is slow," Davis said. "We're going to be the slowest team in pro football."

Rodgers was the Raiders' top-rated quarterback in the draft, and the Raiders were in need of a quarterback. However, Davis was focused, not surprisingly, on Fabian Washington, the fastest player in the draft. Washington, a cornerback out of Nebraska, had ability but not the type of coverage skills that would elevate him into the first round.

Each first-round pick that year would take a maximum of 15 minutes. Davis was going to have to wait as long as 45 minutes to select Washington. He couldn't wait. Even though he was told that Seattle, Green Bay and Washington weren't going to select a defensive back, Davis simply couldn't wait that long to make the pick, so he traded his first- and fifth-round picks to move up three spots for Seattle's first-round pick.

Many teams speculated that the Raiders engineered the trade so that they could draft Rodgers, one pick before Green Bay's turn. The surprising move set off a moment of panic in the Packers' draft room.

> *"Al was mad," Kebric said. "He went into a tantrum, (saying) 'This son of a bitch is slow. We're going to be the slowest team in pro football.'"*

After the draft, Kingdon called Green Bay scout Shaun Herock to compare notes on the draft. Without prompting, Herock related that the Packers were stunned that the Raiders had bypassed Rodgers.

"Why would you trade a fifth-round pick to move up into the first round so that you could take Fabian Washington?" Herock asked Kingdon.

"I told him that Al didn't have the patience to wait to select Fabian," Kingdon replied.

The next year, Davis found himself in a similar situation. The Raiders had two picks in the seventh round, and Davis wanted a little-known wide receiver out of the University of Maine named Kevin McMahan. Angelo Coia had scouted McMahan, and he saw nothing of note beyond McMahan's speed. Davis knew that McMahan ran a 4.41-second 40-yard dash.

When Davis brought up McMahan and started singing his praises, Coia interrupted.

"Al, I got two guys who haven't been drafted who are better than Kevin McMahan," Coia said.

"Who are your guys, Angie?" Davis said.

"Marques Colston and Miles Austin," Coia said.

"What do those guys run?" Davis asked. "Of the three of them, who is the fastest?"

"McMahan is the fastest, but he's third as a player," replied Coia.

"Draft McMahan," Davis said.

"That's what it got down to," Kingdon said. "Al was going to take the fastest player, regardless of performance."

Colston was drafted by the New Orleans Saints at No. 252 and three picks later, the Raiders snapped up McMahan with the final selection of the draft. Austin went undrafted, but he ultimately signed with the Dallas Cowboys.

Coia was the lone Raiders scout that had seen all three players in person. He graded Austin as a fifth-round prospect, Colston a sixth-rounder and McMahan a free agent. It all came down to that single number on a piece of paper.

McMahan never caught a pass or played in an NFL regular-season game. Colston has caught 711 passes for 9,759 yards and 72 touchdowns during a standout 10-year career with the Saints. Austin caught 361 passes for 5,273 yards and 37 touchdowns during his 10 NFL seasons, the first eight of which were spent with the Cowboys.

On special occasions, the scouting department would manipulate a reported 40 time.

Running back Marcus Allen was a complete running back when he won the Heisman Trophy in 1981 and entered the 1982 NFL draft as a top prospect. He rushed for 2,427 yards and 22 touchdowns his senior season at USC. He also caught 34 passes and blocked as well as any collegiate back in the nation.

But, he had clocked a 4.75 40-yard dash. By the time that figure hit Davis' desk, it had been changed to 4.65. The Raiders selected Allen with the 10th pick that year.

Davis hit upon his share of gambles with fast players. However, time and again, he was burned by his fascination with speed.

Davis wanted opposing teams fearful of the Raiders turning any play into a back-breaker on speed alone. He wanted cornerbacks worried about getting beat by Raiders receivers on every play. Davis wanted defensive coordinators so consumed with the Raiders' speed that the Raiders would have a decided edge in game planning.

Of course, this meant that Davis oftentimes overlooked players who could have helped him win more games simply because they didn't run a certain time in the 40-yard dash. There wasn't much Davis' scouts could do once he locked in on a fast player.

"Whenever a player would run fast at the scouting combine, any scout sitting near us would immediately turn to us and say, 'There's your first-round pick,'" Kingdon said.

Davis insisted upon using 40-yard dash times collected at the scouting combine because the invited players were tested for performance-enhancing drugs.

He paid attention to 40 times culled elsewhere, but he was suspicious of them.

"Initially I thought the difference between the combine and the pro day times was probably related to less pressure at the latter," Kebric said. "I decided to investigate Al's theory and after talking to strength coaches at various schools, I learned that substances do exist that can elevate performance for a few hours on a given day. That's what Al was afraid of."

The scouting combine was an event that Davis loved to attend. He sat in the same seat each year and eagerly awaited the 40-yard dash.

Once Davis was seated for the 40, he never moved. He didn't even take bathroom breaks. He generally was joined by such NFL luminaries as Cowboys owner Jerry Jones, long-time head coach Bill Parcells and former Cowboys vice president of player personnel Gil Brandt, the latter considered the originator of many of the modern scouting tests.

"Al sat at the start of the 40, in the first row," Kingdon said.

"Most of us wanted to be at the finish line," Kebric said.

Davis was adamant about being at the starting line. Kebric joked with Davis about that position being the worst seat in the house.

"Why do you sit at the start and not the finish?" Kebric asked Davis.

"I want to see explosion," Davis remarked. "I can get the 40 times from you."

Angie Coia and Kent McCloughan were the Raiders' timers for the 40-yard dash. Both had extensive track backgrounds. Coia had been a 400-meter finalist at the 1960 U.S. Olympic trials, while McCloughan was the Nebraska state record holder in the 100-yard dash.

Davis also insisted upon times other than the 40, so Kingdon and Kebric generally timed the first 10 yards, while Jim and John Otten were stationed at 20 yards.

"The 20 was the most irrelevant time for anybody," Kingdon said. "Everyone would talk about the 10 and the 40."

Former Raiders running back Derrick Jensen, who scouted for the Seattle Seahawks, once said to the amusement of everyone timing at the 20: "Have you ever heard about someone not being drafted because he had a bad 20 time?"

The National Scouting Combine provided each team with two hand-held 10, 20 and 40 times from designated timers on the field, as well as electronic times. Davis chose to ignore the times of others and relied solely upon the ones collected by his Raiders employees, who sat in the stands.

"Al obviously focused on the 40 times," Kingdon said. "He would ask general questions about the other drills — bench press, vertical jump, broad jump and shuttles. He would ask if the player had good numbers, not really wanting to know the specific numbers."

Though he said that he looked for explosion in a player, Davis did not hesitate to dismiss players such as future NFL greats Michael Strahan and Terrell Suggs because neither posted a fast 40 time. Strahan ran 4.93 at the combine and a slower 5.02 when Kebric timed him at his pro day workout. The same goes for Suggs, who ran a 4.85 on AstroTurf.

"Strahan and Suggs were two of the most explosive players I ever scouted, but Al was not interested in either due to the 40 times," Kebric said. "He had told me that he positioned himself at the start of the 40 because he wanted to see explosion. When I mentioned the explosive pass rushing ability displayed by Strahan and Suggs, he ignored me. So, I surmised that explosion and speed were synonymous to him."

When Strahan had a standout week at the Senior Bowl, his name started to rise quickly on NFL scouting boards. He had a school-record 19 sacks his final year at Texas Southern and was perceived to have vast untapped potential given that he had played only one season of high school football. Strahan had moved to Germany with his military family at the age of nine and had returned to Houston only for his senior year of high school.

Strahan, however, was not on Davis' radar that year, even with the outstanding Senior Bowl performance. His 40 times simply were not fast enough. Raider coaches and scouts saw the potential in Strahan, and finally convinced Davis to watch game tape with the group. Not long into this viewing, Davis' attention suddenly turned to another Texas Southern player. He had discovered Kevin Johnson, a 306-pound nose tackle, and his focus on the 253-pound Strahan quickly waned.

"Did you see him (Johnson) do this? Did you see him do that?" Davis exclaimed over and over.

Davis' discovery of another player, or in his mind a "sleeper," had occurred on numerous other occasions, much to the dismay of the Raiders staff members.

The Giants selected Strahan in the second round of the 1993 draft. Strahan went on to achieve an NFL record 22.5 sacks during the 2001 season and was inducted into the Pro Football Hall of Fame in 2014. Johnson, on the other hand, was drafted in the fourth round by New England, cut by the Patriots, played two years for Philadelphia and then joined the Raiders in 1997 after the Eagles waived him.

In the 1996 draft Oakland selected La'Roi Glover, a defensive tackle from San Diego State, in the fifth round. Glover was a favorite of the Raiders scouts, who on three separate occasions had made trips to San Diego to time him in the 40-yard dash. Glover wasn't able to break five seconds on any of the visits, generally a reason for Davis to discard him as a draft prospect.

The Raiders, at the time, were in the midst of returning to Oakland from Los Angeles. An office site had been selected but was not ready at the time of the draft, so Davis along with the coaches and scouts congregated in a room at the Oakland Airport Hilton for the draft proceedings. Davis had been busy overseeing the move and had not had the time to study the lower-round prospects. His knowledge of the draft was exhausted by the fifth round, Kebric said, so he told the scouts to make the pick. Glover was the unanimous selection. Raiders secondary coach Steve Shafer, who formerly had coached at San Diego State, also strongly supported the selection of Glover.

Glover appeared in two games for the Raiders in 1996 and then was sent to the Barcelona Dragons of the World League. By the time Glover returned to the United States, Davis had signed Kevin Johnson, whom he had not forgotten from the Strahan tapes. With Johnson in the fold, Davis felt no need to keep Glover on the roster. Chet Franklin, a former Raiders coach and executive, immediately signed Glover for the New Orleans Saints. Glover, another player who was jettisoned from the Raiders because he couldn't run fast enough, went on to lead the NFL with 17.5 sacks in the 2000 season and was named to the NFL All-Decade team for the 2000s after garnering six Pro Bowl berths and four All-Pro selections. Johnson was out of the league after a short stint with the Raiders in 1997.

When Glover achieved All-Pro status, Davis was asked why he had let Glover go. The line that Davis put out was that the Raiders, at the time, had three top defensive tackles in Darrell Russell, Russell Maryland and Grady Jackson. "Al conveniently left out the fact that Kevin Johnson was also kept on the roster at that time," Kingdon said, "and few people remembered this egregious decision."

"Speed had always been important to Al, but as his health deteriorated, he relied even more upon speed," Kebric said. "He did not have the energy necessary to complete the tedious draft preparation process. The easiest approach for him was to concentrate on the fast players, watch their tapes, read the scouting reports on those individuals and then select who he considered the best of the fastest, which generally meant the fastest."

During the 2004 draft, Davis was interested in selecting a wide receiver and, to the surprise of no one, had zeroed in on Texas Tech's Carlos Francis. The diminutive Francis had recorded the fastest 40-yard dash time at the NFL scouting combine.

"Coach, Francis isn't even the best wide receiver at Texas Tech," said scout David McCloughan.

Naturally, Davis wanted to know the name of the player that McCloughan vouched for as being a better NFL prospect than Francis.

"David, who is the best receiver at Texas Tech?" Davis asked.

"A guy by the name of Wes Welker," McCloughan said.

"David, what does he run?" Davis asked.

When McCloughan related that Welker ran a 4.71 40-yard dash on AstroTurf, which translated to 4.79 on grass, Davis quickly removed Welker's name from consideration, either as a draft choice or as a free agent.

"Oh, fuck it, take Francis," Davis said.

The Raiders selected Francis with the third pick in the fourth round. Welker went undrafted. He signed with the rival San Diego Chargers after the draft.

Welker played one game for the Chargers before he got released. Davis and the league's 31 other teams allowed Welker to pass through waivers unclaimed.

Welker was signed by the Miami Dolphins, for whom he caught 96 passes for 1,121 yards and one touchdown his first three seasons.

Welker showed promise early on, but he didn't develop into an All-Pro receiver until the Dolphins traded him to the New England Patriots for a second-round draft pick in 2007.

Francis' NFL career lasted only one season. He appeared in five regular-season games and didn't catch any passes. Injuries and lack of interest by the Raiders resulted in Francis walking away from the NFL in 2006.

Welker totaled 903 receptions for 9,924 yards and 50 touchdowns in a career that merits consideration for his induction into the Pro Football Hall of Fame.

Davis kept tabs on Welker's career and even questioned how Welker escaped the Raiders drafting net.

"When Welker became a player, Al called me and asked why we didn't like Welker when he came out in the draft," Kingdon said. "I reminded him how we brought up his name and how he immediately dropped him when he heard his 40 time."

"What was it?" Davis asked.

"4.71 on AstroTurf," Kingdon told Davis.

"Bullshit!" Davis yelled into the phone. "Do you believe that time?"

"That's what he ran," Kingdon said.

Later on, Davis instructed his scouts to "find me a Welker," Kebric recalled.

Contrary to widespread belief, speed didn't always win out with Davis. The best example came in 1983, when Davis vacillated on which player to select with his late first-round pick.

Davis was torn between Darrell Green, a lightning-fast cornerback and kick returner from Texas A&I (now Texas A&M-Kingsville), and Don Mosebar, a versatile offensive lineman out of the University of Southern California. Green posted a 10.08-second time in the 100 meters in college, and he is believed to have been one of the fastest ever in the 40-yard dash. When Green ran a 4.35-second 40 on grass, the fastest ever recorded by Kebric, it seemed logical that Green was destined to be a Raider.

"I told Al that Green, at the time, might be the best football player

I had ever scouted," said Kebric. "He not only was a shutdown corner but was a better kick returner than Billy 'White Shoes' Johnson, whom we drafted at Houston and had become the NFL's best returner."

"If he was only two inches taller," Davis said in explaining his hesitation. Green had been measured at 5-foot-8 but carried a solid 184 pounds on his frame.

"Al, if he was two inches taller, he would be a top-five pick," said Kebric.

The Raiders used the 26th pick on Mosebar, who stood 6-foot-6. Green went to the Washington Redskins two picks later, with the final selection of the first round.

After the draft, Kebric was talking with Washington general manager Bobby Beathard.

"There was only one team that we were worried about," Beathard said. "I figured, if he got by you guys, we had him."

Green was an instant success for Washington, as he returned a punt 61 yards for a touchdown the first time he touched the ball in an NFL game and ran down Cowboys running back Tony Dorsett in the regular-season opener to save a touchdown in a nationally televised game. They were just the kind of plays Davis envisioned when he targeted fast players. During a 20-year career with Washington, Green played in 313 regular-season and postseason games, intercepted 60 passes and was a first-year inductee into the Pro Football Hall of Fame in 2008.

Though Green played cornerback for Washington, Davis later related that he envisioned Green as someone who could have had a bigger impact on offense.

"I was going to make him a receiver," Davis said to Kebric a few times. "That shows what a dumb bastard I was."

Passing up Green proved difficult for Davis, and Davis became irate a short time after the draft when he learned that Mosebar was in the hospital, recovering from back surgery.

Kebric had departed for Texas before the first round had been completed so he could get a jump on signing undrafted players. He had no idea whom the Raiders had selected until Kingdon called later that day.

"Guess what? All hell just broke loose," Kingdon said.

"What are you talking about?" Kebric said. "What's going on?"

"Mosebar just recently had back surgery and was in the hospital when we drafted him," Kingdon said.

Davis was furious.

Kingdon had called Mosebar before the draft, as he had numerous other prospects. This was standard procedure so that the team knew where the player could be reached during the draft or for a later free-agent signing. Kingdon and Mosebar spoke by phone. It wasn't until after they drafted him that the Raiders learned Mosebar had injured his back earlier that spring while throwing the shot put for the USC track team. He had a surgical procedure performed just prior to the draft, but neither Mosebar nor his agent, Howard Slusher, had bothered to notify NFL teams.

"[He] called me and asked me where I was going to be on the day of the draft," Mosebar later said. "If he would have asked me how I was doing, I would have told him that I had back surgery."

Mosebar recovered from his back surgery and enjoyed a distinguished 12-year career with the Raiders. Davis moved Mosebar from his natural tackle position to center, and Mosebar was named to the Pro Bowl on three occasions and participated in one Super Bowl victory. His career ended on a sad note during a 1995 scrimmage with the Dallas Cowboys, when Mosebar suffered a freak eye injury while blocking defensive lineman Chad Hennings.

The next time he had the opportunity, Davis wasn't about to bypass an elite speedster, who was shorter than desired. In 1995, his decision of whom to pick in the first round was between running backs — University of Washington's Napoleon Kaufman and University of Michigan's Tyrone Wheatley.

"Kaufman was Gale Sayers-like," Kingdon said. "He could cut at full speed and was really explosive."

Davis was truly enamored with Kaufman's speed and quickness, while Wheatley's assets were strength and power.

"In Al's mind, he wanted to select Wheatley but in his heart, he really wanted Kaufman," Kingdon said. "He never let on who he would choose if it came down to one or the other."

Coincidentally, Wheatley went one pick ahead of the Raiders to the New York Giants and spent the final six years of his 10-year NFL career with the Raiders.

Kaufman was 5-foot-9 and 182 pounds, with 4.4 speed. What he lacked in stature, he more than made up for with his speed and surprising strength. He recorded 24 reps in the 225-pound bench press at the scouting combine, which was the second-best mark among running backs that year.

At a preseason game that year, Kingdon ran into Packers general manager Ron Wolf and asked him what he thought of Kaufman.

"I about fell out of my chair," Wolf said. "I never believed that Al Davis would draft a guy that small."

Davis was equally enamored that draft with Derrick Brooks, a linebacker out of Florida State. Brooks, at 6-foot and 229 pounds, was a bit undersized for his position. Yet he too was fast, having run the 40 in the 4.6s.

Davis devised a plan. He took Kaufman at No. 18 because he thought he could work out a trade with the Dallas Cowboys for the 28th selection.

"Al told us that he thought he had made a deal with Dallas," Kebric said. "But later Jerry Jones told him that Tampa Bay offered the Cowboys more. That one really surprised me because Al had an affinity for Jones. One time I was in Al's office and Jones called. I remember Al saying to Jones, 'There are not many people that I call a friend ... (pause) ... but you're one.'"

When the Buccaneers selected Brooks, Kebric said, "Al went into a total funk. And we did not see him again until just before our second pick."

Davis made another run at Brooks in 2009, six months or so after Brooks was released by the Buccaneers. The Raiders worked out Brooks during training camp, but Brooks no longer had what it took to be an every-down player and Davis passed.

Brooks carved out a stellar 14-year career with the Buccaneers and was elected to the Pro Football Hall of Fame in 2014. He had one of his team's five interceptions in the Buccaneers thrashing of the Raiders in Super Bowl XXXVII at the end of the 2002 season. Two years later, he ended the career of Raiders quarterback Rich Gannon with a neck-crushing tackle in a regular-season game in Oakland.

Kaufman had a productive six-year career for the Raiders before his retirement after the 2000 season. His 4,792 career rushing yards included a career-high 1,294 in 1997, along with a Raider record 227 yards against Denver in an upset win that year. His 5.8-yard average rushing in 1996 topped the league. Kaufman today is an ordained minister who serves as the Raiders team chaplain.

Davis also had a penchant for pursuing former Olympians.

"We always referred to 1993 as Al's double gold medal draft," Kebric said. "In that one, he garnered not only two of the fastest players in the draft, but two world-class sprinters."

With the drafting of James Trapp and the post-draft signing of free agent James Jett, Davis now had two of the sprinters who had represented the U.S. at the 1992 Barcelona Olympic Games.

"He was ecstatic with the acquisition of James Trapp and James Jett," Kebric said.

That draft was a controversial one from start to finish. Davis' first two selections, safety Patrick Bates and quarterback Billy Joe Hobert, both carried personal baggage from their collegiate days. Bates had been on the West Coast previously as a freshman member of the UCLA Bruins football team. He had returned to his home state of Texas at season's end and enrolled at Texas A&M. Hobert had led the Washington Huskies to a Rose Bowl victory and a co-national championship (along with Miami) in January 1992 only to be dismissed from the team a few months later.

"Did you see his workout?" Davis asked Kebric, when the latter questioned taking Bates high in the first round.

"I was in charge of his workout at Texas A&M," Kebric snapped back at Davis. "R.C. Slocum, the Aggies head coach, told me to conduct the workout, so I had organized things and put Jack Stanton, the Raiders secondary coach, in charge of the drills."

Bates' numbers, 6-foot-3, 224 pounds and a 4.49-second 40-yard dash, and his excellent workout were too gaudy for Davis to pass up at the No. 12 pick.

Bates lasted two seasons in Los Angeles this time around and started only nine games for the Raiders. Just prior to the start of the 1995 regular season, Bates walked away from the team, citing incompatibility with his teammates and coaches, as well as what he perceived as a dysfunctional organization.

As he related to Thomas George of the *New York Times* in May, 1996, "I saw a lot of old heads in the locker room who were used to doing things their way and when you spoke up for change, for winning, they looked at you like you were crazy. And then the staff treated me that way. I truly believed I was the best player at my position, and the Raiders just jerked me around, in and out, from starter to backup. I didn't understand it. They didn't understand it. What I saw was a place where there were a lot of Indians and every one of them thought they were the chief."

Davis, however, managed to salvage something from the Bates fiasco when he traded the disgruntled player to the Atlanta Falcons for a second-round selection. At the time of the trade, Thomas George quoted Falcons head coach June Jones as saying, "We picked 10th in the '93 draft and Bates went at 12. We nearly took him then. I can't believe we got him now for a second-round pick to the Raiders. He has more ability than any safety I've seen."

But once again Bates proved to be a big disappointment. He started nine games in his lone season for Atlanta, totaling 61 tackles with no interceptions. At the end of the 1996 season, both Bates and Jones were looking for employment. Jones rebounded as the offensive coordinator and interim head coach for the San Diego Chargers in 1998. Bates, however, had played his final NFL game.

With the first of two third-round selections, the choice revolved around two Washington quarterbacks, Hobert and Mark Brunell. Both had been starters at Washington and both had led the Huskies to Rose Bowl wins. Brunell was one year ahead of Hobert scholastically and had been the 1990 starter. When Brunell suffered a spring practice knee injury, Hobert jumped in and guided the Huskies to the co-national championship. Hobert was the starter entering the 1992 season when it was discovered that he had accepted $50,000 in loans from a friend. Hobert was dismissed from the team and Brunell regained the starting role.

Davis, the decision-maker, had to choose between the bigger and stronger Hobert, the coaches' favorite, or the smaller, faster, more consistent Brunell, who was championed by the scouts. The deciding vote may have been cast by running backs coach Joe Scannella, who, after viewing Hobert's Rose Bowl performance against Michigan, said, "He looks like a fucking first rounder to me, Al."

Finally, the stage was set for the player that most fascinated Davis, James Trapp, the Olympic sprinter from Clemson. The scouts had projected Trapp as a fourth-rounder, but when Davis asked for a guarantee that Trapp would be available at that point, none was forthcoming. Trapp was another player who had experienced some problems during his college career. He had been beaten for two fourth-quarter touchdowns in a loss to Virginia during the fall of his senior season. On the flight back to South Carolina, Trapp and an assistant coach got into a heated argument and nearly came to blows. The next week, Trapp was moved down the depth chart and did not start for the remainder of the season.

"When I visited Clemson, one of the coaches told me that they would be happy to see him go," Kebric recalled.

During a pre-draft video session, Davis and his staff viewed the Clemson-Virginia game tape. Davis, as was his custom, had previously watched the game on his own and knew that Trapp played well for the first three quarters. At the end of the third quarter, Davis conveniently said that he had seen enough of Trapp and told the video operator to turn off the projector.

Kebric, who was sitting next to Davis, said, "Al, we didn't see the part where he gives up two touchdowns."

"Shhh," Davis whispered to Kebric.

"My comment really disturbed him," Kebric said. "He told me that I needed to go find defensive coordinator Fred Whittingham and secondary coach Steve Shafer and tell them that I liked Trapp. I couldn't find either one of them at the time and Al never asked me if I had carried out his request."

Somehow, as the eight-round draft unfolded, Davis managed to lose track of the other speedster he coveted, James Jett.

"After our final selection, I asked Al if he wanted to sign Jett as a free agent," Kebric said.

"Why didn't you tell me about Jett?" Davis screamed at Kebric. "Fuck yes, sign him."

Kebric quickly moved into an adjacent room and asked George Karras, the Raiders pro scouting director, to call Jett's agent, Bruce Allen. Yes, the same Bruce Allen who later worked for the Raiders. Karras dialed the number Kebric had given him and started talking to one of Allen's assistants, telling him that Davis was demanding that we sign Jett. Allen soon joined the conversation, and he was on the verge of agreeing to a $5,000 signing bonus, when Davis stormed into the room and wanted to know if the Jett deal was done. Without breaking stride, Davis grabbed the phone from Karras.

"Ten thousand dollars is my final offer," Davis shouted to Allen.

Allen quickly accepted the $5,000 signing bonus increase, and Davis handed the phone back to Karras.

"Now that's the way you do a deal," Davis told Karras and Kebric.

Jett turned out to be the star of the 1993 Raiders draft, and the $10,000 signing bonus was money well spent. During a 10-year NFL career, all with the Raiders, Jett caught 256 passes for 4,417 yards, a gaudy 17.3 yards per catch average, and 30 touchdowns. The quarterback that got away, Brunell, was drafted by Ron Wolf and the Green Bay Packers. Two years later Wolf traded Brunell to Jacksonville, where as a nine-year starter he established all of the Jaguars team passing records and played in three Pro Bowls. Hobert had an undistinguished three-year career with the Raiders and later stints with Buffalo, New Orleans, and Indianapolis.

The Raiders and the Baltimore Ravens met in Oakland for the 2000 AFC Championship. During the week prior to the game, Kebric was scouting the East-West Shrine Game practices on the Stanford University campus. While walking between drills, Kebric heard someone call out, "Hey, Bruce!" When Kebric looked up, he saw Phil Savage, the Ravens director of player personnel.

"Hi, Phil," Kebric replied.

"Is James Jett going to play on Sunday?" Savage asked.

"No," Kebric said.

"What about Napoleon Kaufman?" Savage continued.

"I don't think so," Kebric said

Savage then smiled, and said, "Great, we will win."

Ozzie Newsome, the Ravens general manager who was standing next to Savage, nodded his approval.

Jett and Kaufman, the Raiders two fastest offensive players, did not play in the game and the Ravens held the Raiders to a season-low three points in a 16-3 win. Two weeks later, the Ravens won the Super Bowl.

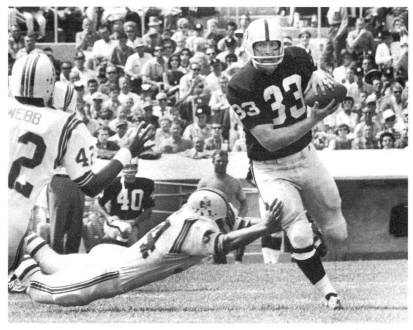

Ron Riesterer

Al Davis had a penchant for converting players from one position to another. His first conversion came in 1964, when he took Billy Cannon (33), one of the AFL's top rushers, and developed him into a productive tight end.

CHAPTER SEVEN

The Experiments

Al Davis loved being portrayed as some magical, wizard-like figure. As a creature of the night, many thought that he spent his time brewing potions to both enlighten and embarrass his NFL colleagues. The "genius" label that was pinned on him in the late 1960s by pundits and friends was well-received. For a 20-year period, the label was most appropriate, as he was the scourge of the NFL both on and off the field.

"When I joined the Raiders, I remember people coming up to me and asking, 'How is the genius?' Or, 'What's it like working for the genius?'" Bruce Kebric said. "One of my biggest surprises came in the Houston Astrodome press box one year, when Hall of Fame coach Sid Gillman, who provided Davis with his first professional coaching opportunity, asked me, 'Do you still work for the genius?'"

Atop the list in Davis' desire to create a legacy was his constant search for a player whom he could convert from one position to another with great success. This displayed his deft touch for player evaluation and foresight.

In the 1960s, he took one of the American Football League's top rushers, Billy Cannon, and successfully converted him into a productive tight end. He saw Nebraska's Kent McCloughan run down Gale Sayers in a college game and immediately thought, "He's a cornerback." McCloughan was a standout running back for the Cornhuskers and had played some at safety in college. But, as McCloughan later told people, he had no idea when he arrived at the Raiders camp that he was to be placed on an island, as a cornerback.

"I was scared to death when Al put me on the corner," McCloughan said.

"Don't worry," Davis said. "I know what I am doing."

The Davis projection resulted in honors for both men, as McCloughan developed into an All-AFL cornerback.

Davis merely had to refine future Hall of Famer Willie Brown when he arrived in Oakland. Brown had played tight end and linebacker at Grambling College and had trials at both running back and defensive back with the Houston Oilers prior to being traded to Denver, where he was moved to the cornerback position. But it wasn't until Davis got his hands on Brown that he became one of pro football's all-time great cornerbacks.

Matt Millen was an All-American nose tackle at Penn State, but Davis pictured Millen as a productive NFL middle linebacker. Once again, Davis was correct as Millen successfully transitioned from the defensive line to linebacker and today is the proud bearer of four Super Bowl rings.

Davis also had a particular affinity for developing tight ends. In 1964, Billy Cannon was the first conversion Davis made and far from the last. Davis converted collegiate quarterbacks Warren Bankston and Derrick Ramsey to the tight end position. He made an All-Pro tight end out of collegiate wingback Ray Chester. He turned Dave Casper, who had been an offensive tackle at Notre Dame until his final season, into a Hall of Fame tight end. He picked up Todd Christensen, who had been dumped as a fullback by two previous NFL teams, and turned him into a prolific, All-Pro tight end. Ethan Horton was a running back whom Davis picked up off the scrap heap, moved to tight end and then was selected to the Pro Bowl.

Davis found clues about players in places others overlooked. Such tips oftentimes were the genesis for Davis' idea to move a player from one position to another.

"Did you know Mike Jones was a linebacker?" Davis asked Kebric one day in 1991.

"As far as I know, he always has been a running back at Missouri," Kebric replied.

"No, not at Missouri, in high school. He had 10 interceptions his senior year," Davis exclaimed.

When Jones was not drafted, Davis immediately set in motion his plan. He was going to take the 6-foot-1, 218-pounder who covered 40 yards in 4.57 seconds and move him to linebacker.

"I was the one Al selected to convince his agent that such a move was a logical one," Kebric recalled.

Kebric knew that Jones had to be upset that he had not been drafted, even though Jones participated in the scouting combine in Indianapolis.

Now, he pondered how to get Jones' agent, Harold Lewis, on board with Davis' proposal.

Kebric began the phone call to Lewis by saying, "Al Davis wants to sign Mike Jones."

Lewis cut Kebric off.

"We already have a nice offer from the Broncos," Lewis said. "What's yours?"

"Harold, I think Al will meet the Broncos' signing bonus offer," Kebric continued, "but before you say 'No' to what I have to say, please hear me out."

Kebric told Lewis that Davis envisioned Jones as a linebacker, and he emphasized that Jones would be an Al Davis project and that Al Davis projects get every opportunity to succeed.

"Harold, Al Davis' projects generally get a lot of grace time," Kebric said as part of his sales pitch. He also added that if Denver really liked Jones, then they would have drafted him in the first place.

Lewis said that he would check with Jones and get back to Kebric. At the same time, he indicated that he wasn't sure that Jones would be receptive to the idea.

"Please ask him," Kebric pleaded. "And please tell him that everything I just said is coming directly from Al Davis."

Lewis called back a short time later and said that Jones was going to sign with Denver. Kebric made a final plea, knowing that Denver was the last place Davis wanted to see Jones wind up.

"Harold, how about Mike flying to Los Angeles tomorrow and meeting with Al?" Kebric said.

Jones and Lewis accepted that offer. Jones flew to Los Angeles the next day, went through some linebacker drills, had a productive meeting with Davis and signed a contract to play for the Raiders.

The transition started immediately. Jones, whom scouts felt was a marginal running back/fullback-type prospect, developed into a starting linebacker. He eventually spent seven years with the Raiders and also had stints with the St. Louis Rams and the Pittsburgh Steelers during a 12-year NFL career.

Jones is best known, however, for a famous play in Super Bowl XXXIV deemed "The Tackle," while a member of the Rams. With the

Rams leading 23-16 and six seconds remaining in the game, the Tennessee Titans were stationed at the St. Louis 10-yard line. On the game's final play, Jones correctly diagnosed a slant route by wide receiver Kevin Dyson, making a sure tackle of Dyson at the one-yard line to preserve the victory, the Rams' only Super Bowl win.

Davis once again had gone beyond the scouting reports in his search for players. His keen eye while going over a player's questionnaire had led to a successful position change for Jones, who participated in 194 NFL regular-season and postseason games, all at linebacker.

Sometimes, it took a while for Davis to pull the trigger on converting players. Sammy Seale was drafted in 1984, and Davis envisioned him carving out a career as a wide receiver on a team that featured speedsters Cliff Branch, Dokie Williams and Malcolm Barnwell.

In preparation for his second season, Seale alternated with Williams at receiver and cornerback at practice one day. Coaches Willie Brown and Chet Franklin happened upon the informal exercise and noticed Seale jamming Williams at the line of scrimmage the way an experienced cornerback might do. They asked Seale whether he had ever played defense.

"Yeah, I was an all-state defensive back in high school," Seale replied.

A few days later, Seale showed off his two-way skills in a scrimmage against the Dallas Cowboys in training camp, with Davis watching. On one play, Seale took a pass in the flat and turned it into an 80-yard touchdown. He then moved to cornerback and intercepted a pass.

"Hey, man, don't worry about going back to offense," Willie Brown told Seale. "Just stay on defense."

Seale also had Davis' blessing.

"You would be a good defensive back," Davis said. "You can run. What do you think?"

The Raiders had just drafted receivers Jessie Hester and Tim Moffett with their first two picks, which added to an already talented receiving corps.

"I wanted to make the football team, so I switched to defense," Seale said.

Seale ultimately played 10 seasons in the NFL and appeared in 121 games. What he learned from Davis' respect for speed and his philosophy of projecting players at positions other than what they played in college is something he employs as a scout for the Green Bay Packers.

"If you really look into most NFL players' backgrounds, I guarantee you will find that most of them played more than one position and
that they were pretty good at it, too," Seale said. "You just have to have an
opportunity. You can't pigeonhole a person into one position — he's this
or he's that. You bring a guy in, and one thing that Al used to always say:
'Speed kills. If you've got speed, you have a lot of things that you can do
with a guy that can run.'"

Davis also coveted potential game-changing players, especially
those who could rush the passer and cover receivers.

The Raiders were fresh from an AFC championship and a Super
Bowl appearance in 2003, and they had the final two first-round selections
in the 2003 draft, Nos. 31 and 32. The latter pick came from Davis' trade of
coach Jon Gruden to Tampa Bay a year prior.

The Washington Redskins called the Raiders before their first selection of the draft and offered their second-round pick in 2003 (No. 44) and
their first-rounder in 2004 in exchange for moving up 13 spots. Davis contemplated the trade but turned down the offer.

"I can't risk losing Nnamdi," Davis told his staff.

He already had committed himself to taking Nnamdi Asomugha,
a University of California safety who had played some cornerback during
his final season, and Tyler Brayton, a defensive end from Colorado. The
scouting staff encouraged Davis to make the trade, with the thinking being
that Asomugha would be available with the Redskins second-round pick.

Terence Newman, Marcus Trufant and Sammy Davis were rated
ahead of Asomugha as cornerbacks by Oakland scouts. Davis really wanted University of Southern California safety Troy Polamalu with one of his
first-round picks, but he knew that was a long-shot. Kebric and Kingdon
were at USC for Polamalu's pre-draft workout. When Davis called to find
out Polamalu's 40-yard dash time, Kingdon told him that Polamalu had
run a 4.36 40-yard dash on the USC track.

"We lost him," Davis said.

Indeed, Polamalu's stock soared even more, and he ended up with
the Pittsburgh Steelers at No. 16. Newman, Trufant and Davis also were
gone before the Raiders made their initial selection. Hence, Asomugha
emerged as the leading candidate among defensive backs.

It was anticipated that Brayton, whom Oakland scouts assigned a third-round grade, might be gone by the time the Raiders selected with Washington's second-round pick. In fact, Kansas City Chiefs coach Dick Vermeil wanted Brayton with the 27th pick, but he was overruled by general manager Carl Peterson, who preferred Penn State running back Larry Johnson.

Things went according to Davis' plan, and he got both of his players.

Not only were the scouts upset that Davis had not made the trade with the Redskins, but NFL officials at the New York draft headquarters had to rally to commissioner Paul Tagliabue's rescue when Davis selected Asomugha in the first round. Each year, the commissioner announces all the first-round selections. He gets prepped by his associates as to name pronunciations. The NFL was not prepared for Asomugha to be selected in the first round and Tagliabue was baffled when handed the Raiders' draft card. After consultation, he still pronounced the name incorrectly, saying As-o-mu-gha instead of As-som-wa. Of course, conspiratorialists called it an Al Davis ploy to embarrass the commissioner.

Asomugha had all the skills Davis valued in a cornerback, and he developed into one of the NFL's best and highest-paid players, though it took him until his third season to become a full-time starter. Davis had envisioned Brayton as a 10-sack-a-season player. That one did not turn out as Davis had planned. Brayton notched only 17½ sacks in a 141-game, nine-year NFL career, the first five with the Raiders.

When it became obvious that Brayton was unable to play end in the NFL, Davis could not concede his mistake. He moved Brayton to outside linebacker, where he struggled even more.

The drama that year continued into the second round, with a linebacker out of Fresno State named Sam Williams emerging as a central figure.

While the in-room debate centered on two players, Stanford's Teyo Johnson, a projection from wide receiver to tight end, and USC running back Justin Fargas, Davis interjected: "Let's do this. Let's draft Sam Williams here and then we'll trade for another pick and take either Fargas or Johnson."

Anticipating where Davis was going, those in the room quickly galvanized support for Johnson and rammed through that selection before Davis could gain traction with his out-of-the blue idea.

"Al was really simmering, as he felt he was being ignored," Kingdon said. "He told Bruce Allen to trade next year's second-round pick to get a 2003 third-round pick so he could take Sam Williams."

Allen made a deal with Houston Texans general manager Charley Casserly and snared the extra third-round pick Davis requested, as well as a 2003 seventh-round pick, in exchange for the Raiders' 2004 second-round pick.

Kingdon had scouted Fresno State players that season. Williams was listed as a prospect and certainly looked the part. He stood 6-foot-5, weighed 250 pounds and ran a 4.62 second 40-yard dash.

Aside from Williams' fast 40, his workout was unimpressive. There was little to recommend Williams besides his height and 40 time.

"I had no idea that he could run that fast, so I immediately went to watch more tape," Kingdon said.

Kingdon had given Williams a free-agent grade based off the tape he watched during the season. He watched tapes of three more Fresno State games and focused on Williams. After having done so, Kingdon moved Williams from a free-agent grade to a seventh-round prospect.

"Did you see his workout numbers?" asked Mike Lombardi, a Raiders personnel executive. "Those are numbers like the guy I drafted at San Francisco, Charles Haley."

Kingdon responded by telling Lombardi, "Even though Williams had Charles Haley's workout numbers, he was nowhere near Charles Haley."

Soon after, Kingdon received a call from Al Davis, asking about a player named Sam Williams.

Kingdon saw where this was headed. Davis loved comparisons, especially when they involved former Raider greats or standout NFL players that he admired from afar. Davis loved Haley, who starred for the 49ers and Cowboys. He said many times that he regretted not being able to trade for Haley when the 49ers grew tired of Haley's questionable behavior. Davis strongly recommended to Cowboys owner Jerry Jones that he trade for Haley since Davis was unable to and told Jones that Haley would help the Cowboys get to the Super Bowl.

Maybe now, Davis thought, he could get the next Charles Haley, who played a key role as a linebacker on two 49ers Super Bowl-winning teams and as a defensive end on three Cowboys title-winning teams. Haley was inducted into the Pro Football Hall of Fame in 2015.

"When he heard the comparison made between Sam Williams and

Charles Haley, he made it his mission to get Sam Williams," Kingdon said.

Since Kingdon was the only scout who had been to Fresno State and written a report on Williams, he asked the other scouts to watch three Fresno State game tapes and evaluate a linebacker who wore No. 40. He made no further comments about No. 40 so as not to influence the other scouts' assessments.

The next day, David McCloughan came up to Kingdon and asked, "Did you give us the correct number?"

"Obviously, they did not care for Williams, either," Kingdon said. When Williams' name came up in a meeting in which Davis attended, the scouts were unanimous in their disaffection for Williams as a player. However, defensive line coach Mike Waufle backed Davis.

"That was all that Al needed," Kingdon said.

Davis envisioned converting Williams from linebacker to defensive end, similar to what Haley had done midway through his NFL career. Hence, the Raiders invited Williams, who lived close to the team's practice facility, and worked him out solely as a defensive end. He performed drills such as taking off from a three-point stance (Williams always had played in a two-point stance in college), running toward a designated bag, making a short cut and then bursting to the quarterback.

"He really looked tight and stiff," Kingdon said, "and no one felt as if he could make the transition to defensive end."

"Did you see it?" Davis asked to those in attendance. "Did you see that?"

Davis was beaming.

"Did you see it, Kent?" Davis said to veteran scout Kent McCloughan.

"Al, I didn't see it," McCloughan replied, as he looked forlornly at Davis.

"Kent, you used to be able to see it," Davis countered, not discouraged in the least. "I'm telling you, he's good for 10 sacks a year."

Davis got his man, Williams, with the 19th selection of the third round. Coincidentally, Davis also got Fargas 13 picks later.

"At the end of the day, Al was ecstatic," Kingdon said. "The first three rounds had his handprints all over them. He got good athletes and he got what he thought would be the second coming of Charles Haley."

Davis even prevailed upon head coach Bill Callahan to refer to

Williams as "the gem" of the Raiders' 2003 draft class in Callahan's post-draft news conference.

Four players, three position projections (Asomugha, Johnson, Williams). That was Al Davis' type of draft. He would show the football world that he still had it.

As people headed home for the night at the conclusion of the third round, Kingdon and Davis ended up alone in the draft room.

"Boy, we really gave up a lot for Sam Williams," Davis said to Kingdon.

"You didn't give up anything for Sam Williams. You gave it up for Fargas," Kingdon said.

Davis picked up on what Kingdon meant.

"Oh, so you think Sam would have been there at the end of the third round?" Davis asked.

"He would have been there at the end of the sixth round," Kingdon replied. "I wanted to say the seventh, but thought that would be pushing it."

"We'll see," Davis said, as the conversation ended.

Davis immediately converted Williams to defensive end, intending to take advantage of Williams' speed. The spotlight was on Williams in his first mini-camp, with Davis and the scouts eager to see how the rookie looked.

There weren't the limitations on contact in the camps that are in place today. Therefore, it was easier to get a pretty good feel for a player's ability.

"As it turned out, we saw it all too quickly," Kingdon said. "He showed no feel for pass rushing and could not get off any blocks."

Williams did develop into a core special teams player and one of the most-liked players in the organization. Each year, the public relations department hoped the personable Williams was a member of the Raiders team because he never turned down a public appearance request. At the end of an 84-game NFL career, Williams' sack total stood at one, far from the 10 sacks a year that Davis had predicted.

Some of Davis' best conversions occurred with players he acquired after they had played in the NFL.

In 1986, Ethan Horton was out of the NFL and unsure what he was going to do with the rest of his life. He was back at the University of North Carolina, counseling student-athletes about the importance of completing their education. He used his story as a cautionary example.

Horton had been selected by the Kansas City Chiefs in the middle of the first round of the 1985 draft and released before training camp in 1986. Twelve other teams worked out Horton, none offered him a second NFL contract. Davis signed Horton in 1987 out of curiosity, but the Raiders released Horton after eight games. The Raiders cut Horton again in 1988 after he didn't pan out as a slotback, a receiver that lines up in the backfield.

Horton returned to North Carolina and was prepared to find another line of work. Davis wasn't giving up on Horton as an NFL player. Late in the '88 season, Horton received another call from Davis.

"Mr. Davis said he had an idea," Horton recalled.

Davis wanted to convert Horton from a running back into a tight end. He laid out a plan in which Horton worked out with strength coach Marv Marinovich, who had played for Davis in 1965 and was the Raiders' strength and conditioning coach from 1968-70. Horton added 15 pounds to reach 240 before the 1989 season.

"I didn't have anything to lose," he said. "He was giving me an opportunity."

Davis told Horton that he had plenty to gain.

"In the midst of that conversation, he told me that he thought I could play the position and play it very well," Horton said. "He thought that I could excel because of my size and speed."

Horton, who had been recruited to North Carolina as a quarterback, caught only four passes for 44 yards and one touchdown his first season at tight end, as he learned the nuances of the position from coach Terry Robiskie. He was named to the Pro Bowl in 1991 and caught 169 passes over six seasons with the Raiders.

"Without Al Davis, there's really no Ethan Horton. He took a number one draft choice, who was out of the league, considered a bust, then the man pretty much resurrected my career," Horton said.

When Horton was selected to the Pro Bowl, Davis congratulated him and reflected on the decision he made three years prior that benefited both the player and the team.

"I knew you could do it," Davis told Horton as they exchanged a handshake.

Davis wasn't afraid to miscast a player. The times he succeeded in projecting a player to a different position emboldened him to keep toying with the idea of taking a player who played one position well in college and seeing how well he could do at another position in the pros.

While watching the 1997 East-West Shrine Game practices, Davis noticed a fast running back from Colorado State by the name of Calvin Branch. Scout David McCloughan, once an NFL defensive back, had earlier mentioned that he thought Branch could make the transition to defensive back. Branch was fast, smart and tough.

During the 1996 season, Branch rushed for 1,297 yards (153.7 per game) and scored 21 touchdowns, third in the nation. Branch also returned 19 kickoffs for a 22.7-yard average, including a 96-yard touchdown vs. Colorado. When Branch, 6-foot, 200 pounds, ran the second-fastest 40-yard dash (4.44 seconds) among the running backs and recorded the second-best marks in the vertical jump (39 inches) and standing broad jump (10 feet, 7 inches), Davis was all too happy to go along with McCloughan's projection, selecting Branch in the sixth round.

The highlight of his career came one year later, when Branch chased down Deion Sanders, the Dallas Cowboys' speedy punt returner, to save a potential game-winning touchdown in a 13-12 Raiders victory. Davis knew he had his man. Branch was a reliable backup and special teams player for four years.

After Branch suffered a knee injury playing in NFL Europe, Davis asked Kingdon to work with Branch and see if he had the ability to eventually become a scout. Branch showed a natural feel for player evaluation and was signed to be a scout full time after the 2000 season.

However, Davis never forgot about Branch's speed or the play in Dallas. During the 2005 season, with a sudden need for a safety, Davis asked Branch to return to the gridiron, this time as a safety.

After Calvin returned to the field as a player, various scouts would come up to Kingdon and ask, "Didn't I just scout with Calvin last week? Because I just saw him in your game the other day."

Kebric heard many of the same things. "A few weeks ago, I was scouting with Calvin, and now I am scouting Calvin," a scout from another team said.

After one game that year, Branch gathered some of his teammates for a group picture. When asked why the picture was being taken, Branch explained that he wanted a picture with all the players that he had previously scouted.

Time and again, Davis reveled in the opportunity to display that he knew more than everyone else.

Ronald Curry was a record-setting college quarterback who also starred on one of the nation's top basketball teams at North Carolina. Curry's prep resume included first-team All-American honors in both football and basketball, as well as being named the national high school scholar-athlete of the year. While at North Carolina, Curry had established school records for career passing yards and total yards.

But Davis noticed on a questionnaire that Curry had high school experience as a defensive back and kick returner. Raiders special teams coach Bob Casullo, who had extensive East Coast contacts from his collegiate recruiting days, was asked to obtain tapes of Curry's Hampton, Virginia, high school games.

"I remember Al being all excited one day and asking us to watch Curry's high school tapes," Kebric related. "I had never seen anything like it before. Every time he touched the ball, he scored a touchdown, whether running the ball, making an interception or returning a kick."

Kebric had scouted Curry in college and reported that Curry appeared to be more of a pure athlete than an NFL passer.

"Al told me that he agreed with my evaluation and that he projected Curry to be an NFL safety and returner," Kebric said.

Though he was excited about the prospects of Curry becoming a Raider, Davis was concerned about the 4.60 40 time that Curry ran at the scouting combine. So Davis held off until the seventh and final round before he drafted Curry. At his first mini-camp, Curry lined up at safety, a position he had not played since high school. He struggled at safety in training camp, so Davis suggested that Curry move to wide receiver. Late in training camp, Curry suddenly blossomed at his new position. After two position changes, Davis had his player. The Raiders had two first-round and two second-round picks in the 2002 draft, but this seventh-round project of Davis proved to be the best of the bunch.

> *Time and again, Davis reveled in the opportunity to display that he knew more than everyone else.*

Three serious injuries — two Achilles tears and a broken foot — are the only things that stood between Curry and NFL stardom. Curry's nine-year NFL career included 193 receptions for 2,347 yards and 13 touchdowns. Curry's most memorable play was a remarkable one-handed touchdown catch during a Denver snowstorm. The catch led to a 25-24 Raiders upset win over the Broncos. For years, the photograph of that catch was prominently displayed in the Raider offices.

Not all of Davis' position change projects succeeded. In fact, one of the players involved in such a move lasted just one day at his new spot. Davis had seen Rod Coleman, a defensive end from East Carolina, at the East-West Shrine Game practices and immediately imagined a Matt Millen transition from defensive line to middle linebacker. Coleman was a 6-foot-2, 262-pound player who had run a 4.80 at the combine and posted a sensational 35-inch vertical jump. Coleman also had been a collegiate terror as a pass rusher, notching 15 sacks his senior season. Despite Coleman's pass-rushing talent, Davis was going to turn him into a middle linebacker.

Coleman did not have the physique or tools to make the transition to linebacker. When this was pointed out to Davis, his response was to defend his decision by saying he had seen Coleman physically and that his body style would not be an impediment to the position change.

The Raiders drafted Coleman in the fifth round of the 1999 draft, as a middle linebacker. It took everyone, including Davis, only one mini-camp session to realize that Coleman had neither the body nor the movement to play in space as a middle linebacker. Without stating he was wrong, Davis quickly and astutely moved Coleman back to his natural position as a defensive tackle.

Davis' quick change of course on Coleman proved to be prescient, as Coleman developed into one of the NFL's top inside pass rushers. During the Raiders' road to the Super Bowl in 2002, Coleman accounted for 11 sacks, even though he started only two games. After five years in Oakland, in which he accumulated 28½ sacks, Coleman moved on to Atlanta, where in 2005 he was named second-team All-Pro and was selected to the Pro Bowl. A 2008 injury ended his career.

As the decades passed, however, Davis seemed to lose a bit of his magic, But, his last position change projection was one of his best.

Jon Kingdon had pushed hard for the Raiders to draft Marcel Reece, a 6-foot-1, 231-pound wide receiver who covered 40 yards in the excellent time of 4.45 seconds. Reece was a two-year player at Washington and had not been invited to the scouting combine in Indianapolis.

Davis, however, had his mind on two other receivers in that draft. He selected the talented, but injury-prone Arman Shields in the fourth round and then his "sleeper," speedster Chaz Schilens in the seventh.

Reece went undrafted.

After the draft each year, there's a mad rush by the league's 32 teams to sign free agents. High-profile free agents typically receive multiple offers, which affords them some leverage. Due to Kingdon's persistence, Davis gave him permission to sign Reece as a free agent.

The Raiders soon found out that other NFL teams were aware of Reece's physical ability, and Reece's agent requested a sizable $10,000 signing bonus to obtain his client's signature on a contract. When Davis was informed of the request, he said that the maximum bonus he would permit was $5,000. The Raiders learned the next day that Reece had signed with the Miami Dolphins for an $8,000 bonus, which still was more than Davis was willing to spend.

Miami conducted its rookie mini-camp one week after the draft, while the Raiders mini-camp was slated for two weeks after the draft. The Dolphins unexpectedly cut Reece after their camp, and Reece once again was on the open market and available for the Raiders camp. Kebric later asked Jeff Ireland, the Dolphins general manager, why the Dolphins had cut Reece so quickly. Ireland told him that Bill Parcells felt that Reece was too big to be a receiver.

Kingdon again pushed for Reece.

"Ah, fuck," Davis said. "Yeah, bring him in. He's your guy."

On the first day of the mini-camp, Reece lined up at wide receiver and performed very well. The problem was, at that position, he was going be a threat to Schilens, so the coaches were directed by Davis to move Reece to tight end. Once again, Reece shined at his position. Once again, he was a threat to a Davis favorite in John Madsen, a wide receiver who was transitioning to tight end. Thus, Reece was moved to his third position in three days, this time to fullback and proved to be a serious prospect at that position, as well.

He performed so well that head coach Lane Kiffin selected Reece as the standout offensive player, one of two players singled out for their play. Reece received the recognition, but he still didn't have a contract.

As the players walked off the field following the award session, Kebric sidled up to Reece and said, "You're going to sign with us this time, right? We really wanted you after the draft but could not afford what your agent asked."

Davis also was impressed with Reece's performance, but he was in a quandary as to what to do with him. Where would Reece fit? Davis pondered. He did not envision Reece competing with either Schilens or Madsen.

Tight ends coach Kelly Skipper wanted Reece.

"Nah, no, no, no," Davis responded. "I don't think so."

There weren't many more options.

"We can use him at fullback," Davis said.

Davis really liked the potential of Reece, but placed him at fullback simply because he did not want to upset the development of Schilens or Madsen.

Five years later, Reece was a Pro Bowl selection. Once again, Davis had seen something that others had missed.

At his final draft, Davis still was trolling the draft board and conjuring up images of players he could move from one position to another. That year, he envisioned fourth-round selection Taiwan Jones moving from running back to cornerback, sixth-round pick Richard Gordon moving from tight end to fullback and seventh-rounder David Ausberry moving from wide receiver to tight end.

As Davis frequently said to his scouts, "Don't you see it?"

A little less than four months after the 2011 draft, Ohio State quarterback Terrelle Pryor declared for the supplemental draft. Kingdon, Kebric and Calvin Branch wrote up reports on Pryor, with Branch attending his workout in Pittsburgh.

Kingdon recalled general support for Pryor:

"We all gave Pryor fourth-round grades, and Branch came back with a glowing report on Pryor's athleticism at the workout. It was not a sure thing that Pryor could play quarterback at the next level but at the very least he would be able to contribute at any number of positions having played both quarterback and wide receiver at Ohio State. This was someone who had led Ohio State to 34 wins and only six losses in his three years there. There were also positive reports on Pryor from his coaches in spite of his leaving Ohio State, and ESPN analyst Jon Gruden, a former Raiders head coach, also spoke highly of Pryor."

The feeling among Raiders scouts was that Pryor would be taken before the Raiders' pick in the fifth round. That meant the Raiders would need to use their third-rounder, given they already had traded away their first-rounder for quarterback Carson Palmer, their second-rounder for offensive tackle Joe Barksdale and their fourth-rounder for quarterback Jason Campbell. Picks made in the supplemental draft count against a team's draft the following year.

Hue Jackson was in his first season as the Raiders' head coach. He made it clear to Kingdon that he wanted Pryor at any cost.

"Hue was very much in favor of the pick, telling me that he was staying up nights thinking of things that he could do with Pryor in his offense."

It wasn't anywhere near as easy getting Davis on board, mostly because of his failing health, Kingdon reasoned.

"Three times I tried to speak with Al about the upcoming supplemental draft and what we thought of Pryor and each time I was told that we would talk about it later.

"Finally, the night before the supplemental draft, Al called me and asked if we had any opinion about the players in the draft. I said that Terrelle Pryor was a player that we had in the fourth round but should consider taking in the third round. Al snapped at me.

"When the hell were you going to bring this up?" Davis said. "After the draft?"

Rather than pointing out how often he had tried to bring it up with him previously, Kingdon settled for: "Tonight would be the right time."

In turn, Kingdon shared all the information the scouting department had on Pryor. Davis told Kingdon that he would think about it and get back to him.

"I did not hear from Al that night, and early in the morning I had still not heard from him," Kingdon said. "Coach Jackson was particularly concerned and kept asking if I had heard from Al."

Davis finally called back later that morning and agreed to select Pryor in the third round. The Raiders submitted their selection.

Pryor was Davis' final draft pick of any kind, as Davis died 47 days later.

Pryor was drafted as a quarterback, his preferred position. However, his height, speed and athleticism made him an intriguing prospect at other positions. Pryor refused to entertain the notion of playing anything other than quarterback when he was with the Raiders. He succeeded as a quarterback in high school and at Ohio State, and he was intent on doing so in the NFL.

For all of Hue Jackson's creative plans for Terrelle Pryor, his playing time that season was extremely limited. Pryor was on the field for only one play the entire regular season, and he drew a penalty prior to the snap and was pulled out of the game and did not see the field again.

The Raiders gave Pryor a shot in 2013 after presumptive starter Matt Flynn performed so poorly in training camp that head coach Dennis Allen had no other realistic option. Pryor enjoyed moderate success during his nine starts — he had seven touchdown passes and 11 passes intercepted and set an NFL record for the longest run by a quarterback, 93 yards against the Pittsburgh Steelers — but he was traded to the Seattle Seahawks before the 2014 season after the Raiders had traded for veteran quarterback Matt Schaub, and drafted quarterback Derek Carr in the second round.

Pryor failed to stick with the Seahawks, Kansas City and Cincinnati after he was traded from the Raiders. In June 2015, the Cleveland Browns claimed him off waivers. By that time, Pryor had been converted to wide receiver by Bengals offensive coordinator Hue Jackson, Pryor's head coach with the Raiders in 2011.

Pryor developed into Cleveland's top receiver in 2016, using his dynamic talents to join Marlin Briscoe as the only players in NFL history with 1,000 receiving yards in one season and 1,000 passing yards in another, marking a promising future for Al Davis' final experiment.

Ron Riesterer

John Matuszak was jettisoned by three NFL teams prior to finding a home with Al Davis and the Raiders in 1976. He played in 96 games for the Raiders, including two Super Bowls, but "The Tooz" became just as well known for his "Wildman" tendencies off the field.

CHAPTER EIGHT

The Tooz

It didn't take Jon Kingdon long to discover that working for the Raiders was going to be quite a unique experience.

Soon after he was hired in 1978, Kingdon was asked by team executive John Herrera to attend a booster club meeting. Herrera told Kingdon that defensive lineman John Matuszak and kicker Errol Mann would be representing the Raiders as well.

Kingdon felt as if attending such a function would be a good way to "get into the Raider mentality."

He had no idea.

Kingdon was instructed to drive to Matuszak's residence in Berkeley and then follow him to the function. When he arrived at Matuszak's house, Matuszak was very cordial upon greeting Kingdon. Matuszak then drove off in a big car with an eight-cylinder engine. Kingdon followed in a Toyota Camry, which had a manual transmission and far less horsepower.

"I still did not know where to go and tried very hard to follow him," Kingdon said. "John was going about 90 miles per hour on the freeway, and my car was beginning to vibrate and struggling to keep up."

Eventually, Matuszak pulled over into a parking lot, where there were a number of shops. Kingdon assumed that they had arrived at the site of the booster club meeting.

"As John opened the door, a major waft of smoke came out of the car," Kingdon said. "I immediately recognized it was not tobacco smoke."

Matuszak told Kingdon that he wanted to get something to drink and that they should proceed together in Matuszak's car. Kingdon jumped at the offer because of his concern for his car's ability to keep up.

Before they left, Matuszak emerged from a store with an eight-pack of beer in large-sized cans. He offered Kingdon one of the cans.

"I politely refused," Kingdon said, "and he then insisted that I take one. I don't really like beer but figured it would be one less beer that John might drink."

Kingdon sipped his beer on the drive to the booster club function that eye-opening night. Matuszak had polished off the seven other beers by the time they arrived.

As Matuszak walked in the door, an admiring fan exclaimed, "Hey, it's The Tooz! Great to see you. Let me buy you a drink."

Matuszak, who no doubt had become accustomed to such adoration, asked for a triple Crown Royal, without hesitation. The fan seemed a bit taken aback about the price of a triple shot, but nonetheless paid for the drink.

Over and over, throughout the night, the same scene played out.

"Tooz, let me buy you a drink."

"Make it a triple Crown Royal."

"I counted 10 times this occurred, though there may have been other instances as well," Kingdon said.

Eventually, the time came for Matuszak to speak.

"I wondered how he could stand," Kingdon said, "but he got up and gave a fantastic talk that got the people in the room really excited."

Kingdon and Matuszak left the function together. Kingdon marveled at Matuszak's ability to function so well after having imbibed so much.

Kingdon wasn't comfortable getting into the car with Matuszak, but he had no alternative since he had no idea where his car was and Matuszak insisted upon driving. Unsure whether Matuszak knew where Kingdon had parked, Kingdon innocently asked where they had left his car earlier that evening.

"Don't worry about it," Matuszak said.

Kingdon, indeed, worried about finding his car. In an attempt to mollify Matuszak, Kingdon talked about how nice the place was so that he could go back again one day.

"I know where your car is," Matuszak said in a stern voice, as he glared at Kingdon.

Sure enough, Matuszak drove Kingdon right to the spot where they had left his car earlier that night.

Unsurprisingly, Matuszak said, "Let's go into that bar over there and have a drink."

As soon as they walked into the bar, someone yelled, "Hey, it's The Tooz. Let me buy you a drink."

Equally unsurprising, Matuszak responded: "Make it a triple Crown Royal."

Men and women flocked to the bar, where Matuszak was seated, so that they could spend some time with the larger-than-life figure. Matuszak spent most of the 30 minutes or so he was in the bar talking to a young woman. The two of them eventually walked through a door at the back of the bar. After a few minutes passed, Kingdon went through the door as well to see what was back there.

"Rather than another room, all that was there was an open field," Kingdon said.

Kingdon then checked the parking and discovered that Matuszak's car was gone.

"I took this as a signal that I should leave as well," Kingdon said.

Naturally, Kingdon was concerned about Matuszak's well-being, even though he realized that there wasn't much he could have done to prevent him from doing as he pleased.

To that end, Kingdon turned on the news as soon as he got home, concerned that Matuszak might have made headlines. There wasn't any mention of Matuszak.

The next day, Kingdon made a point of going to practice to see if Matuszak was there and, if so, what condition he was in. Sure enough, The Tooz was on the field in his No. 72 uniform.

"I was relieved to see him out on the field," Kingdon said.

Kingdon wandered over for a closer look at Matuszak, who seemed fine and showed no lingering effects from the night before.

Kingdon and Matuszak hit it off from the outset. At the same time, their first night out made one thing abundantly clear.

"I never would have wanted to hang with him in any type of manner after our evening at the booster club," Kingdon said.

Still, Kingdon always made it a point to say hello to Matuszak, who seemed to enjoy his company and the opportunity for some light-hearted banter.

At one Saturday morning practice, Matuszak walked over to Kingdon.

"Jon, I know you like pussy," Matuszak said. "I want to show you these pictures."

Matuszak pulled out two graphic Polaroid pictures of naked

women. Kingdon asked Matuszak about the story behind the pictures.

"I was with them last night. You know, there are women out there that want to fuck a giant," he said in a matter-of-fact tone. "I'll accommodate them."

"It was never a dull moment with John," Kingdon said.

By this time, Matuszak had become a Raiders legend, both for his on-field and off-field exploits.

Matuszak, 6-foot-8 and 272 pounds, had a personality and zest for life that matched his mammoth stature. In many ways, he personified the Raiders during their rise to glory in the 1970s and early 1980s. Before long, he became known simply as "The Tooz."

Davis populated his roster with flawed individuals like Matuszak. Most times, those players repaid Davis in spades for his blind faith in them.

"Al would just tell him, 'This is your last chance, John. If you do what I tell you to do, you're going to be successful. If not, you're done,'" Bruce Kebric said. "These players had no alternatives. They had no leverage. Al did a really good job taking advantage of that."

Davis first targeted high-profile free agents a year before he signed Matuszak, when he signed linebacker Ted Hendricks and tight end Ted Kwalick.

> *Davis populated his roster with flawed individuals like Matuszak. Most times, those players repaid Davis in spades for his blind faith in them.*

"Al actually started what became today's free agency when he signed Hendricks and Kwalick," Kebric said.

At that time, there was an unwritten rule that you weren't going to sign other teams' players.

"Basically, if you wanted to retain a player, there were limited options for that player," Kebric said.

Davis changed it all when he signed Hendricks and Kwalick. He viewed free agents as a quick and easy way to bolster his roster — gentlemen's agreement be damned. Teams complained, Kebric said, but Davis just said, "Hey, stop me."

Kwalick had played for the San Francisco 49ers his first six seasons and earned Pro Bowl selections from 1971-73. After a brief stint with the

World Football League, Kwalick eyed a return to the NFL. It was assumed Kwalick would rejoin the 49ers, because that's how things worked at the time. Instead, Davis lured away Kwalick and talked him into wearing the Raiders' silver-and-black gear.

"Al had his own rules, along with the support of a top attorney, Joe Alioto," Kebric said. "He felt very secure with any legal challenge."

Davis used this strategy more and more to great advantage. Perhaps it's not a coincidence that the Raiders got over the hump and started winning Super Bowls at about the time Davis employed this philosophy.

NFL players gained full freedom in 1993 with the advent of unfettered free agency. That placed the rest of the league on a level playing field with Davis and others who had followed his lead of breaking the unwritten code of signing other teams' free agents.

The new rules didn't deter Davis from going after other teams' cast-offs, busts and problem children. In fact, that remained one of Davis' central tenets. Most years, Davis had only one first-round pick in the NFL draft. Ultimately, he wound up with several players drafted in the first round by other teams.

"The worst we can do is cut them," Davis often said. "If they turn out, great. If they don't turn out, maybe we learn in our evaluation where we went wrong."

This was Davis' way of getting his hands on players he coveted in previous drafts. Even better, the players came at a reduced price. Their original teams had doled out the huge signing bonuses that were customary through the 2010 season. Now Davis had a way to get a first-round talent at a lower-round price.

Davis also relished the opportunity to get the kind of production out of players that their previous employers expected, and paid for, in terms of a high-round draft pick and exorbitant salary.

According to Kingdon, "Al felt he could show that he was smarter than everyone else by making something out of someone else's draft pick that had not lived up to expectations."

Quarterback Jeff George was selected by the Indianapolis Colts with the first pick of the 1990 draft. He spent four years with the Colts and three with the Atlanta Falcons before he joined the Raiders in 1997. George led the league in passing yards and finished second in touchdown passes that season.

In 1994, Davis signed quarterback Andre Ware, who was the seventh pick of the same draft that produced George. Unlike George, Ware didn't enjoy any success in the NFL before Davis signed him to a low-risk, low-salary contract.

Ware had won the Heisman Trophy in 1989, when he was a highly touted prospect out of the University of Houston. All that was more than enough to pique Davis' interest.

"Let's find out what's wrong with him," Davis said. "On these high draft picks, you want to be the second team that they're with because they're humble by now. Sometimes with these guys, their second team is their best one because they go into the first team, they're highly regarded, highly paid and such, they're a little bit spoiled, then they get cut and realize that, 'Hey, I'm going to have to work.'"

Matuszak joined the NFL in 1973. He was the first pick of the draft, taken by the Houston Oilers. He started all 14 games that season. The Oilers ultimately traded Matuszak to the Kansas City Chiefs for defensive lineman Curley Culp and a first-round draft pick. Matuszak played for the Chiefs for the next two seasons.

Davis snared Matuszak soon after the 1976 season started. Matuszak became available once he was set free by the Washington Redskins, who had cut him a couple of weeks after they had acquired him via trade.

Matuszak realized he had run out of chances and that the Raiders likely were the last team he was going to play for. He played a key role in the Raiders winning their first Super Bowl in 1976 and was a linchpin for the Raiders during his six-year tenure with the club, though he never came close to being the dominant player many thought he was destined to be. He retired after the 1981 season because of a back injury and took up acting. Matuszak played a lead role in *North Dallas Forty* and several other movies and appeared in numerous TV shows before he died in 1989 at the age of 38 as a result of a prescription drug overdose.

The Raiders were Matuszak's fourth team. Fifth, if you count a brief stint with the Houston Texans of the World Football League.

Long before he played a game in the NFL, though, Kebric became acquainted with the man who broke a guy's jaw in Missouri and was subsequently kicked out of college, broke girls' hearts from coast to coast and broke curfew on a regular basis.

Kebric was scouting for the Houston Oilers in 1972 when he heard about this freakishly big and talented player who made as much news for his off-field behavior as he did for his on-field exploits.

Matuszak was born in Oak Creek, Wisconsin, in 1950. By the time he reached 21 years of age, he had spent a year at Fort Dodge Junior College in Iowa and a year at the University of Missouri, prior to being dismissed by head coach Dan Devine before the team's first game in 1970.

"John told me that he got in a fight at a fraternity party and broke a guy's jaw," Kebric said.

Matuszak transferred from Missouri to the University of Tampa after his sophomore season, which he said "was the best school I could find at the time."

That was in 1971. Kebric scouted Matuszak at Tampa a year later; he found The Tooz to be quite engaging, very smooth and plenty intelligent.

Kebric, Tampa head coach Earle Bruce, Matuszak's defensive line coach and Matuszak talked over lunch before practice one day.

"I was extremely impressed with John," Kebric said. "During the season, I had the opportunity to visit with him, watch him on game films, in practice and in a game where Tampa upset the University of Miami."

Matuszak was invited to the prestigious Senior Bowl in Mobile, Alabama, but opted to play in an all-star game in Tampa instead. Kebric later learned that Matuszak had been paid $10,000 to play in that game, far more compensation than the Senior Bowl participants received at that time.

After attending the Senior Bowl game, Kebric drove through the night to Tampa so that he could watch Matuszak play. To no one's surprise, Matuszak was the star of the game.

Houston owned the rights to the No. 1 pick in the draft as a result of its 1-13 finish in 1972. Louisiana State University quarterback Bert Jones was regarded as the top overall prospect, but the Oilers already had two young quarterbacks, Dan Pastorini and Lynn Dickey, on their roster, so they weren't in the market for another quarterback. Hence, the Oilers attempted to trade away the top pick.

The Baltimore Colts were so certain the Oilers weren't going to take a quarterback that they traded with the New Orleans Saints, who had picked quarterback Archie Manning two years before, for the No. 2 spot so they could take Jones.

With the Oilers on the clock and nearing the time to make their pick, the Miami Dolphins offered a number of backup players for the Oilers No. 1 pick, Kebric said.

In turn, the Oilers asked for center Jim Langer and running back Mercury Morris.

The Dolphins refused to trade those two players and, with trade talks stalled, the Oilers opened the 1973 NFL draft with the selection of Matuszak.

Despite an auspicious beginning, Matuszak's transient nature continued once he arrived in the NFL.

The Oilers brought in all their players for a mini-camp at the Houston Astrodome shortly after the draft. Head coach Bill Peterson wanted to see how well his players ran, so he instructed them to do a 40-yard dash. Matuszak clocked a jaw-dropping 4.65 seconds.

"Those were the days when 4.6 was fast," Kebric said. "Guys didn't train for the 40 like they do today. If a receiver ran a 4.6, that was fast. So, everybody was excited about John."

Even with Matuszak in a starting defensive end role, the Oilers went 1-13 his rookie season, just as they had the previous season. Sid Gillman replaced Peterson after the Oilers lost their first five games. In 1974, Gillman brought in Bum Phillips to be his defensive coordinator, and Phillips changed to a three-man front in an attempt to model his defensive scheme after the Dolphins' famed "53" defense. With that same 3-4 defensive scheme, the Dolphins, in 1972, had won 17 consecutive games and the Super Bowl.

Phillips moved Matuszak from defensive end to nose tackle and installed Elvin Bethea, a future Pro Football Hall of Fame selection, and Tody Smith, a first-round draft pick of the Cowboys in 1971 and the younger brother of defensive standout Bubba Smith, as the defensive ends.

"I said, 'Wait a minute, the guy is 6-foot-8, how is he going to play in there? They're just going to chop his legs,'" Kebric said.

Kebric's concerns were borne out two nights after an exhibition game against the Chicago Bears in which Matuszak played "poorly."

The night after the Bears game, Matuszak was nowhere to be found. The players had the day off, but they were required to report back by 6 p.m. on Sunday.

Phillips said Matuszak didn't show up at the position meeting, probably because he was embarrassed by how poorly he played against the Bears.

Someone asked equipment manager Johnny Gonzales if he had any idea what happened to Matuszak.

"No," Gonzales said. But, he went on to add, that after the game, Matuszak had asked Gonzales if he could keep his uniform, so he could take a picture with his family, which was in town for the game, the next day. "I thought it was OK," Gonzales said.

Adrian Burk was the general counsel for the Oilers. He had been a first-round draft pick of the Baltimore Colts in 1950. He gained fame for throwing seven touchdown passes in a game in 1954 as a member of the Philadelphia Eagles, an NFL record he shares with seven others. A day later, Burk called Gillman with this news: "I just got word that Matuszak has signed a contract with the Houston Texans."

The Texans were in the World Football League, a league competing with the NFL for players.

Gillman then instructed Kebric to contact Burk and assist with the pressing matter.

"Adrian, that makes sense, because he's not here in camp and he's got his gear," Kebric remarked when he contacted Burk.

Kebric surmised that Matuszak had taken his Oilers equipment because the Texans probably didn't have any big enough to fit a player of his stature.

On Wednesday, Kebric drove from the Oilers training camp in Huntsville to Houston. By the time he arrived, Burk had taken care of the legal aspects and the two of them departed for the Astrodome to see if Matuszak actually was on the field in a Houston Texans uniform. Sure enough, when they entered the stadium, along with the process server, they spotted "The Tooz" with his new teammates.

Burk pointed out Matuszak to the process server, who waited until after Matuszak had played in the Texans' first defensive series to hand him a restraining order that prohibited Matuszak from further participation in the game vs. the New York Stars. The Texans' legal team countered soon thereafter by presenting a subpoena that required all the Oilers players and coaches to attend a court hearing the next week on the temporary injunction. This subpoena forced the Oilers to miss a day of pre-season practice and travel to Houston for the hearing.

Matuszak, when asked by judge Arthur Lesher whey he had signed the contract with the Texans, innocently replied: "This is America, the land of motherhood, apple pie and freedom. Why can't I just go and play for the Texans?"

Prior to this episode, Matuszak had been one of the most visible and vocal players who picketed the practice field each day during an NFL strike that lingered into the exhibition season, but ended before the Bears game.

"Our players appeared both amused and annoyed during the proceedings," Kebric said. "Future Hall of Famer Elvin Bethea, obviously not a fan of Matuszak's, turned to me and remarked: 'Can you believe this guy?'"

The court ruled that Matuszak had a valid NFL contract with the Oilers and that he had violated the contract.

By this time, Gillman and Phillips didn't want Matuszak around, so they suspended him. When he received news of the suspension, Kansas City Chiefs coach Hank Stram called Gillman and inquired about Matuszak. Gillman was all ears.

"Hank wanted Matuszak," said Kebric. "He was willing to part ways with Curley Culp. It worked out for both teams. We got Culp, a future Hall of Famer who really set the standard for the nose tackle position, along with the Chiefs first-round draft pick that turned out to be linebacker Robert Brazile, a seven-time Pro Bowler and a member of the 1970s All-Decade Team."

The Oilers went 6-2 their final eight games in 1974 and improved to 10-4 the next season. Matuszak wore out his welcome in Kansas City in short order, and Stram was fired after the 1974 season. Matuszak was now Paul Wiggin's problem.

"Paul told me a number of years later that the Kansas City police had said, 'Get this guy out of town, or he's going to jail,'" Kebric said.

Wiggin did just that. He traded Matuszak to Washington. A few weeks later, Washington head coach George Allen was forced to cut Matuszak when his players told him that they didn't want "The Tooz" around.

"By the time that Al got John, he had no options," Kebric said of Matuszak.

Matuszak had signed a four-year, $175,000 contract with the Oilers, the largest ever doled out for a defensive lineman. The contract included a $50,000 signing bonus. His legendary temper and penchant for on- and off-field brawls outlived that contract.

He had been kicked out of one college, punished for moonlighting with a rival league, discarded after one season by the team that used the top pick in the draft on him, and later was jettisoned by two other teams.

"If a guy had talent, Al didn't care about his background," Kebric said. "Al felt that, as long as the player showed up for practice and showed up on Sunday, he could do what he wanted to do the rest of the time."

As if by fate, Matuszak ended up where he belonged in the first place. Davis welcomed Matuszak with open arms and offered him a clean slate. Matuszak, in turn, became part of the package that gifted Davis with his first Super Bowl ring.

Brad Mangin

Raiders scouts had quarterback Brett Favre as their sixth-highest-rated player in the 1991 NFL Draft, but owner Al Davis was fixated on another quarterback and ignored the advice of his scouts. Favre went on to a Hall of Fame career, while Davis spent the next 20 years searching for the next Daryle Lamonica, who Davis deemed his prototypical quarterback.

Al Davis selected quarterback Todd Marinovich in the first round of the 1991 NFL draft out of the University of Southern California. Marinovich was drafted by Davis, even though Raiders scouts had informed Davis that Marinovich was plagued by drug problems and a questionable work ethic in college. Marinovich played in only nine games during his two-year NFL career.

Rob Brown/Getty

CHAPTER NINE

The Hall of Famers Who Got Away

One of Al Davis' first masterstrokes as a talent evaluator was securing quarterback Daryle Lamonica from the Buffalo Bills in 1967. Lamonica was a backup to Jack Kemp in Buffalo his first four seasons. During that time, he earned the nickname "The Fireman" for bailing out Kemp on occasion and guiding the Bills to several come-from-behind victories. With the Raiders, he became known as "The Mad Bomber" for his penchant for throwing deep passes on a regular basis, a key to Davis' plan to "stretch the defense."

Lamonica was a sensation his first three years in Oakland, going 36-4-1 as a starter and guiding the Raiders to three AFL Championship Games and one Super Bowl appearance. He was the prototypical quarterback for an Al Davis offense, with the ability to strike deep, strike fast and strike fear into opposing defenses.

The vertical passing game remained a tactical opiate to Davis for the rest of his life. But he never found another Lamonica. In some ways, his search for the next Mad Bomber defined the Raiders in the final four decades of his ownership, especially late in his life when instead of outsmarting everybody else, he began to outsmart himself. And in his increasing desperation, he saddled the team with some major disappointments while turning a blind eye to future Hall of Famers.

This was epitomized in the 1991 draft, in which he wasted a first-round pick on Todd Marinovich even as his scouts advocated for someone who would become one of the most charismatic, successful, daring and prolific quarterbacks in NFL history.

A fellow named Favre.

That draft provided the perfect platform, with the Raiders interested in a long-term solution at quarterback and the kind of shutdown cornerback they had lacked since the days of Mike Haynes and Lester Hayes.

The Raiders scouting department outlined to Al Davis how it expected the first two rounds of the draft to play out and, based upon that projection, which players the Raiders could select if things went according to expectation.

The draft played out perfectly for Raiders scouts and Al Davis, though they seemed to be working at cross purposes. Instead of taking strong-armed quarterback Brett Favre and cornerback Aeneas Williams, as the scouts recommended, Davis opted for Marinovich and running back Nick Bell.

When Davis would make a pick that went against the advice of his scouting department, one could only hope that he saw something in the pick that others did not see. Kingdon termed the Marinovich pick as a double negative selection:

"Marinovich proved to be a major disappointment that was further exacerbated because of the player the Raiders did not pick — Brett Favre. Not only did Favre have a rifle for an arm, he had unquestionable toughness, coming back from a car accident where he ended up losing part of his intestines."

Favre was the Raiders scouting department's top quarterback, and its sixth-rated player overall. Yet Favre remained undrafted through the first 23 picks. The Raiders had the 24th selection.

In an ESPN documentary, then-Raiders quarterbacks coach Mike White said it was a unanimous decision to take Marinovich with the team's first-round pick. That was far from the truth. Besides the fact there was disapproval from the scouts, White's preference among the available quarterbacks was, in fact, University of Louisville's Browning Nagle. White had worked out both Favre and Nagle before the draft and expressed his opinion that the latter was the better choice.

Coincidentally, Ron Wolf, who had left the Raiders for the New York Jets prior to the 1990 season, also hoped to get Favre.

While scouting Favre during an East-West Shrine game practice at Stanford University a couple of months before the draft, Kebric felt a tap on his shoulder.

"That guy is your best quarterback?" the fellow evaluator asked, after witnessing a number of poor passes by Favre.

"Yeah, I guess I blew another one," Kebric replied.

"He's mine, too," Wolf said, as he walked away.

As it turned out, Favre went to the Atlanta Falcons, one spot ahead of the Jets, and Wolf had to settle for Nagle.

Adding to the ignominy for the Raiders, Wolf, after moving to the Green Bay Packers, traded for Favre in 1992, before Favre had started a regular-season game in the NFL. Wolf benefited from the stellar play of one of the all-time great quarterbacks, while Davis was saddled with the short and disappointing career of Marinovich.

Many of those in the Raiders draft room were disappointed in Davis' decision to take Marinovich, but the selection was not a surprising one.

According to Kingdon, Davis often had his mind set on a player he wanted to select long before the draft and would not allow himself to be swayed.

Marinovich's father, Marv, had both played and coached for the Raiders. After his playing career ended, Marv embarked upon a career as a personal trainer and was widely known for his array of unconventional training methods. He used many of his out-of-the box theories on his son, Todd, who had been nicknamed "Robo QB" for the way he had been forced to follow a lifestyle designed by his father from the day of his birth — he was born July 4th, 1969, on Davis' 40th birthday. When Todd's strict dietary program was being discussed during the Raiders draft preparations, scout Kent McCloughan, a Raiders teammate of the elder Marinovich, told the story of how Todd had brought his own cake to a birthday party at the McCloughan household. He then went on to tell about Todd's excitement when the McCloughan family permitted him to sample some of the birthday cake that the other kids were enjoying at the time.

Marinovich developed into a solid quarterback at Southern Cal and played his home games on the same field used by the Raiders at the Los Angeles Memorial Coliseum. Hence, Davis was keenly aware of Marinovich's talents. At the same time, he would not allow himself to see the all-too-obvious flaws.

The scouting staff had given Marinovich a second-round grade, but Kingdon saw Davis move him to the first round:

"Todd did have ability, but we had issues with his arm strength. He was more of a finesse passer, one who did a good job in leading the receivers and was fairly accurate. The concern was that he was able to get away with things at the collegiate level that he would not be able to do on the professional level, as well as his off-field issues."

As for Favre, Kebric had been the lone Raiders scout to visit Southern Mississippi during the regular season and was very impressed with Favre's talent and toughness.

"The guy just had so much moxie," Kebric reported. "He was a linebacker playing quarterback. He had a great arm and he wasn't afraid to take chances."

Kebric also noted that Favre had some alcohol-related problems, and he had been seriously injured in a car accident prior to his senior season, which forced him to miss his team's opening game.

The concerns about Marinovich, however, were much greater than those about Favre.

There were well-founded questions about Marinovich's overall demeanor as well as his consistency on and off the field. Kingdon did his best to illuminate these issues in hopes of getting Davis to steer clear of Marinovich and draft Favre.

Davis asked to see video of a game in which Marinovich did not perform well. The scouts selected a game in which Marinovich had several of his passes intercepted. Davis watched as a handful of Marinovich's passes belied his status as a first-round prospect. Then came an eye-opening, head-turning throw on a deep out route, an impressive throw that not all quarterbacks can make on a consistent basis, even in the NFL.

"Turn the machine off," Davis said after Marinovich's deep route. "I've seen enough."

Davis didn't allow the video to run long enough to get to the Marinovich throws that resulted in interceptions.

"Al wanted to see what he wanted to see," Kingdon said, "and he did not allow himself to see what he did not want to see. He would repeatedly run over and over a good play and then skip past bad plays."

All-Pro cornerback Albert Lewis discovered Davis' penchant for selective hearing soon after he signed with the Raiders in 1994 after an 11-year career with the Kansas City Chiefs.

"Mr. Davis can hear you, he can understand what you're saying, but if he doesn't agree with you, he might not tell you that he doesn't agree with you," Lewis recalled. "He'll just kind of change the course of the conversation."

This point was driven home one day when Davis summoned Lewis to his office.

"Albert, I want you to rate the receivers," Davis said upon Lewis' arrival.

"So, I started going down the list," Lewis said. "When I didn't put

James Jett where he wanted me to, he just abruptly ended the conversation."

"Ah, fuck. Who asked you?" Davis snapped in response to Lewis overlooking the speedy Jett, a Davis favorite.

"That's just how he was," Lewis said. "All I could do was laugh. I said, 'You brought me here and you asked me.' He only heard what he wanted to hear."

Marinovich's off-field problems were a major concern and brought to Davis' attention, with examples of his undisciplined behavior and tardiness for meetings at USC, as well as legal issues presented. The USC coaches had told Kingdon that they had locked the door to the quarterbacks meeting room, on more than one occasion, when Marinovich was a late arrival. An even bigger concern to the scouts was Marinovich's arrest on cocaine charges, exactly three months prior to the draft.

During a meeting, at which time all these negatives linked to Marinovich were being detailed, Raiders assistant coach Steve Ortmayer spoke up and defended Marinovich. Ortmayer said that his contacts assured him that weren't any problems with Marinovich.

Later, Kingdon and Kebric approached Ortmayer and asked him for the name of his source.

"Marv," Ortmayer said.

"Todd's father?" Kingdon asked, in an incredulous manner.

"Yes," Ortmayer said. "Marv said there are no issues with Todd."

Davis usually took a lawyer's tack, where he seldom asked a question unless he knew the answer that would be forthcoming. When he asked defensive line coach Earl Leggett what he thought of Todd Marinovich, he assumed Leggett would sing Marinovich's praises.

Why would Davis ask a defensive line coach about a quarterback? As it turned out, Leggett's son, Brad, played guard for Southern Cal and was a teammate of Marinovich's.

"What do you think we should do about Marinovich?" said Davis, whose attendance at Marinovich's private workout had prompted Marinovich to run over and shake Davis' hand.

In his deep southern drawl, Leggett said, "Coach, the best thing that could happen to Marinovich would be for him to be drafted by a team like Green Bay or Buffalo. He needs to get out of Los Angeles. There are just too many distractions for him here."

Davis was a little taken aback about the candor and negativity of

Leggett's response but, in the end, Leggett's critique fell on deaf ears.

Besides Ortmayer, head coach Art Shell backed Davis' endorsement of Marinovich and the deal was sealed.

The decision had long been made. Davis simply had gone through the charade of debating which player to take in the first round, while searching for at least one person in the room to support his view.

Davis operated in a way that shielded him from potential criticism.

"He sought out one person to support him," Kebric said. "He searched the room for that one person so that if his guy didn't make it, he had someone else to assume the burden."

Davis had Shell and Ortmayer on board. So, in this case, nothing else mattered.

Kebric and others were upset with the selection and there was some tension existing in the room. It took Joe Madro, a former Raiders assistant coach and scout, to alleviate the situation.

Madro was retired at this time, but he still attended the draft at Davis' invitation. Most of the time he was seen, not heard.

"Hey, Bruce!" Madro blurted out.

> *Davis operated in a way that shielded him from potential criticism. "He sought out one person to suuport him. He searched the room for that one person so that if his guy didn't make it, he had someone else to assume the burden."*

"What do you want, Joe?" Kebric replied.

"Is Todd a redhead?" Madro asked.

"Yeah, what's the big deal?" Kebric responded.

"Al's always been queer on redheads," Madro said.

Davis, after hearing Madro's comment, turned and said, "Fuck you, Joe," though he did smile at Madro's comment.

With Marinovich a member of the Raiders, Davis and the others in the room shifted their focus toward the second-round pick. As the draft evolved, it appeared as if the Raiders were going to be in position to take Southern University's Aeneas Williams.

Kebric felt that Williams had the potential to be a top player, but he also expected Williams to fall into the second round due to two factors: Williams played for a small college, and he didn't run a very fast 40-yard dash during a pre-draft workout at Tulane University in which Kebric timed Williams at 4.55 seconds. He had watched Williams extensively during the season and also thought that Williams had an excellent showing at the Senior Bowl.

Yet Davis wasn't moved by Kebric's presentation. He could appreciate the talent in a player, but Davis simply could not allow himself to look past a player's 40-yard dash time if it did not meet his minimum standards.

When it came time for the Raiders second-round pick, Davis opted for University of Iowa product Nick Bell, a big back with excellent speed. Williams later was drafted by the Phoenix Cardinals in the third round, No. 59 overall. He enjoyed a stellar career and was inducted into the Pro Football Hall of Fame in 2015. Once again, Davis had ignored the pleadings of his scouting department.

Prior to the second-round selection, Davis handed Kebric the running backs report book and told him to look at the Nick Bell report by Raiders' running backs coach Joe Scannella. Kebric had watched some tape on Bell, but he had not seen him in person. "Our scouts said that Bell was a big, fast back who lacked toughness and consistency," Kebric remembered.

As Kebric read the report, Davis said: "This is the best report this coach has ever written on a player."

"That statement upset me even more," Kebric said, "and I not only replied, 'Consider the source,' but threw the book back at Al. When Bell was drafted, I was on the verge of quitting."

Kebric and Davis disagreed quite often in future drafts, but the tone wasn't the same.

"We frequently had differing opinions on players," Kebric said. "After that episode, however, I realized that he was the boss and it was my duty to give full support to the player once the decision had been made. On a number of occasions, I actually prayed that I was wrong in my evaluation."

Marinovich started nine games, including a playoff game his rookie season. In his two NFL seasons, both with the Raiders, he finished with a 3-6 record and had more of his 228 passes intercepted than those that resulted in touchdowns.

He was regarded as a free spirit and someone with varied interests. That came to light one night, when Davis offered to give Kebric a ride from team headquarters in El Segundo to the local hotel where he was staying.

"We walked downstairs and there's this big, long thing wrapped up," Kebric said. "It's right by the receptionist's desk. Al almost tripped over the thing."

"What the fuck is that?" Davis said.

Kebric walked over to the mysterious item and saw that it was addressed to Todd Marinovich and had been sent from Portugal.

"Al, I think it's a surfboard," Kebric said, as he felt the package in search of clues.

"Ah, fuck," Davis replied.

"I don't know if that was the crowning blow or not. Al never said it. But it was clear that, if Todd is in Portugal in the offseason," Kebric said, "he's not here working out, then he's probably not as committed as he needs to be."

Marinovich was out of the league after the 1992 season, while Favre's career was just taking off. By the time he retired after the 2010 season, Favre had established a reputation as one of the best and toughest players in the league's history. He started 321 straight games — regular-season and post-season — was named the league's most valuable player three straight seasons, earned 11 Pro Bowl selections and retired having owned or shared numerous NFL records.

The Raiders, meanwhile, were back in the market for a quarter-back in 1993 and spent most of the time during Favre's career trying to find a long-term answer.

Davis still hadn't managed to draft a franchise-type quarterback since 1968, when Kenny "The Snake" Stabler was selected in the second round and went on to a Hall of Fame career.

Davis had selected Tennessee State quarterback Eldridge Dickey in the first round of that draft. Dickey, the first African-American quarterback ever picked in the first round in pro football history, was the player Davis envisioned as the successor to Lamonica. It was Wolf who prevailed upon Davis to draft Stabler.

"Ron told me that Al didn't like Stabler from Day One," Kebric said. "He didn't want him around, initially."

To that end, Davis and the Raiders concocted a story about Stabler and his wife having marital problems that necessitated Stabler returning to Alabama, Wolf told Kebric. Later, Stabler was shipped off to Spokane in the Continental League.

Stabler didn't play for the Raiders until 1970, and even then he appeared in only three games and attempted seven passes. He started one game in the 1971 and '72 seasons. It wasn't until 1973 that Stabler became the full-time starter, three games into the 14-game season.

Stabler bore little resemblance to Lamonica. He was left-handed and was a precision passer with modest arm strength, while Lamonica completed fewer than half his passes over his career, and possessed a strong arm.

The things Lamonica possessed and Stabler lacked, Davis could have had in Favre. Through it all, Davis kept searching for another Lamonica. He enjoyed differing levels of success with the likes of Jim Plunkett — who directed the Raiders to two Super Bowl titles — Dan Pastorini, Marc Wilson, Jeff Hostetler, Jay Schroeder and Jeff George.

Strangely, Davis enjoyed more success with average-arm-strength quarterbacks such as Stabler and Rich Gannon than he did with his favored strong-armed quarterbacks.

According to Kebric, Davis had to be persuaded to sign Gannon in 1999, at a time when he was fresh from having employed Schroeder, Hostetler and George as his starting quarterbacks the previous 11 seasons. "Jon Gruden was the one who wanted Gannon," Kebric said. "The whole thing started with Gruden."

But Gruden had to convince Davis.

That wasn't the only time Gruden got his way when it came to quarterbacks that didn't fit Davis' standards.

In 2001, Davis called Kebric during the Rose Bowl being played by Purdue University and the University of Washington and asked if he was watching the game.

"The Washington quarterback looks great," Davis said of Marques Tuiasosopo, who was an equally effective passer and runner.

A few months later, Davis told Kebric of Gruden's affinity for Tuiasosopo, when he said, "If I don't take the Washington quarterback, the head coach will never talk to me again."

The Raiders selected Tuiasosopo, who was the MVP of the 2001 Rose Bowl, in the second round of the 2001 draft with the intent of having him run Gruden's West Coast Offense. He started two games during his six-year NFL career, none in his lone season with Gruden. He wasn't deemed a good fit for Norv Turner's vertical offense, so Davis drafted strong-armed Andrew Walter in 2005. By the time Lane Kiffin, another West Coast Offense advocate, arrived in 2007, Tuiasosopo was a member of the New York Jets.

Coincidentally, Tuiasosopo and Washington played against Purdue and Drew Brees in that Rose Bowl. Brees passed for twice as many yards as Tuiasosopo in that game, and later picked apart the Raiders defense time and again as a member of the San Diego Chargers and New Orleans Saints.

"Al never liked Drew Brees," Kebric said. Brees, selected 27 spots before Tuiasosopo, lacked the size and arm strength that Davis loved.

"As long as he is the quarterback, we will beat them," Davis remarked to Kebric after a Raiders win over the Chargers during the early phase of Brees' NFL career.

Davis believed he had found his next Lamonica in 1983, long before anyone had heard of Favre. That year, Davis thought he had engineered a trade with the Baltimore Colts for the rights to John Elway, the No. 1 pick in the 1983 NFL draft. Elway was the consensus top quarterback that year among a group that included future Hall of Famers Jim Kelly and Dan Marino, along with three other first-rounders in Todd Blackledge, Tony Eason and Ken O'Brien.

He was big, fast, athletic and possessed one of the strongest arms ever for a quarterback.

Elway's father Jack, a former head coach at Cal-State Northridge, San Jose State and Stanford, wasn't fond of then-Colts coach Frank Kush, and he advised his son not to play for the Colts.

In turn, John Elway informed the Colts that he wouldn't play for them. Furthermore, if he didn't get his wish to be traded, he would continue playing baseball for the New York Yankees, who had drafted him as an outfielder in the second round of the 1981 Major League Baseball draft. Elway already was playing for the Yankees in their minor-league system.

Davis told Kebric that he pounced on the opportunity and offered a trade package that satisfied the Colts. Kush was thrilled, as well.

"That night, I went to bed thinking I had Lester Hayes and Rod Martin," Kush told Kebric during their time together with the Arizona Outlaws of the United States Football League, "and I woke up with Chris Hinton and Mark Herrmann."

Kush had no idea at the time that NFL commissioner Pete Rozelle had conspired against Elway being traded to the Raiders.

"Al always said that John Elway was supposed to be a Raider, but Pete Rozelle told the Colts that they could trade Elway to any team except for the Raiders," Kebric said.

Elway, too, enjoyed a stellar NFL career. He guided the Broncos to five Super Bowls during his 16-year career and exited the game as one of the best quarterbacks in football history.

Herrmann started 12 games during an 11-year career in which he spent most of his time as a backup. Kush was fired by the Colts after the 1984 season.

A year later, Kebric and Kush were jogging in the desert, when Kush confided in Kebric how the Elway saga unfolded.

"Were you disappointed?" Kebric asked.

"I was damn disappointed," Kush said.

"Even though Stabler won a championship for him, he wasn't the big, strong-armed guy," Kebric said. "He wanted Daryle Lamonica-type guys. So he traded Stabler for Dan Pastorini because Dan had the big arm."

Kebric spent five years with Pastorini in Houston, when both were with the Oilers. He called him the most physically gifted quarterback he had been around.

"If Sid Gillman (who coached Pastorini in 1974) had him from Day One, Dan Pastorini would now be in the Pro Football Hall of Fame," Kebric said.

Instead, Pastorini endured coach after coach after coach. Davis acquired Pastorini in 1980 in hopes of winning another Super Bowl with a strong-armed quarterback at the helm. That's precisely what happened, but it was Plunkett who carried the bulk of the load after a broken leg ended Pastorini's season early on.

Davis' final shot at landing a big-armed quarterback came in 2007, when the Raiders used the number one pick of the draft for Louisiana State's JaMarcus Russell.

"He didn't listen to us in 1991," Kebric said. "And he didn't listen to us in 2007. His loyalty to a former Raider clouded his judgment in the Marinovich selection, while in 2007, Al wanted to return to his 'roots,' drafting the biggest, strongest quarterback he could find."

Brad Mangin

Jon Gruden was hired over Bill Belichick in 1998, though Raiders owner Al Davis had his concerns about Gruden's age. Like Davis had done at a young age, Gruden succeeded as a head coach in his early 30s and led the Raiders to prominence.

CHAPTER TEN

Jon Gruden: Striking Gold

On December 21, 1997, Jon Kingdon sat in his car at the Oakland Coliseum on the morning of the Raiders' regular-season finale against the Jacksonville Jaguars.

Kingdon watched as the fans streamed past. He knew what was about to happen. He knew that the Jaguars were going to beat the Raiders. It was just a matter of how badly.

"I had to force myself to get out of the car," Kingdon said. "I didn't want to go inside. I was embarrassed at the product that was being put out to this very loyal fan base, all dressed in silver-and-black gear."

Kingdon finally summoned the energy to get out of his car, trudging into the stadium to stomach yet another loss.

The Jaguars jumped to a 14-0 lead in the first quarter and cruised to a 20-9 victory as they finished 11-5 and the Raiders concluded a 4-12 campaign, the worst in the Al Davis era up to that point.

The next day, Davis called Kingdon.

"What do you think?" Davis asked.

Kingdon replied: "Do you really want to know?" Davis said, "'Yes.'"

"This was the first time where I went into a game knowing that there was no chance we would win," said Kingdon, who began working for the Raiders in 1978. "The whole season has been a disaster. I've seen the players quit and there were coaches on the staff that have long since quit. I've never been more embarrassed to be associated with this team. These fans deserve a lot better than what we've been giving them. It's not worth the effort if this is the product we're putting out."

"You're right, you're right," Davis said. "I'm going to turn this thing around."

Davis had to do something drastic. All the momentum the Raiders had built upon their return to Oakland in 1995 had dissipated. The players had turned on the coaches, many fans stopped going to the games and whispers about the game having passed Davis by reverberated.

"Al realized that it was essential to make the right decision in choosing his next head coach," Kingdon said. "He knew his legacy was at stake."

Davis interviewed Jon Gruden, Bill Belichick and Jim Haslett after he fired Joe Bugel.

Gruden had become the league's youngest offensive coordinator when he was hired by the Philadelphia Eagles in 1995 at the age of 31.

Belichick was two years removed from having been fired by the Cleveland Browns after a 36-44 record in five seasons. He was an assistant coach for the New York Jets when Davis called.

Ultimately, it came down to Belichick and Gruden.

Davis had interviewed Gruden on three different occasions from 1995 to 1997 and came away impressed each time. He confided in Bruce Kebric that there was just one thing about Gruden that prevented Davis from taking the leap.

"Bruce, I want him, but he looks like he's 18 years old," Davis said of Gruden in 1997.

"What did a 32-year-old Al Davis look like?" Kebric replied.

"Yeah, you have a point," Davis said.

Davis also liked Belichick. Yet it was assumed by those who were close to Davis that Belichick would not be the one hired because of his defensive pedigree. Even Belichick felt that way.

"It was a good experience for me," Belichick said years later of his interview with Davis. "We had a good couple days of conversation. It was good because we talked a lot about football, and he's very, very knowledgeable about the game, personnel, schemes, adjustments and so forth. He was asking a lot of questions about what we did defensively."

Davis coached the Raiders from 1963-65, and in the 30-plus years afterward, he had earned a reputation as a hands-on owner. In particular, Davis fancied himself nonpareil when it came to defense.

"You kind of don't want to give too much information because, you know, he's running the defense," Belichick said. "He wasn't really too interested in talking about offensive football. He's a great mind. It was unlike any other interview I've ever had with an owner because he was so in-depth. His interview was so in-depth, really, about football, about Xs and Os and strategy and use of personnel and acquisition, all the things really that a coach would talk about, that's really what he talked about. That made it pretty unique."

Belichick indulged Davis, though all along he expected Gruden to get hired.

"It really seemed like a waste of time," Belichick said, "because I felt pretty certain that he wouldn't hire a defensive coach. ... It's a parade of offensive coaches out there. He's really a defensive coordinator."

In time, everyone associated with the Raiders learned that Davis presided over the defense.

Hall of Fame defensive tackle Warren Sapp realized as much soon after he signed with the Raiders. He was enlightened by veteran teammate Derrick Gibson, who had been indoctrinated several years prior. At the time, Sapp was in the locker room after a Raiders loss to the Philadelphia Eagles and frustrated by his inability to make the kind of impact that he had become accustomed to as the linchpin to the Tampa Bay Buccaneers defense from 1995-2003.

"I was at my locker about to just lose my mind," Sapp said. "Derrick Gibson looked over at me and goes, 'Go tell Al.' I'm like, 'What?'"

"Dog, you're like one of them geese that laid a golden egg," Gibson said. "If you go tell Al you want a 4-3 defense, you're going to get a 4-3 defense on third down."

"What?" Sapp said, incredulous at the suggestion.

"Dog, go tell him," Gibson implored.

"Are you kidding me?" Sapp replied.

"Do you want it?" Gibson asked.

"Yeah, I need it, or else I'm going to die here," Sapp said.

"Well, you got to go tell the man that makes everything move around here," Gibson explained to Sapp, who played collegiately for the University of Miami.

"This was a Florida State Seminole telling me this, so I'm like, 'All right. Derrick Brooks (another Florida State product and Sapp's teammate with the Buccaneers) is always giving me good advice, so let me go with this one, too.'"

Thus emboldened, Sapp walked over to Davis in the locker room.

"We lost a tough one," Davis said to Sapp.

"Yeah, Mr. Davis," Sapp answered. "I need to talk to you."

"Let's talk," Davis said.

"Well, I don't whisper, so here we go," Sapp started off. "You brought me in to do my thing on third down, right? Because I'm a quarterback hunter."

"Yeah," Davis said.

"Then, why the hell are we in all these crazy-ass defenses rushing three men?" Sapp responded. "Put Tommy Kelly beside me, Derrick Burgess on the outside and I can teach DeLawrence Grant to fucking be the end on the other side."

"What are you saying?" Davis asked Sapp.

"I need a four-down rush," Sapp said, in reference to wanting four defensive linemen in obvious passing situations. "Rob Ryan can play all this rinky-dinky, crazy shit all he wants on first and second down, but I've never had man-to-man behind me. Trust me, I don't give the quarterback that amount of time to be back there drinking tea."

Davis looked at Sapp and paused.

"You'll get it, Warren," Davis assured Sapp.

"OK," Sapp replied.

The next day, defensive coordinator Rob Ryan conducted his standard day-after-game meeting.

"Oh, my god," Sapp said. "Rob Ryan was cursing me out in front of the whole defense. 'I can't believe one of my players would go and ask ...' Just motherfucking me up and down, in front of everyone. But he didn't say my name. I had told Burgess, 'We're getting a 4-3 defense around here.' Burgess leaned in to my chair and said, 'What?' I said, 'Mr. Davis said he's getting me a 4-3 defense on third down? You ready?'"

"'I'm ready, Big Homey,'" Burgess replied.

"Trust me, we're going," Sapp said.

Sapp recorded a sack of Drew Bledsoe the next game, then three sacks of the Tennessee Titans' Steve McNair four games after he went to Davis with his request. Three weeks after the Titans game, Sapp suffered a season-ending shoulder injury in a Raiders win that upped their record to 4-6. The Raiders lost their final six games without Sapp.

"We were going to take off," Sapp said. "We were going to win 9 or 10 games, I promise you this."

Davis liked Belichick and Gruden equally, and he wasn't sure which way to go. He sought advice from Kebric as it came time to make a hire, largely because Kebric had done extensive research on Gruden, at Davis' request, during the previous two years.

"Al told me to talk to my friends and ask them what they thought of Gruden," Kebric said. "I had never met Jon Gruden but I told Al that the general consensus from my contacts led me to believe that Gruden was energetic, passionate, confident, competitive and a natural leader. I left out one thing in my report to Al, however; that Jon had a very strong personality."

Two of the most interesting comments Kebric received came from Philadelphia Eagles scout Dan Shonka and Tampa Bay Buccaneers player personnel director Jack Bushofsky, who knew the Gruden family well since Jon's father, Jim, had worked for the Buccaneers as a coach and a scout. Shonka told Kebric that Gruden basically was the head coach with the Eagles.

"If you attend one of our practices, you would think that Jon is the head coach," Shonka said.

When Kebric asked Bushofsky to compare Jon to his father, Jim, whom Kebric had scouted with, Bushofsky said that Jon had his mother's personality.

"She is one of the most competitive individuals I have even been around," Bushofsky said. "She is so competitive that she was banned one year from participating in the wives' golf competition."

That background factored into Kebric's recommendation.

"The vote is 1 to 1," Davis told Kebric in a call. "Bruce Allen wants Jon Gruden. Amy Trask wants Bill Belichick. Who do you want?"

Allen was the Raiders' senior assistant. Trask was the team's chief executive officer.

"You know something", Kebric told Davis that day, "Bill's intelligent and a good coach but from what I've heard, I would go with Gruden."

This time, Davis offered Gruden the job, and Gruden jumped at the opportunity rather than wait for a better one that might not come. Another motivating factor at the time: All the other NFL head coaching openings had been filled.

The Raiders weren't high on the lists of many prospective coaches when Davis hired Gruden. An organization that prided itself on stability for most of the 1960s, all of the 1970s and through the mid-1980s had become the epitome of instability. John Madden and Tom Flores were the only Raiders head coaches from 1969-87. Two coaches, three Super Bowl titles and great continuity for 19 seasons. The Raiders head coaching job was a coveted position during that time.

In fact, A-list candidates lobbied for the job even when there wasn't an opening.

Madden's final year coaching the Raiders came in 1978, which coincided with Kingdon's first year with the Raiders. One day, Davis summoned Kingdon to his office.

"He asked me if I knew George Allen," Kingdon said.

"The coach?" Kingdon replied. "I certainly know who he is."

Davis then informed Kingdon that Allen, who was not coaching at the time, wanted to visit Patriots wide receiver Darryl Stingley in the hospital. Stingley had just suffered a broken neck in an exhibition game against the Raiders in Oakland, and he was hospitalized in the Bay Area.

Davis handed over the keys to his black Lincoln and instructed Kingdon to pick up Allen at the Oakland Airport and take him to the hospital. Kingdon and Allen enjoyed a nice conversation on the ride. As Allen visited Stingley in his private room, Kingdon waited outside with Stingley's mother.

From there, Kingdon drove Allen back to the airport.

"I was going to drop him off at the curb," Kingdon said, "but he insisted that I come in and have some ice cream with him."

Fortunately, for Kingdon, everyone was familiar with Davis' car, so he was able to just leave it at the curb.

"I thought it was very cool having ice cream with George Allen, and he began to share with me his philosophy of coaching," Kingdon said. "He then told me how well he knew the teams in the AFC West."

As Allen's flight time neared, he asked Kingdon to get Davis on the phone so that he could thank him for helping set up the Stingley visit. Kingdon overheard Allen thanking Davis, and then telling Davis about his coaching philosophy and a bit about the other AFC West teams. After talking to Davis, Allen thanked Kingdon and boarded his flight.

Madden announced his retirement at the end of that season, and there was a lot of speculation as to who would be his successor. Flores was the natural favorite and eventual choice.

During the process, Kingdon was driving with Davis, when, out of the blue, Davis asked, "Who do you think is really interested in becoming the head coach of the Raiders?"

Kingdon thought for a second, then said, "George Allen?"

"How did you know that?" Davis responded, after giving Kingdon a double take.

Kingdon reminded Davis of the time he spent with Allen on his Stingley visit and that it was obvious how much he wanted to get back into coaching.

"Very interesting," Davis said, as he nodded.

Kingdon asked Davis if he would consider hiring Allen, who had winning records in every one of his 12 seasons with the Los Angeles Rams and Washington Redskins from 1966-77, and was inducted into the Pro Football Hall of Fame in 2002.

"No, there's no way that he and I could work together," Davis said, though he had a great deal of respect for Allen.

But by 1998, Davis had blown through Mike Shanahan, Art Shell, Mike White and Joe Bugel since Flores stepped down. This rapid turnover made it difficult to hire quality coaches, as did Davis' heavy-handedness in shaping coaching staffs.

When Shanahan was hired as the head coach in 1988, Davis allowed him to bring in only three coaches, offensive line coach Alex Gibbs, receivers coach Nick Nicolau and special teams coach Pete Rodriguez. Davis forced Shanahan to keep the remaining coaches from Flores' staff.

Shanahan, who was eager for his first head coaching job, accepted the arrangement. As a result, he was stuck with a number of coaches who resisted many of the changes that he wanted to implement. Predictably, he regretted the forced marriage and filed it away for when he got his next opportunity.

Shanahan, whom Davis referred to as "the high school coach," turned down the Broncos' head coaching job when it was offered to him in 1993 because owner Pat Bowlen attached "conditions related to pay and hiring coaches," as reported by *Boston Globe* writer Will McDonough. Bowlen ultimately promoted defensive coordinator Wade Phillips, who won half his games the next two seasons, while Shanahan remained with the 49ers and received a contract extension that made him the NFL's highest-paid coordinator. In 1995, Bowlen replaced Phillips with Shanahan and allowed him to hire his own staff.

After Davis fired Shanahan, he asked Kingdon what he thought of Shanahan.

"I told him that I thought he was really a bright coach but that he did not have a chance," Kingdon said.

Davis quickly picked up on what Kingdon was going to say.

"You mean the assistants?" Davis said.

"Yes," Kingdon said. "I don't know how you can win if you have coaches on your staff that want to see you lose."

Davis didn't argue the point.

With the Raiders, Shanahan faced an uphill battle. He instituted a rule that prohibited players from sitting on their helmets while on the field. That didn't go over well with a veteran-laden team set in its ways.

He implemented a playbook used by every NFL team except the Raiders. Quarterbacks coach Larry Kennan once told Kingdon that the Raiders' playbook made no sense, that the approach involved memorizing the plays, but the numbers on the play did not show any real pattern.

"The problem was that the team was successful and would not change," Kingdon said.

Shanahan also commented about the Raiders playbook being out-moded. In fact, even earlier, Flores wanted to make the changes during his reign as head coach from 1979-87, but Davis overruled that suggestion.

Shanahan succeeded in changing the way practices were conducted. In particular, the Raiders ran far more plays than they had in the past. Changes, corrections and comments took place in meetings instead of on the field.

He also tried to bring some different ideas to the Raiders coaching staff. He liked to get the offensive staff together on a Friday afternoon so that the coaches could eat pizza, watch tape and bounce ideas off each other in a casual and relaxed environment.

Art Shell, the assistant offensive line coach, refused to stay, saying, "That's not how it's done with the Raiders."

Naturally, Shell succeeded Shanahan when Davis fired him four games into the 1989 season.

By the time 1997 season finally ended, the Raiders had developed into one of the most undisciplined teams in any sport. The tail was wagging the dog. Defensive tackle Chester McGlockton watched practice in his raincoat one day. Wide receiver Tim Brown threatened to call his own plays. The Raiders were last against the pass and the run. The team pretty much had hit rock bottom, a precipitous fall in a short period of time.

Under Shell's guidance, the Raiders had played the Buffalo Bills in the 1990 AFC Championship Game. The Bills throttled the Raiders 51-3 in that one, yet it seemed only a matter of time before the Raiders reached another Super Bowl.

The players loved Shell, who came off as a players' coach compared to predecessor Shanahan. Davis reveled in his team's sudden success, seeing it as validation for his decision to replace Shanahan with Shell.

Shell was one of Davis' all-time favorite players and a loyal lieutenant. Davis had the man he wanted as his coach, the Raiders just needed a player or two to get back to the Super Bowl for the first time since the 1983 season.

Or so Davis thought.

Seven years later, the Raiders were as far from the Super Bowl as they had been at any time during Davis' 35 years. As a result, he endured increasing chatter and stories about the game passing him by, that it was time for Davis to sell the team or bring in an infusion of younger people with fresh ideas.

This infuriated Davis. He always functioned as if he had a decided edge on the rest of the league based upon his keen eye for talent, his penchant for taking chances on players that others deemed toxic or too risky and, simply, because he was smarter than everyone else.

Yet Davis' well-earned reputation for doing things his way, and succeeding, no longer carried much cachet among his peers, the fans and the media. The Raiders' sustained lack of success — they went 54-58 from 1991-97 — painted Davis as someone whose unorthodox ways no longer worked in an ever-changing league.

Shell departed after the 1994 season. The Raiders won less than half their 32 games under White in his two seasons. The next year, the Raiders reached what was then the lowest point in the Davis era — four wins.

Davis needed to make a splash, create some buzz and get his listing franchise righted and headed in the right direction. Gruden offered all of this to Davis.

Gruden had been told what to expect long before he arrived in Oakland, and he had a plan in place. After the team's first practice, Kingdon and Gruden crossed paths and Kingdon remembered a conversation between the pair: "I told him how much I really enjoyed watching the practice, how much different it was from the prior seasons and how he wasn't putting up with any of the little mistakes."

Gruden stopped in his tracks, looked at Kingdon, and, in a gruff, gravelly voice, said: "Jonnn (drawing out Kingdon's name), I'm going to make the players hate my fucking guts."

That's not the response Kingdon expected, but it caught his attention and portended things to come.

Kingdon and others didn't have to wait long to see what Gruden had in mind.

During Gruden's first mini-camp — a time when coaches get a chance to assemble most, if not all, of the players on the roster for practices over a three-day period — veteran cornerback Larry Brown marched into Gruden's office after one practice.

Brown had joined the Raiders in 1996 — parlaying a two-interception, Most Valuable Player performance in that year's Super Bowl as a member of the Dallas Cowboys, into a five-year, $12.5 million contract with the Raiders.

> *Gruden stopped in his tracks, looked at Kingdon, and, in a gruff, gravelly voice, said: "Jonnn (drawing out Kingdon's name), I'm going to make the players hate my fucking guts."*

That made Brown one of the highest-paid defensive backs in the league. It did not make him immune from Gruden's master plan.

Brown played in 12 games his first two seasons with the Raiders, and he performed at a level not commensurate with his lavish contract.

Yet, he still felt emboldened, be it as a result of his shining moment in the Super Bowl, his contract or the fact Gruden was new to the job.

On this day, Brown entered Gruden's office and launched into a tirade. He informed Gruden that he wasn't pleased with the way his predecessors, Bugel and White, treated him and instructed Gruden, in no uncertain terms, about how he wanted to be used from that point.

Gruden stoically listened as Brown ranted. Once Brown finished,

Gruden calmly called Mark Arteaga, his assistant, into his office.

"Mark, would you please buy him a ticket and send his ass back to Dallas?" Gruden said to Arteaga.

Just like that, Gruden jettisoned Brown from the roster. It wasn't until that afternoon's practice that the players learned of Brown's absence. It suddenly became clear to all when rookie cornerback Charles Woodson, whom the Raiders selected with the fourth pick of the 2008 NFL draft, showed up at practice wearing the No. 24 that Brown had donned earlier that day.

Roster moves were Davis' domain. Gruden had cut Brown without consulting his boss.

Later that day, Kebric saw Gruden in the coaches' locker room.

"He was really dejected," Kebric said.

"Well, I think I'm gone," Gruden said.

"What are you talking about?" Kebric replied.

"I think I'm going to be fired," Gruden said.

"Why?" Kebric asked.

"I just put Larry Brown on a plane back to Dallas," Gruden said.

"You did what?" Kebric said.

"Yeah, Brown came in, he started complaining, and I told him, 'If you don't like the way we're doing things, Mark Arteaga will get you a ticket back to Dallas,'" Gruden said.

"Does Al know about this?" Kebric asked.

"No, that's why I think I'm going to be fired," Gruden said.

"Jon, this is the best move that you could make because the players don't care for Brown," Kebric said. "They know he's around here only for one reason. He's one of Al's scholarship guys. You have a contract, right?"

"Yeah," Gruden said.

"This will be the first big move that you make in this organization," Kebric said in an attempt to reassure Gruden.

Davis was upset, but there was nothing he could do. Veteran players, such as wide receiver Tim Brown, quickly warmed to Gruden as well.

"They jumped on Jon's side because they thought, 'Hey, he's not going to put up with keeping all of Al's scholarship guys,'" Kebric said.

Davis had a penchant for keeping players around longer than he should, if for no other reason than to save face and avoid admitting he had made a mistake. Larry Brown simply was the latest, most high-profile example.

"It was difficult for Al to concede his mistakes in his choice of free agents or drafted players that he personally and often individually selected," Kingdon said. "He was a victim of 'pride of authorship.' There was a double negative with this attitude. He was throwing good money after bad and tying up roster spots with players that simply could not help the team."

That Gruden survived getting rid of Brown showed not only that there was a new sheriff in town, but that Davis would give Gruden some latitude. Just the same, Davis had been adding assistant coaches to the Raiders staff. This did not deter Gruden, who had a plan in place when he arrived in Oakland.

One day Kebric asked Gruden, "Jon, how do you coordinate 16 assistant coaches?"

"Bruce, I tell them to stay the fuck out of my way," said Gruden, who also served as his own offensive coordinator and quarterbacks coach.

"They may have had others listed in those roles," Kebric said, "but Jon ran the whole offensive show."

Around this time, veteran defensive back Albert Lewis went to Davis with a proposition: He would retire as a player after 15 seasons and take on a role as a conduit between Davis and the players.

Lewis explained to Davis that he wasn't sure if he wanted to play anymore, given how badly things had gone under head coach Joe Bugel in 1997, and that he felt he could be of more value to the Raiders in a front-office capacity. He reminded Davis that he would save the team quite a bit of money, too, by moving from the locker room to the front office.

"If it hadn't been for 1997, I probably wouldn't have retired in 1998," Lewis said. "I still had three years left on my contract. But, emotionally, I was spent. That was Al's worst year in all his time being there, and it was certainly mine. It was like a bad cut that you couldn't stop from bleeding. Worse, you didn't know what really caused the wound."

Lewis felt as if he could be part of the healing. He shared his ideas with Davis, and Gruden, who wanted Lewis in uniform. Ultimately, Davis rebuffed Lewis' overture, and Lewis played one final season.

"I went most of the off-season preparing to say I wasn't going to come back," Lewis said. "After going through a season like we had, all you have is reasons for not coming back. Coach Gruden promised me a difference in approach and a difference in attitude."

As it turned out, Gruden recognized the glaring issues that Lewis felt were holding back the Raiders, and he effected change from the outset. With Gruden in charge, Lewis sensed that the Raiders' downturn was short-lived.

"I realized it right away," Lewis said. "Unfortunately, he came at the end of my career rather than the beginning. He had this approach that really brought people together. He had a real intense approach to his coaching style, which was needed because all the other coaches were just too laid back. It's not that they were bad coaches, but they were just too laid back for that talent group, for that group of young men.

"They needed somebody that would be stern, be consistent and push. They needed to be pushed all the time. Once they got that, and the right combination of veterans and young guys, I knew Gruden was going to turn it around. He didn't really give himself any other options. He had one thing in mind; that was success."

"It didn't start off easily for Jon," Kingdon said. "The Raiders' reputation was sinking rapidly. It had reached a point where coaches did not want to come to the Raiders."

Mindful of that experience, Davis realized the need for Gruden to bring in his coaches. Still, Davis insisted upon keeping the likes of mainstays Willie Brown and Fred Biletnikoff.

Davis tried to impose some of his other favorites on Gruden, too. When the name of one coach was broached, Kingdon went to see Gruden. "I asked Jon if I could speak with him," Kingdon recalled.

"Sure," Gruden replied.

"Jon, I heard that there is a coach who Al wants you to hire and, to be honest with you, when I heard the name, I got nauseous," Kingdon said. "He's a good person, a hard worker and a bright guy, but he has never been successful with any position he has coached here."

Gruden looked at Kingdon.

Gruden responded: "Jonnn, when I heard this guy's name, I became nauseous, too."

"Jon then brought up a couple of other names which Al had recommended and I again had a similar reaction," Kingdon added. "Jon thanked me and said that his door was always open to me."

Gruden brought with him Bill Callahan, who went from the tight ends coach to the offensive coordinator.

"That's a pairing that worked to perfection," Kingdon said.

Gruden called the passing plays and Callahan called the running plays.

Gruden was a football lifer, someone who grew up at the foot of a father who coached football. Just like Shanahan, though, Gruden was untested as a head coach. Davis gave both a chance, one of the many things that made Davis so successful over the years. Davis was twice Gruden's age, but Gruden impressed Davis with his football intelligence and boundless energy.

Yet Davis still was concerned about Gruden's age and youthful appearance, whether Gruden could command the respect of players far closer to him in age than most head coaches.

Gruden won over Kebric right away. Kebric was so intrigued by Gruden that he attended Gruden's introductory news conference, the first time that Kebric felt compelled to attend such a Raiders event.

Kebric sat in the front row of the auditorium at team headquarters in Alameda, when Gruden was introduced as the Raiders' head coach.

"I focused on Jon the entire time, never taking my eyes off him," Kebric said. "I was looking for the confidence, the intensity, the leadership that my friends had talked about. At the end, I concluded, this is one guy who can cope with Al Davis.

"Everything he said at the press conference, there was a conviction. I thought I saw something special that day and as I got to know him and worked with him, I saw it more and more."

For Gruden to get the Raiders back to their winning ways, he felt he needed to shake things up. Getting rid of Larry Brown in 1998 was one thing, but targeting the quarterback proved a sure-fire way to get the other players' attention.

Ultra-talented quarterback Jeff George had a way of impressing coaches with his natural ability and strong arm.

He bounced from team to team, never able to cement his status as a team's unquestioned starter. Infatuation always seemed to be closely followed by frustration with George for the five NFL teams he played for during a career that spanned from 1990-2001.

He was the first pick of the 1990 NFL draft by the Indianapolis

Colts, but rarely was viewed as an elite quarterback. His best season came in 1997, when he started all 16 games in his first season with the Raiders. George recorded 29 touchdowns, passed for a career-high, and a league-best, 3,917 yards, and had only nine of his 521 passes intercepted.

"Jeff had a truly magnificent arm, and he could make any throw from anywhere on the field," Kingdon said.

Few questioned George's physical ability. The question marks centered on his commitment to being a well-rounded quarterback.

He was the "anti-Gruden," as Kingdon said. Gruden inherited George as his starting quarterback in 1998, and it became apparent early on that George soon would be looking for another team.

"Jon couldn't understand Jeff's lack of commitment to being more than just a quarterback," Kingdon said. "He didn't have the intangibles that separate the good from the great."

Gruden felt George lacked the traits that quarterbacks such as Brett Favre and John Elway possessed, particularly for being a leader. At various times, George had been labeled aloof, self-absorbed and intractable.

One time, Gruden asked George if he ever thought about taking his offensive linemen out to dinner.

"No," George said.

"Jeff, take your linemen out to dinner," Gruden said. "I have a lot of money. I'll pay for the dinner."

George ignored Gruden's suggestion.

Soon thereafter, while the Raiders waited out a delay at an airport, Gruden spotted George seated with a group of front-office employees at a bar.

"Look at that Jeff George," Gruden said, with obvious disdain. "Sitting with my assistant Tommy Fucking Jones. Do you think Brett Favre would be sitting with him if he was here? Fuck no! He would be buying drinks for his linemen."

George suffered a groin injury early in the 1998 season. Gruden used journeymen Wade Wilson and Donald Hollas in George's eight-game absence and the Raiders limped to an 8-8 record. That set the stage for Gruden's next big move.

The Raiders brought in Jeff Garcia, who had starred in the Canadian Football League for five years out of college but yearned for a shot in the NFL. Davis and Gruden were intrigued.

"Garcia was a dominant player in the Canadian League," Kingdon said, "but when he had his private workout with the Raiders, he simply had an awful day."

That left open the door for Rich Gannon, a talented player who had yet to start more than 12 games or pass for more than 16 touchdowns in any of his 11 NFL seasons.

Gannon came highly recommended by Paul Hackett, who had been Gannon's offensive coordinator with the Kansas City Chiefs from 1995-97.

Hackett convinced Gruden, who passed along his endorsement of Gannon to Davis.

"The head coach wants to sign Rich Gannon," Davis said to Kebric in a phone call. Interestingly, Davis always referred to Gruden as "the head coach" when Gruden was with the Raiders.

"You have to be kidding me," Kebric said. "The only time we ever beat the Chiefs was that Monday night game when Gannon was at quarterback."

Kebric later related: "Boy, was I wrong on that one."

Gruden prevailed. Davis signed Gannon. In Gannon, Gruden had found his match. Gruden finally was paired with someone who was going to work just as hard as he did.

"Rich needed a Jon Gruden, and Jon Gruden needed a Rich Gannon," Kingdon said.

Gannon just wanted a chance to succeed. He sensed this was his best opportunity and he would not let anything get in his way, even his teammates. The quarterbacks' meeting room was situated next to the players' lounge. One day, the players discovered all the balls missing from the pool table in the players lounge. That ended the pool games, though the table remained. The sound of the pool balls banging into each other bothered Gannon while he was watching game tape, so he solved the problem.

A Raiders team devoid of leaders found the ideal in Gannon. Shortly after he signed with the Raiders, Gannon complained about being the only player who came in on Saturdays to put in the extra work.

"Who the hell is he to bring that up?" Davis snapped to Kingdon.

"He's your quarterback," Kingdon said.

"Ah, bullshit," Davis said. "He's the new guy."

Davis viewed Gannon's questioning the dedication of his new teammates as an indictment of the way things were on Davis' watch.

No one watched more film than Gruden. He had the perfect foil in Gannon. They each had very strong egos and would take no crap from the other. Neither would hesitate to yell at the other.

The verbal battles over the headphones were classics. Gruden asked the video staff to record the verbal exchanges between him and Gannon during an exhibition game so he could hear how it sounded after the fact.

The back-and-forth conversations were full of profanity, but it all worked in the end because they shared the common goal of wanting to win, and neither would allow their ego to get in the way.

Davis had succeeded in finding his coach and "turning it around." Gruden had found the quarterback to help engineer that turnaround. The question was, could Davis and Gruden coexist long enough for the Raiders to win another Super Bowl?

Bob Larson

Head coach Jon Gruden and Raiders quarterback Rich Gannon (12) were known for their unrivaled intensity, and it was Gruden who pushed for signing Gannon in 1998.

CHAPTER ELEVEN

Jon Gruden: The Rock Star

Al Davis reveled in the Raiders' newfound success, but two major obstacles were now looming. Could he continue to co-exist with head coach Jon Gruden, who, in Davis' words, had become "bigger than the Raiders?" And would Davis be willing to pay Gruden a salary commensurate with the team's success?

It took a mere three years for Gruden to turn around a program that had not experienced a winning season since 1994, nor earned a playoff berth since 1993. Under Gruden's guidance, the Raiders improved from a four-win season prior to his arrival, to 12 victories and a berth in the 2001 AFC Championship Game. Gruden's popularity skyrocketed. Suddenly, with his boundless energy and his ceaseless intensity, he became something akin to a rock star, not only in the Bay Area but nationally as well.

His many snarls and facial contortions earned him the nickname "Chucky" for his resemblance to the menacing doll possessed by the soul of a serial killer in a string of similarly titled movies. Women loved his blond, blue-eyed, surfer looks. Men admired Gruden's kick-ass, eat-drink-and-sleep football attitude. Everyone reveled in the results. *People Magazine* even joined in, naming Gruden one of the "50 Most Beautiful People" in 2001, alongside Hollywood luminaries such as George Clooney, Johnny Depp, Hugh Jackman, Jude Law and Heath Ledger. The magazine commented, "With his boyish looks, football coach Jon Gruden makes us instant fans."

Al Davis was 33 when he was hired to coach the Raiders. Jon Gruden was 34 — half Davis' age at the time — when the Raiders owner provided him with his first NFL head coaching job.

"Jon was a younger version of Al," Jon Kingdon said.

Often, Davis would make suggestions to his coaches about plays or schemes or personnel groupings. Most would listen intently and promise to implement them in the near future. With Gruden in charge, it was different. Every time Davis recommended something, Gruden fired back with, "I did that the other day," or "We're doing that today."

Rather than be impressed, Davis seemed "frustrated" by Gruden's prescience, Kingdon said.

There also was a time when it was questionable if Gruden would even make it to his third season as the Raiders' head coach. The team entered the 1999 regular-season finale with a 7-8 record and was playing the 9-6 Kansas City Chiefs at Arrowhead Stadium, where Oakland was 0-11 since 1988, including a 1991 playoff game. Midway through the first quarter, Oakland trailed 17-0, but Gruden rallied the team to a 41-38 overtime victory. The win not only solidified Gruden's position, but denied the Chiefs sole possession of the AFC West title.

"More than once, Al said that if the Raiders had not beaten the Chiefs that game, he would have fired Gruden," Kingdon said.

Davis conceded that Gruden, like so many of the coaches that preceded him, did not have great job security: "Jon's first two years, he was in tough. He won a big game that kept him alive."

It was not long after the Raiders' stirring upset of the Chiefs that Gruden's meteoric rise from unknown assistant coach to a national celebrity took off.

"Al had problems with all the attention that was being bestowed upon Jon," Kebric said. "When you drove on the Nimitz Freeway, there was Jon Gruden pictured on the billboards. You had the catchy 'Chucky' moniker, and signs like 'I love you, Jon' and 'Marry me, Jon' in the stands at our games."

Raiders quarterback Rich Gannon, who became a star under Gruden's tutelage, was moved to remark in the *People Magazine* article, "Our fans have a love affair going with Jon."

Longtime Raiders fans knew all too well what was happening. They witnessed this in the 1980s, when running back Marcus Allen became wildly popular and threatened Davis' standing. Out of nowhere, the dynamic Gruden had burst onto the scene, reinvigorated the Raiders and gained widespread credit.

"I don't think Jon intentionally tried to become the personality he evolved into," Kebric said. "But all of a sudden, this team turned the corner and his fame had spread way beyond the Bay Area.

The Raiders came within one victory of reaching the Super Bowl in 2000, losing at home to the Baltimore Ravens in the AFC Championship Game. A year later, Gruden had the Raiders back on the cusp as they defeated the New York Jets, 38-24, in their first playoff game and then traveled east for their next game.

The Raiders and the New England Patriots met in the AFC Playoffs semifinal January 19, 2002, at Foxboro Stadium, with the winner to play the following week in the AFC Championship Game against the Baltimore Ravens or Pittsburgh Steelers.

In a heavy snowstorm, the game featured 172 plays — one standing head-and-shoulder-pads above the others. That play would have wide-ranging and long-lasting ramifications that no one could have imagined.

That one play launched the Patriots' dynasty that remained dominant 15 years later. That one play set in motion the demise of the Raiders, which lingered for 13 years. That one play helped make Patriots quarterback Tom Brady a household name. That one play introduced the world to a rule that went from unknown to almost everyone outside the close-knit community of NFL game officials to a combination catchphrase and punch line that instantly became ingrained in the NFL lexicon.

That game now is known as "The Tuck Game" as a result of that one play.

With one minute, 50 seconds left in the fourth quarter, the Patriots had a first-and-10 at the Raiders 42-yard line.

Raiders cornerback Charles Woodson blitzed Patriots quarterback Tom Brady, and drilled Brady as he attempted to secure the ball against his body.

Woodson's hit knocked loose the ball from Brady's right hand, at which point Raiders linebacker Greg Biekert recovered the fumble for what appeared to be a game-clinching play.

Raiders senior executive John Herrera watched from the sideline.

"As soon as Biekert fell on the ball, everybody was just ecstatic," Herrera said. "I was already on the phone with Pittsburgh contacts, checking out hotels in Pittsburgh. I was already on to the next week."

Not so fast.

The NFL's replay assistant at the game, Rex Stuart, ruled that the play should be reviewed, as he could do inside the final two minutes of the game. An interesting footnote is, if the play had happened with more than two minutes left in the game, the Patriots would have been unable to challenge the ruling and ask for a review as they were out of time-outs. Not until 2012 did NFL owners approve instant replay review of all turnovers.

Referee Walt Coleman presided over the review in the Patriots-Raiders playoff game.

"One minute became two, and two became three and then, a four- or five-minute delay," Herrera said. "All of a sudden we started getting a little antsy. What's going on here? What's happening? There's no way they can screw us on this deal. What's going on?"

The Raiders had good reason to be wary. Or, at least that's the theory they subscribed to after years of questionable calls and crucial plays seeming to conspire against them.

Real or imagined, the Raiders expected the worst at such times. Davis believed that the league had it out for his team based upon his numerous run-ins with commissioner Pete Rozelle and other NFL owners.

Davis fostered this belief. His players ultimately converted into full-blown believers. Herrera didn't need to be convinced.

"Just this bad kind of feeling came over us, like, 'What could they possibly do to take the game from us?'" Herrera said of Coleman and the NFL. "You have to remember at that point in time, we had never seen that play, or heard of the rule, and the Raiders had a history at that time, for whatever reason, mysterious calls seemed to go against our team. That wasn't something we imagined or dreamed up.

"I know in the media, they always kind of mocked us about how paranoid we were about things being done, but there were a series of really strange calls. Stuff like that happened to us on a regular basis. So we're thinking, 'What in the world could they possibly come up with?'"

Davis and other front-office employees, some assistant coaches and scouts fidgeted in the press box as Coleman sorted out the play. Everyone wondered what was taking so long.

Brady had pulled down the ball toward his midsection after he decided not to follow through with an attempted pass. Woodson arrived as the ball neared Brady's stomach region, and he knocked it loose with a clean hit.

The Raiders had a photograph of the ball touching Brady's left hand, an act that could have been interpreted by Coleman to mean that Brady had gone from a passer to a runner and, therefore, the tuck rule no longer applied. Raiders senior assistant Bruce Allen would use a snapshot of the moment when the ball touched Brady's left hand on the cover sheets of faxes he sent out.

Biekert fell on the ball and secured it at the Raiders 48-yard line. Both teams seemed resigned to their fate.

Gruden had worked hard the previous four years changing the team's victimization mentality. He instructed his players to ignore those who perpetuated the belief that there was a conspiracy by the league to screw the Raiders at every turn.

For the most part, Gruden succeeded in changing that mind-set. Yet, as time went on during the review of the Brady fumble, even Gruden sensed that something was about to happen that would undo a hard-earned, favorable outcome.

After a lengthy delay, Coleman made his way toward the middle of the field so he could announce the verdict of the review. Gruden intercepted Coleman before he heard the ruling. Herrera overheard the one-sided conversation.

"You're going to fuck me, Walt, aren't you?" Gruden yelled. "You're going to fuck me. I know you're going to fuck me. You're going to fuck me, aren't you? Tell me you're not going to fuck me."

Sure enough, Coleman invoked the "tuck rule" and overturned the fumble, declaring this play an incomplete pass. The seldom-cited rule stipulated that an attempted pass doesn't conclude until the ball makes contact with the body. Hence, the rule's name.

The Tuck Rule had been instituted in 1999, as Rule 3, Section 22, Article 2, Note 2 of the NFL rulebook. The rule stated:

> "When a Team A player is holding the ball to pass it forward, any intentional forward movement of (the passer's) arm starts a forward pass, even if the player loses possession of the ball as he is attempting to tuck it back toward his body. Also, if the player has tucked the ball into his body and then loses possession, it is a fumble."

Raiders employees stationed in the press box vented their anger by cursing out loud, slamming their fists on desktops and kicking the wood that separated them from the row below where they were seated.

Patriots kicker Adam Vinatieri tied the game at 13-13 when he booted a 45-yard field goal with 27 seconds left in regulation. Vinatieri's 23-yard field goal midway through the overtime period gave the Patriots the win and kept alive their season. Just before his game-winning kick, in a thinly veiled admonishment directed at Raiders employees, the Patriots made an announcement in the press box for everyone to show class and comport themselves in a professional manner however the play turned out.

In his postgame speech, Gruden impressed upon his players how he would not blame the loss on the officials and that he didn't want them to, either. Herrera remembers little else that Gruden said, other than it was so quiet that "you could hear a pin drop."

At the same time, Coleman issued his response through a pool reporter.

"Obviously, what I saw on the field, I thought the ball came out before his arm was going forward. Then, when I got to the replay monitor and looked at it, it was obvious his arm was coming forward. He touched the ball. And they just hooked it out of his hand. His arm was coming forward, which makes it an incomplete pass."

Davis eventually made his way from the locker room to the team buses. Herrera watched as Davis approached in a cart, with his bodyguard behind the wheel.

"He looked like a ghost," Herrera said of Davis. "He was as white as a ghost."

Davis instructed his bodyguard to pull the cart alongside Herrera, at which point Davis went off.

"They stole it from us, didn't they?" Davis said.

"They absolutely stole it from us, without any question," Herrera responded.

Davis kept shaking his head in disbelief. He was just getting warmed up in the sub-freezing night.

"They fucked us," Davis said. "They fucked us, didn't they?"

Davis' anger and disgust were so intense that he didn't even notice exiting Patriots fans cursing and flipping off Raiders players and coaches as they boarded buses.

"All this chaos was five feet away, but Al was totally oblivious to it because he was so devastated from what had just happened in the game," Herrera recalled.

Jon Kingdon didn't fly home with the team. Instead, he headed to Florida to scout the Florida-USA College All-Star Game. Many fellow scouts came up to Kingdon at the first practice and expressed their sympathy for the Raiders, particularly in the manner they lost. Baltimore Ravens scout Terry McDonough and Kingdon discussed the Raiders-Patriots game.

Davis and Terry McDonough's father, Will, had been close for many years because of Will McDonough's distinguished career as a sportswriter for the *Boston Globe* and a TV broadcaster. However, as a Boston native, Terry McDonough harbored a grudge against the Raiders because of a controversial call in a 1976 playoff game in which the Patriots lost to the Raiders.

Patriots defensive tackle Ray "Sugar Bear" Hamilton, whom Davis hired as the Raiders defensive line coach in 1993, was penalized for roughing the passer, Kenny Stabler, turning an incomplete pass on third-and-18 from the Raiders 28-yard line into a first down with a little more than a minute left in the game. The Raiders parlayed their good fortune into a game-deciding touchdown and went on to win their first Super Bowl.

"That should have never been a penalty," Stabler told Will McDonough in 2002. "I got hit a lot worse than that in my career and it was never called. Hamilton just went for the ball and landed on me. That's all that happened."

Terry McDonough agreed with Stabler. He told Kingdon that he would never forgive the Raiders, who conveniently dismissed the call that went their way against the Patriots. At the same time, he wanted Kingdon to know that in the Tuck Game, "the Raiders had gotten screwed and he really felt bad for them."

Later that day, Kingdon received a call from Davis. As Kingdon shared with Davis what was taking place at the all-star game in Florida, Davis interrupted.

"Forget that for now. What are people saying about the call yesterday?" Davis asked.

"I related what Terry had said and since Al had been close with Terry's father, Will, it carried a lot of weight," Kingdon said.

"That's what Terry said?" Davis responded "They all felt we got fucked?"

"Yes," Kingdon replied. "That was the consensus."

Two months later, "The Tuck Game" controversy was a primary

subject when the Competition Committee convened at the NFL Annual Meeting in Palm Desert, California. When Raiders general counsel Jeff Birren returned from the meeting, he reported that two head coaches, both former collegiate quarterbacks with NFL quarterback coaching experience, appeared to side with the Raiders during "The Tuck Game" discussion.

Mike Holmgren, the Seattle Seahawks head coach who earlier in his career had led the Green Bay Packers to back-to-back Super Bowls, put it very simply when he said, "If you're in a bar and fifty guys see the play and they all say it's a fumble, it's a fumble."

Jim Fassel, the New York Giants head coach who had mentored his team in the 2001 Super Bowl, exclaimed that he knew of no quarterback coach who ever taught his quarterback to reload from the hip.

The NFL's vice president of officiating, Mike Pereira, jumped in to defend the call by saying that it was not clear that Brady wasn't trying to throw the ball as he brought it to his other hand. Of course, he could not clarify if the right-handed Brady would have been able to throw the ball with his left hand.

No one in the room agreed with Pereira's explanation, Birren said, so NFL commissioner Paul Tagliabue brought an end to the discussion by saying he did not want to put an asterisk by Robert Kraft's Patriots Super Bowl victory.

The loss to the Patriots marked the end of Gruden's tenure with the Raiders, four years after he had arrived and masterfully resurrected the franchise.

"The Tuck Rule Game was the undoing of a lot of things," Davis said years later.

The Raiders won 23 of 32 regular-season games in Gruden's final two seasons and endured excruciating playoff losses to teams (Baltimore and New England) that went on to win the Super Bowl. Gruden had turned the Raiders into a team that players wanted to play for and coaches wanted to coach for.

"Gruden related to me how, when the Raiders hired him, it was a battle to get good coaches and players to come to the Raiders," Kingdon said.

It didn't take long for that to change. In a short period of time, free-agent players were putting the Raiders on their list, some placing the Raiders at the top. Suddenly, big-name talent such as wide receiver Jerry Rice, safeties Rod Woodson and Eric Turner and running back Charlie

Garner signed free-agent deals with the Raiders.

With the success generated by Gruden, Davis realized that soon he would have to compensate his head coach with a new and more lucrative contract.

Gruden had signed a three-year contract in 1998 that included two one-year team options, and his salary was one of the lowest in the league. The original contract's option clauses meant that the Raiders were in control of two additional years (2002 and 2003) at the terms originally agreed upon. It was apparent, however, by the end of the third season that Gruden had outperformed the original contract and a substantial raise was well-deserved.

Kebric was watching an East-West Shrine Game practice at Stanford University in January 2001, three days after the Raiders 27-0 playoff victory over the Miami Dolphins, when a familiar voice called out:

"Hey, Bruce. What are they doing to my boy?"

"I looked around, and it was Jim Gruden, Jon's father, who was scouting for the San Francisco 49ers," Kebric recalled.

"What are you talking about, Jim?" Kebric replied. "Jon is the toast of Oakland. I saw a billboard with his picture on it while I was driving over here today. I heard fans screaming 'Chucky, Chucky, Chucky' at Saturday's game. Everything is great in Oakland."

Bob LaMonte, Jon Gruden's agent, was standing alongside Jim Gruden.

"Everything is not great," LaMonte said. "Al is low-balling Jon."

"I don't know what you are talking about," Kebric responded. "I don't have anything to do with contracts but I'll tell Al what you said when I get back to the office."

"Be sure to tell Al that Jon wants to be there," Jim Gruden requested. "Jon loves the team."

As promised, Kebric called Davis upon his return to the team's facility in Alameda and told him about the conversation he had with LaMonte and Jim Gruden.

"They are disturbed about Jon's contract," Kebric said.

"Thanks for calling me," Davis said, and then he asked questions about the East-West Shrine Game practice.

Eight years later, Kebric was visiting with Gruden and former

Raiders senior assistant Bruce Allen at the Avila Country Club in Tampa, Florida, where both resided at that time. During their visit, Kebric learned much more about Gruden's 2001 contract situation.

According to Gruden, Davis came up with an extension which he had Allen present to Gruden. A few days passed. By that time, Allen was in Hawaii for the Pro Bowl. Gruden was summoned to Davis' office, where he met with Davis and Raiders chief executive Amy Trask.

"Jon explained to me that he was ready to sign the contract that he had been presented by Allen," Kebric said. "But when he met with Davis and Trask, the contract figures differed from those he had been given by Allen."

When Gruden pointed out the difference, Kebric was told, Davis and Trask placed the blame for the change on Raiders general counsel Jeff Birren.

Gruden, thinking that Birren was being made a scapegoat, told Davis: "I'll sign the contract if you fire Jeff Birren."

Davis did not fire Birren, nor did he sign Gruden to a contract extension.

In 2008, Davis had this to say about Gruden: "Jon was a good coach, but don't forget, I took Jon [when] no one else even knew who he was."

Gruden, with two one-year team options remaining on his contract, had little leverage. He coached the Raiders for one more season, which ended with the loss to New England. The consensus was that, had the Raiders won in New England, then Davis' only option would have been to sign Gruden to a long-term contract extension. But Davis had other plans and only a small window of time to capitalize on the leverage he possessed. His plan: to move on without Gruden, while getting something in return. In 2008, Davis had this to say about Gruden: "Jon was a good coach, but don't forget, I took Jon (when) no one else even knew who he was."

Not long after the New England game, Davis asked Kingdon,

"Would you take a first-, third- and fourth-round draft picks for Gruden?"

"No," Kingdon said.

"Why not?" Davis said.

"We're getting ready to go to a Super Bowl and Gruden's a great coach. Why make a change like that?" Kingdon said.

Davis, as always, had an answer.

"He's only going to stay for one more year, and then he's going to leave," Davis said.

"Fine, I'll take the one year," Kingdon said. "Maybe we can change his mind."

"Yeah, but what if he goes to the 49ers?" Davis asked.

Then, without prompting, Davis added: "Would you take three No. 1s?"

"That I might consider," Kingdon said.

Soon, Davis received a blockbuster offer from Tampa Bay.

"Al called me late one night," Kebric said, "and he said, 'I can get two 1s and two 2s for Gruden. Would you do it?' I said, 'I would trade Vince Lombardi for two 1s and two 2s.'"

"Good," Davis said.

Ultimately, the Raiders received a first-round pick and a second-round pick in the 2002 draft, a 2003 first-rounder and a 2004 second-rounder, plus $8 million, from the Tampa Bay Buccaneers. This was a coup, in Davis' mind, in relation to what other teams had received for trading coaches. Acquiring Bill Belichick from the New York Jets in 2000 cost New England a first-, a fourth-, a fifth- and two seventh-round selections, while the Jets had sent four of their draft picks, including a first-rounder, to the Patriots for the rights to Bill Parcells in 1997.

Davis wanted more, but Buccaneers owner Malcolm Glazer refused to include perennial All-Pro defensive tackle Warren Sapp as part of the compensation.

"The Glazers said that was the only thing that they wouldn't part with," said Sapp, who was inducted into the Pro Football Hall of Fame in 2013. "They said they would give Al the money, the draft picks, everything, 'but he can't have Warren. We're keeping him.'"

Glazer held firm, and Sapp played an integral role in helping the Buccaneers to a Super Bowl victory over the Raiders in Gruden's first season in Tampa.

Gruden made a believer out of Sapp long before the Super Bowl win, though Sapp initially viewed Gruden as an interloper, of sorts. The Buccaneers had been successful before Gruden arrived, and head coach

Tony Dungy was popular among the players before he was deposed. Hence, Sapp visited Gruden at his office soon after the trade was consummated.

"You don't have to knock on that door," Gruden told Sapp. "You open that door."

"I looked and said, 'Huh?' " Sapp recalled.

"You open that door. You're my captain, ain't you?" Gruden asked.

"Yeah," Sapp said, as the two fierce competitors with fiery personalities commenced a feeling-out process.

Sapp quickly made visits to Gruden's office part of his routine.

"Every morning, I bullshit you not, I used to walk into that office and sit for an hour, from 7 a.m. to 8 a.m.," Sapp said. "That's where I used to eat my breakfast at, and it wasn't food I was eating. I was eating the knowledge of my head coach because this son of a bitch loved the game.

"I was like, 'How in the hell did Al Davis let him out of Oakland, with an MVP (Rich Gannon), Charlie Garner, with fucking Jerry Rice and all them boys? They're crazy. How in the hell did they let him get out of there?' And they let him get to me? I said to him, 'I promise you, every person in this building is going to pay attention to what you got going.'"

"Either that, or I'll run 'em out of here," Gruden said.

The Raiders parlayed the four picks they received from the Buccaneers into University of Miami cornerback Phillip Buchanon, University of California offensive tackle Langston Walker, Colorado University defensive end Tyler Brayton and Virginia Tech center Jake Grove, respectively. None made up for the huge void created by Gruden's unceremonious departure.

"Jon Gruden was a Pyrrhic victory to Al Davis," Kebric said. "Al won the battle, but he lost the war. I supported the trade and was giddy thinking about all those draft choices. I later realized that the draft picks were just expensive pieces of paper. If you have a special coach, you just don't let him go."

Just like that, Davis had jettisoned a successful young coach and turned over the reins to an unheralded assistant coach, Bill Callahan. Once again, Davis was the face of the franchise. Davis' bold move validated a belief held by former Raiders pro personnel director Rich Snead, who was fond of saying: "Al would rather lose his way than win someone else's way."

Brad Mangin

Raiders coach Lane Kiffin frequently used the media as a means of taking shots at owner Al Davis, who fired Kiffin "for cause" four games into his second season in 2008. Davis ultimately retaliated with a memorable news conference in which he referred to Kiffin as a "flat-out liar" and outlined Kiffin's "mistakes" on an overhead projector.

CHAPTER TWELVE

Lane Kiffin:
The Search for the Next Gruden

Al Davis was under immense pressure to make the right hire in 2007 after erring so badly in bringing back Art Shell for a second stint as head coach. The Raiders won only two games under Shell in 2006, the fewest in any season during Davis' reign. Everything Davis counted upon that season went downhill in a hurry. Star wide receiver Randy Moss tuned out Shell and offensive coordinator Tom Walsh. Moss simply went through the motions in what served as a perfect metaphor for the season. Oakland's offense was historically bad under Walsh, who had been lured out of retirement from operating a bed-and-breakfast inn in Idaho. Pro personnel director Mike Lombardi undermined Shell at every turn and was banned from attending practice by Shell, who called Lombardi "a fox in the henhouse."

This came on the heels of Bill Callahan's two-year tenure as Raiders head coach which ended in disaster in 2003. A surreal scene — even by Raiders standards — unfolded in the pregame locker room before the season finale, as players fumed at Callahan, with some contemplating a boycott of the game after Callahan's suspension of star cornerback Charles Woodson and lead running back Charlie Garner for missing curfew the previous night. Norv Turner, Callahan's successor, won only nine games in the 2004 and '05 seasons combined, and was fired in favor of Shell. People couldn't wait to see whom Davis would hire in 2007. Davis had confronted this situation before, having had four disappointing seasons under Shell, Mike White and Joe Bugel. Davis had struck gold with the hiring of Jon Gruden. It was his intense desire to see history repeat itself.

Davis wasted no time. He phoned Jon Kingdon on New Year's Day after the college bowl games had been played and asked Kingdon if he no-

- 191 -

ticed any former Raiders coaches on the field that day.

"I brought up Steve Sarkisian's name," Kingdon said of the assistant head coach and quarterbacks coach at the University of Southern California who had been the Raiders' quarterbacks coach in 2004.

The Raiders had passed for more than 4,000 yards in 2004 and finished eighth in offense that season, with Sarkisian recognized for his role in that success.

That's precisely who Davis had in mind. He instructed Kingdon to contact Sarkisian and interview him for the Raiders' head coaching job, without telling Sarkisian that was the job for which he was being interviewed.

Kingdon tracked down Sarkisian's cell phone number and prepared a list of 20 questions. He reached Sarkisian in his car.

Kingdon told Sarkisian that he wanted to ask him a number of questions about his coaching philosophy, theories, what he thought was wrong with the Raiders and how he would set up his coaching staff.

The interview lasted for 30 minutes. Kingdon faxed the information to Davis.

"Al called me back immediately," Kingdon said. "He was very impressed with all of Steve's answers."

Kingdon mentioned to Davis that Sarkisian's answers came while he was driving, which made it all the more impressive because of the lack of preparation.

"This is fantastic," Davis said. "Bring him in for an interview."

Davis had other candidates in mind, but he was especially intrigued by Sarkisian. His fascination with Sarkisian only grew after each of their first two interviews. Davis was so impressed that he brought Sarkisian back for a third and final interview. This time, Sarkisian brought along two USC cohorts, Lane Kiffin, his prospective offensive coordinator, and Mark Jackson, his choice as the administrative assistant to the head coach.

Davis informed Sarkisian that he would have to keep incumbent defensive coordinator Rob Ryan, who dutifully employed Davis' preferred scheme. Sarkisian told Davis that that was fine, but he wanted to meet with Ryan first. Davis balked.

Still, Davis wanted to consummate the deal with Sarkisian, who had returned to Southern California after his last interview with Davis.

Kingdon called the USC football office and reached receptionist

Irene Puentes, who told Kingdon that Sarkisian was in a meeting but that she would let him know that Kingdon called and have Sarkisian call back as soon as possible.

A couple of hours passed without any word from Sarkisian. So Kingdon phoned USC again.

"Irene was surprised that he had not called me back," Kingdon said.

She paused and then pointed out that the coaches were busy with signing day.

"I called Al and said that something was going on with Steve and that he seemed to be avoiding me," Kingdon said.

Kingdon worked the phones in an attempt to find out what was going on with Sarkisian. He phoned Sarkisian's agent, Gary Uberstine — coincidentally, Uberstine also represented Kiffin at the time — who assured Kingdon that there wasn't anything to worry about, that Sarkisian wanted the Raiders head job.

When Kingdon called Davis to pass along the update, Davis informed him that Sarkisian had just called and removed his name from consideration for the position.

"Now it was very hectic," Kingdon said. "There are no secrets about these job interviews, so Al was really concerned about it getting out that he was turned down by Sarkisian."

The news of Sarkisian's rejecting the Raiders offer did get out, so Davis and Sarkisian went into full spin-control mode. The Raiders said Sarkisian had not been offered the job and, in fact, had removed his name from consideration.

"The Oakland Raiders were not ready to offer the position and wanted to wait until after the weekend as the organization is still doing its due diligence," the Raiders said in a statement.

Davis prevailed upon Sarkisian's camp to play along with the concocted story line.

"I thank them for their interest in me," Sarkisian said of the Raiders in a statement released by USC. "While the job was never offered to me, at this time in my career, I've told them I want to stay at USC. I strongly believe that the Raiders job is a great opportunity for whomever their next head coach is going to be."

The seemingly agreeable Sarkisian even tipped off Davis to a solid fallback candidate: Lane Kiffin.

Davis earlier had ordered senior executive John Herrera to make a beeline to Southern California and track down Sarkisian.

A few hours later, Herrera landed at the Los Angeles Airport and immediately headed to the USC football office.

Much to Herrera's dismay, Sarkisian, Kiffin and just about everyone else from the USC football program were unavailable.

Herrera found a campus worker, asked that person where he might find Sarkisian and was told that Sarkisian and the rest of his coaching staff were at Universal Studios as part of a hosting event for USC recruits.

Herrera failed in his attempt to get Sarkisian on the phone. Finally, he was able to get Kiffin on the phone.

"What the hell is going on with Sarkisian?" Herrera asked Kiffin.

Kiffin said he didn't want to speak for Sarkisian but did concede that Sarkisian "maybe got cold feet."

At that point, Herrera sensed that Sarkisian had second thoughts about following through on his verbal commitment to Davis.

Herrera already was in full-on scramble mode and shifted gears once he sensed Sarkisian wasn't in play anymore. He altered his strategy.

"Are you still interested in being the Raiders offensive coordinator?" Herrera asked Kiffin.

Herrera's time was running out. He was booked on the last flight back to Oakland that night. Davis wanted something concrete by night's end.

"Well, I don't know about that," Kiffin said. "I would be coming up with some coach that I don't know. I don't think that I would be all that interested in that."

Herrera called Davis with the update.

"I've talked to Lane. He's still interested but not as much if Steve isn't involved. What do you want me to do? I've got to try to catch this flight to get back tonight," Herrera said.

"Call me from the airport," Davis said.

Herrera rushed to the airport and barely made his plane. Before the plane departed, Herrera called Kiffin once again.

"I would like you to think about joining us," Herrera said. "Al and I are both impressed with you when you're up on the whiteboard. We think you would be an asset."

Kiffin knew that Davis had interviewed Ryan, former New York Giants head coach Jim Fassel and former Raiders wide receiver James Lofton.

"I don't know," Kiffin said. "Without Steve, I'm not sure."

Herrera wasn't deterred.

"I would like you to fly up tomorrow and talk to us again," Herrera said.

"Well, I don't know," Kiffin said. "I guess I could do it. I'll talk to Pete (Carroll, USC head coach) and make sure it's OK with him. But I don't think I would be interested in being the offensive coordinator for somebody else."

Herrera kept thinking about how Davis wanted him to return with something. He also recalled how he and Davis had been so impressed with Kiffin during his interview.

"I had told Al the night before that, if a guy walked into a room, you would have thought that Lane was the guy interviewing for the head coaching job because Lane had more of a presence," Herrera said. "He kind of lit up the room."

"Yeah, I thought so, too," Davis said.

Herrera trusted his instincts.

"Just come up," Herrera said. "How would you like to interview for the head coaching job?"

An awkward silence filled the next 30 seconds or so.

"Yeah, I would be interested in that," Kiffin said.

"OK, I'll talk to you in the morning, and we'll go from there," Herrera said.

As soon as Herrera landed in Oakland, Davis wanted another update.

"Where are we?" Davis asked. "What's going on?"

"I talked to Lane a couple of times, and he's interested in continuing the discussion about coaching," Herrera said, "but I tossed it out there that maybe we would interview him for the head coaching job."

That was news to Davis.

"There was a long silence," Herrera said. "I'm thinking, 'Oh, shit.' At one point, I said, 'Al, are you still there?' "

Finally, after a minute or so, Davis said, "Well, when is he coming up?"

"I haven't made that arrangement yet, but we'll talk about it in the morning," Herrera said.

"OK, have him come up," Davis said.

Herrera contacted Kiffin the next morning. Once again, Kiffin wasn't quite ready to commit.

"I have to clear it with Pete Carroll," Kiffin said. "I don't want to do anything to alienate Pete."

"Fuck Pete!" Davis said, when Herrera informed him of Kiffin's stonewalling. "Tell Lane to get his ass up here. Don't tell me about Pete. You call Pete and tell him that we want to talk to Lane about the head coaching job."

The sooner Davis hired someone, the quicker they would forget about Sarkisian.

"Lane had gone from not even being a thought to 'Let's get him in here right away,'" Herrera said.

Kiffin received Carroll's blessing, and he boarded a plane to Oakland the next morning. Herrera picked up Kiffin at the airport, briefed him on what he was going to be asked by Davis during the interview and then watched as the process played out. Davis interviewed Kiffin well into the night. He and Herrera discussed the matter afterward.

"Fuck Pete!" Davis said, when Herrera informed him of Kiffin's stonewalling. "Tell Lane to get his ass up here. Don't tell me about Pete. You call Pete and tell him that we want to talk to Lane about the head coaching job."

"What do you think?" Davis asked Herrera.

"Well, he's a presence and you like his football acumen, but he's really young," Herrera said. "But you were really young when you took it over. So were Gruden and Madden. We've had success with young people before."

Everything Herrera said supported Davis' feelings about the matter.

"What do you think, Al?" Herrera asked.

"I think the guy is fantastic," Davis said. "Let's get him in here."

Davis was convinced that hiring Kiffin was a "fantastic" move. Kiffin, in many ways, reminded Davis of himself. Davis was 33 when he was chosen as the Raiders' head coach in 1963. Davis also mentioned the names of two of his most successful head coach hires, John Madden and Jon Gruden, both in their early 30s when he appointed them. Kiffin was 31 at the time.

"Al was looking for a bright young coach that would be able to re-peat what Jon Gruden had been able to do a few years earlier," Kingdon said.

Davis wanted the next Gruden, someone who had a youthful ap-pearance, an aggressive personality, football intelligence and inexhaust-ible energy.

Davis actually was convinced that Kiffin was an even better coaching candidate than Gruden at similar stages of their careers.

"Right now, (Kiffin) is much more of the whole [package]," Davis said after he hired Kiffin. He reminded everyone that the Raiders went 8-8 in each of Gruden's first two seasons. "Jon had to grow into it."

The 2006 season had a profound effect on Davis, who said the constant losing and unparalleled ineptitude wore him down.

"It was a tough year," Davis said. "It was week by week, and it hurt. And as time went on, I realized, or at least I felt, that we had to go in a dif-ferent direction. We have to move the clock back. We have to get youth in the organization, and we have to go ahead and attack. (Kiffin) is someone who really means that he will attack."

As it turned out, most of Kiffin's attacks were directed at Davis.

Gruden and Kiffin did possess many of the same qualities. Besides being young, smart, energetic, well-spoken and engaging, football was their singular passion. It consumed them from the time they awakened until they passed out at night while watching game tape.

Both also had the temerity to stand up to Davis, though Gruden did it much more diplomatically.

"Gruden is the only other coach that I saw stand up to Al," Kebric said.

That manifested itself early on in Kiffin's term. Kiffin faced a daunt-ing task in turning around a Raiders team that had the NFL's worst record. He had one huge advantage, though — the first pick of the draft to work with. The Raiders didn't pick until No. 4 in Gruden's first year, which elimi-nated them from contention in the quest to land either of the two high-pro-file quarterbacks — Peyton Manning or Ryan Leaf — available in that draft.

Gruden would have been thrilled by the prospect of landing a quarterback his first season. Kiffin wanted no part of a quarterback at No. 1 because it likely would have saddled him with JaMarcus Russell, whom Davis coveted in a big way. Kiffin fought Davis long and hard over Russell. To no avail.

Kiffin had been a recruiting coordinator in college, so he felt comfortable and confident in his evaluations. The scouting department, along with Kiffin and his coaches, felt that Georgia Tech wide receiver Calvin Johnson was the best player in the draft and a better option for the Raiders than Russell.

"Lane was the best head coach I ever worked with when it came to college player evaluations," Kebric said. "He and his coaching staff really worked hard on draft preparations that year."

Kiffin might have known personnel, but he didn't know Davis very well. He received a crash course on his boss a few months after he was hired when Davis insisted upon Russell.

Kiffin wasn't one to back down from a challenge. After all, he already had worked for Pete Carroll at a top football program at an age when most coaches his age were toiling at lower-level positions.

Perhaps emboldened by his rapid ascent, Kiffin acted as if he was unimpressed by the fact that the 77-year-old Davis was more than twice his age. Kiffin referred to Davis as "Al" in his introductory news conference, whereas those far closer to Davis' age than Kiffin, such as Bill Belichick, Art Shell and Hue Jackson, called him "Mr. Davis" or "Coach Davis" in a deferential manner.

Davis gained a small measure of revenge by calling Kiffin "Lance" during the same news conference, subconsciously or otherwise coming up with a moniker that soon took on a derisive meaning and has stuck with Kiffin.

Kiffin's arrogance and cocksure attitude were on full display the day he was announced as Davis' new coach, which rubbed some the wrong way and portended what was to come.

While Davis and others in the Raiders organization were just learning about their new head coach, Hall of Fame defensive tackle Warren Sapp had an established relationship with Kiffin. Sapp was first introduced to Kiffin in 1996, one year after he was selected by Tampa Bay in the first round of the draft, when Kiffin's father, Monte, was hired as the Buccaneers' defensive coordinator. Eleven years later, Sapp and Kiffin were reunited in what would be Sapp's 11th and final year in the NFL, and Kiffin's first as a head coach on any level.

"He was too arrogant at the time," Sapp said. "Too arrogant, because he had just left USC, and they had, what, seven straight Pac-10 titles, two national titles, some shit like that? Three Heisman Trophy winners, some shit like that? He could do no wrong calling plays out there."

Yet Sapp felt as if he had some sway over Kiffin. Four games into the season, the Raiders were fresh from a resounding victory over the Miami Dolphins on the road. The win evened their record at 2-2 as they headed into their bye week atop their division. But Sapp sensed change was needed before Oakland's next game against a San Diego Chargers team that revolved around running back LaDainian Tomlinson.

"I pleaded and begged him as we were leaving Miami, 'Please, Kiff, do me a favor. Ask Rob Ryan to fix this defense. We got two weeks. Please, help me fix this defense because we sit in an eight-man front all day long, so the only thing that we got to do is assign two As, two Bs, two Cs and we're home. If we don't do this, LaDainian Tomlinson will run for 200 yards.'"

Sapp was confident that he would get what he asked for, just as he had two years earlier when he pleaded with Al Davis to have Ryan go with a four-man rush on certain downs. He hadn't taken into account the ongoing feud Kiffin was waging with Davis.

"LaDainian ran for 198 yards and four touchdowns. I walked on the bus and told Lane, 'Aw, shit, I missed by two yards.' I swear to God. It was unbelievable."

Kiffin was quite serious. He cared more about defeating Davis than he did the Chargers or any other team on the Raiders schedule.

"He didn't want to hear it," Sapp said. "He didn't want to say anything to Rob. He wanted to show Al that the defense wasn't good with Rob coaching, and he wanted his dad. That was part of the pissing match. I'm watching him like, 'Dude, you ain't going to help me fix this defense? I can't just sit here. I can't sit here and play bad football, lose 12 games. I didn't lose that much in Tampa. I was sick."

Kiffin was just getting started, even though he had given up on the season.

"He was in a full-blooded pissing match with Al at that point," Sapp said. "So, he had checked out."

Kiffin struggled to grasp where he stood from the outset with Davis and the Raiders. Shortly after he was hired, he was in Indianapolis to take part in the NFL scouting combine. Each team is permitted 60 pre-scheduled, one-on-one interviews with prospects. The head coach, the coordinator, the position coach and the scouts generally sat in on these interviews for the Raiders.

At one point, the Raiders brought in a top-tier defensive tackle from the University of Florida named Marcus Thomas, who had drug issues his senior season and was placed on a contract and closely monitored by the school. Thomas violated the contract, which had drug rehabilitation class attendance and curfew requirements, and was kicked off the team.

That might have scared off some teams, but Davis viewed such situations as an opportunity to get a first-round talent with a mid-to-late-round draft pick, not to mention at a financial discount. That's how Davis ended up with defensive tackle Tommy Kelly in 2004 as an undrafted free agent and defensive tackle Anttaj Hawthorne in the sixth round of the 2005 draft. Both players were linked to marijuana and plummeted in the draft. Hawthorne was projected as an early-round pick by some draft experts until he tested positive for marijuana at the scouting combine.

"I figured that Marcus Thomas would be a guy that Al would be interested in," Kebric said. "So, we set up the interview."

Thomas' interview with the Raiders ended after 12 minutes or so of the 15-minute allotment.

"We're done," Kiffin said, as he thanked Thomas and walked him to the door. Kiffin then closed the door and announced to those in the room, "We have only 60 of these, and they're precious. We can't waste our time on somebody like that."

"Lane, if you don't like what we're doing, there's the door," Kebric shot back.

"What did you say?" Kiffin responded, as he glared at Kebric.

"We do everything for a reason," Kebric said to Kiffin, who had a stunned look because he thought he was in full control of the process. "If you don't want to sit in with the guy, that's the door right there."

"This guy is talented and is going to be drafted (Thomas was drafted in the fourth round by the Denver Broncos)," Kebric continued. "Al is going to see how talented the guy is. We took Kelly, who flunked the drug test, and he worked out. We took Anttaj Hawthorne, who flunked the drug test. This is what the combine is for, for us to find out why we do or don't like a guy."

Kiffin and Kebric didn't speak the rest of the night. They ran into each other the next day and engaged in a conversation.

"Lane, I imagine Al has told you that you're going to pick the players, you're going to cut the players and you're going to run the team," Kebric said, "but there's only one guy that's going to do that. That's Al."

Davis refused to be swayed by Kiffin or anyone else, and he drafted Russell — long on athleticism, short on discipline and maturity. He then spent the next 18 months or so demonstrating to Kiffin who wielded the power within the organization.

Toward the end of training camp in Kiffin's first year, Davis cut third-round draft pick Quentin Moses, even though few agreed with the decision, including Kiffin.

"Moses shouldn't have been cut," Kebric said. "He was good enough to be a backup."

Moses was the first player picked in the third round that year, and he became the highest-drafted player from his class not to make the opening-day roster. The Miami Dolphins quickly pounced on Moses.

Davis soon asked Kingdon what he thought of the controversial move. Kingdon said once again that he didn't agree with the decision to release Moses.

In response, Davis instructed Kingdon to watch film on Moses and provide him with another report.

"This was ridiculously superfluous at this point. He had already been cut," Kingdon said, "but I went over every play Moses was in and came up with way more positives than negatives."

Davis called back a short time later, and Kingdon gave him his report, again saying that Moses should not have been cut from the team.

"What about Moses' lack of strength?" Davis inquired.

Kingdon reminded Davis of a play in an exhibition game against the 49ers where Moses had dragged down a running back with one arm, while engaged with an offensive tackle.

Davis remembered the play, Kingdon said, and he dourly replied, "I'll see ya," and hung up.

Kiffin had characterized Moses' play in training camp and exhibition games as "outstanding." He tried to get back at Davis by expressing his desire to cut offensive tackle Mario Henderson, whom Davis had selected with the second of Oakland's three third-rounders that year. Davis forced Kiffin to keep Henderson on the roster.

"Well, we should bring Moses back," Kiffin said.

Davis prevailed on both counts.

Kiffin stewed. Resentment lingered.

Unfortunately for Henderson, he was caught in the middle. Kiffin took every opportunity to castigate Henderson and constantly made him the butt of a running joke, always referring to him as "Super Mario."

The owner-coach relationship was beyond repair.

On and on it went. Midway through the season, Kiffin's name was linked to the University of Arkansas head coaching vacancy. Kiffin denied having any interest in the job that ultimately went to Bobby Petrino.

By this time, Sapp had decided that he was going to retire at season's end. He had one final bit of wisdom to impart upon Kiffin, which Sapp shared before the last game.

"I walked in his office and said, "Lane, you've walked around this office and this place all year long yelling, 'Do what we do. Do what we do.' What is that, as a head coach? Do you know what your team does?"

"Lose," Kiffin responded.

"Whoa, I didn't expect you to say that," Sapp said.

Sapp then went over to the grease board and continued with his lesson.

"From 1996 to 2002, when we won a world championship with your father, you walked in the building at the same time, what was our points per game that we gave up as a defense?"

"Ah ... ," Kiffin said, as he processed the question.

Sapp jumped to his aid, saying, "16.02 points per game. That's why I always said, 'Give us 17 points, and we'll make it stick.' That's what we did. We held people to 16 points a game. That's what we did.

"So, the next time you stand in front of your football team and you yell, 'Do what we do on the way out to the field, know what the fuck that is. And definitely don't say it's 'lose' when somebody asks you after the fact. And I walked out of his office."

The tension level spiked during the offseason when Kiffin attempted to fire defensive coordinator Rob Ryan.

"Guess what? The young guy just asked me if he could hire his father (Monte Kiffin) as defensive coordinator," Davis told Kebric.

"What did you tell him?" Kebric said.

"I told him that I didn't think his father was a very good coach,"

Davis said.

"I don't think Al really believed that," Kebric said, "but he was going to show Lane who was the boss."

With Tampa Bay, Kiffin's father had masterminded the league's top defense in 2002. The crowning achievement of that year's defense came in the Super Bowl against the Raiders, when the Buccaneers intercepted Rich Gannon five times and returned three of those interceptions for touchdowns in a 48-21 victory.

"That loss still stung Al," Kebric said.

Kiffin also wanted to fire offensive coordinator Greg Knapp, whom Kiffin referred to as a "blackboard coach" in conversations with Davis. In 2007, Kiffin sat in on almost every one of the 60 interviews the Raiders conducted with players at the scouting combine in Indianapolis in his first season. In 2008, Kiffin participated only in the interview of running back Darren McFadden, who the Raiders picked at No. 4. At the Senior Bowl that year, Kiffin refused to wear Raiders gear.

"He was looking for another job the whole time," Herrera said. "He was madder than hell when he didn't get the Arkansas job. That lingered into training camp, where he was bad. Every day he was firing a salvo at Al and the team."

Kiffin complained openly about not being able to bring in additional players, even though he had a roster with 90 players. He talked about not being able to conduct practice the way he wanted because he didn't have enough healthy players.

"It was unbelievable," Herrera said. "I would say, 'Al, you have to hear what Lane just said.' He was ready to fire him before the season even started."

Instead, Davis kept silent and let Kiffin build a convincing case for being fired.

"That was just kind of Al's style," Herrera said. "He was not quick to make decisions like that. He always kind of waited. It was just his personality. It was just his way. He didn't want to be reactionary and do something rash. He always reacted that way on just about anything like that.

"Part of it was, he would let people kind of twist in the wind and see if maybe he could force something without having to do it, force somebody to make a move. I'm not saying that was true in Lane's case because

Lane wasn't going to voluntarily quit when he had a contract and walk away from the money."

Davis offered a reminder every now and then who was in charge.

Early in 2008, Davis instructed Kiffin to interview James Lofton for the receivers coaching position.

"Why would I want to interview the guy who wanted the job I got last year?" Kiffin replied. Davis had interviewed Lofton before he hired Kiffin, just as he had in 2006 before he hired Art Shell as the head coach. Twenty years earlier, Davis had traded for Lofton and watched the Hall of Fame-bound receiver average 20.7 yards per catch over two seasons.

"Just do it," Davis ordered Kiffin in regard to interviewing Lofton. When Lofton arrived, Kiffin refused to conduct the interview. Lofton ended up meeting briefly with offensive coordinator Greg Knapp, and then Herrera. Lofton and Herrera spoke for an hour or so, and then Herrera escorted Lofton to see Davis. Lofton and Davis exchanged pleasantries, then Herrera walked Lofton out to the parking lot.

A short time later, Davis told Herrera, "Oh, you can let Lane know that I hired James."

There were two seminal moments that sealed Kiffin's fate. One came September 8, 2008, when Kiffin suspended Randy Hanson, the assistant defensive backs coach, for critical remarks he made on the heels of the Raiders 41-14 loss to the Denver Broncos in the regular-season opener at the Oakland Coliseum.

"It's a good thing that Shanahan didn't have our players," Hanson snapped after the Broncos game, "or else he would have beaten us 1,000 to zero." That was in reference, of course, to Broncos head coach Mike Shanahan, who was fired by Davis four games into the 1989 season.

Hanson said he first upset Kiffin during the Broncos game by providing Raiders defensive players with what one assistant coach deemed too much information. He lashed out after the game in the midst of fellow coaches, within earshot of Kiffin.

Kiffin suspended Hanson for five days and reduced his role, both without Davis' consent. Furthermore, Kiffin lied about the suspension when asked by Steve Corkran in a one-on-one interview.

"Randy had some personal issues going on," Kiffin said nine days after the flare-up. "Randy still did some work for us, but he spent some time at home to get some things straight in his personal life."

Kiffin's half-baked explanation for Hanson's absence pissed off Davis and Hanson because it was nothing short of a bald-faced lie.

"Oh, fuck, that ain't true," Hanson said when asked by Corkran if he had any personal issues. "I was fine. I've been working late and staying up late. They said that I was tired and this and that. The bottom line is, they're trying to move me, they're trying to get me out of the way, is how I feel. They're just trying to reduce my role and make things a little harder on me."

Davis also was incensed that Kiffin ordered Hanson to take a full physical to make sure that he wasn't suffering from any underlying issues.

"Can you imagine that?" Hanson asked. "Look at me, I'm fine."

Corkran called Herrera in an attempt to secure an interview with Al Davis. After speaking with Davis, Herrera called back, with chief executive Amy Trask patched in to the conversation.

"Mr. Davis said that he does not want to be quoted in your story," Trask said. "However, he wants you to know that you have his blessing."

The message was clear: Kiffin had acted without Davis' consent and Davis was content with the story running, regardless of how dysfunctional it portrayed his team.

That same week, Kiffin made it a point to tell the media that Davis and Ryan conspired on the defensive scheme each week. That contention infuriated Davis. Ryan conducted an unscheduled news conference to shoot down Kiffin's assertion.

A day after the story broke about Kiffin suspending Hanson, Kiffin had public relations director Mike Taylor summon Corkran for a face-to-face meeting in a room typically off limits to anyone other than coaches and players.

Corkran entered a room where players routinely met with their position coaches and encountered Kiffin, who was standing at the head of the room.

"I thought I told you that Randy was excused for personal reasons," Kiffin said.

"You did," Corkran replied. "And you lied."

"What do you mean, I lied?" said Kiffin, who acted surprised by the accusation.

"You told me that Randy was excused for personal reasons, when, in fact, you suspended him for comments he made after the Broncos game," Corkran replied.

Corkran had reminded Kiffin that his initial comments about the Hanson matter were being recorded and on the record. Kiffin acknowledged that he understood and that he stood by his comments. Kiffin wanted to know why Corkran didn't come back to him with an opportunity to change his account of how things unfolded.

"My job entails giving you an opportunity to tell your side of the story," Corkran told Kiffin. "My job isn't to keep giving you chances to tell the truth after you've been caught in a lie."

One day after this exchange, Davis fired Kiffin.

The other flashpoint transpired September 21, 2008, after Oakland's third game. Kiffin made several questionable decisions during that game, including failing to call time-out in time to ice Buffalo kicker Rian Lindell before his game-winning field goal.

"After the game, we were at the airport, and Al was just furious," Herrera said. "He was pissed out of his mind. He was hollering, complaining and bitching about the way Lane had coached that game, how Lane had blown the game and why would he do this and that?"

Davis reached the jetway and prepared to get on the plane for the cross-country flight. He still hadn't calmed down. He started "bitching about Kiffin like nobody's business" to assistant coach Willie Brown, Herrera said, while Kiffin stood nearby, around the corner.

"Why in the hell would he do that?" Davis asked Brown. "Why in the hell did he do this? What the hell was he thinking?"

No one could board the plane because Davis stood in the doorway. Therefore, everyone listened in as Davis rattled off the reasons why Kiffin shouldn't be a head coach. Davis didn't know that Kiffin was within earshot. Kiffin heard the whole thing.

"Al, I'm right here," Kiffin said. "If you want to tell me this stuff, I'm right here."

Davis glared at Kiffin and didn't say a word.

Herrera surmised that Davis had said what he wanted to say, and that Kiffin had heard everything by that point.

"So, Al stared him down and walked right past him like he was a nothing," Herrera said. "It was like, 'Get out of my way, I don't even want to see you.'"

Kiffin's response to Davis' words on that airport jetway came a week later, when he trotted out Sebastian Janikowski for a 76-yard field goal attempt — the NFL record for longest field goal at the time was 63 yards — on the final play of the first half. Janikowski's kick didn't even reach the goal line.

It was just a matter of time by that point. Davis' case had been bolstered by a series of events, and he decided to fire Kiffin in a news conference in which Davis famously outlined his case on an overhead projector.

Herrera arrived to work that morning and was greeted by a voice mail from chief financial officer Marc Badain, who relayed the message that Davis wanted Herrera to call him as soon as possible.

"I'm going to let Lane go," Davis told Herrera. "Get with Marc, and you guys go let him know that I want to talk to him. Have him call me."

Herrera found Badain and informed him of Davis' instructions.

"We look at each other like, 'Oh, boy, this is great. We have to go in and fire the head coach,'" Herrera said.

Herrera and Badain made their way to Kiffin's office and knocked on the door.

Kiffin answered the door, looked at Herrera, then looked at Badain and then looked back at Herrera.

"Al wants you to call him," Badain said.

"OK, so that's it, huh?" Kiffin said. "It's over?"

"I'm afraid so," Herrera said.

It's a moment that everyone knew was coming, even Kiffin.

"Knowing who the owner is, you know from Day One there's no job security," Kiffin said in a conference call with Kansas City media earlier that month.

Kiffin was fired four games into his second season. He lasted 20 games and departed with a 5-15 record.

Once Herrera and Badain went into Kiffin's office, Kiffin started asking a series of questions.

"Look, you just need to pick up the phone and call Al," Herrera said. "He's waiting for your call. Call him, and he'll let you know exactly what the situation is, what we're doing."

Kiffin wasted no time. He picked up the phone and called Davis, with Herrera and Badain still in his office. Davis answered.

"Without a lot of fanfare, Al said, 'I'm letting you go ... with cause,'" Herrera recalled.

"With cause? You mean, you're not going to pay me?" asked Kiffin, who had $3.5 million remaining on his contract.

"He never asked about his assistant coaches," Herrera said. "It was just, 'What about me?'" Badain informed Kiffin that Davis permitted him three hours to pack up his belongings and say his good-byes. As he was about to depart Kiffin's office, Herrera glanced at the desk and caught sight of a newspaper article that speculated about Kiffin's future with the Raiders.

Later that day, Davis dismissed the notion that he didn't properly vet Kiffin.

"He conned me," Davis said, "like he conned all you people."

This is the full text of a letter from Al Davis to Lane Kiffin, less than three weeks before Davis fired Kiffin. The letter, which informed Kiffin that he would be fired for cause if he violated the terms of his contract, came four days after the Denver Broncos beat the Raiders 41-14 in the teams' regular-season opener at the Oakland Coliseum:

September 12, 2008

By Hand Delivery and Federal Express

Dear Lane:

Over the past months, you have made a number of public statements that were highly critical of, and designed to embarrass and discredit, this organization, its players and its coaches. I left you alone during training camp in hopes that you would cease your immature and destructive campaign.

However, you continue to make public statements that are critical of the organization, its players as a whole as well as individual players. Such statements constitute conduct detrimental to the Raiders and I will no longer stand silently by while you continue to hurt this organization.

Further, your contract is quite clear that you work "subject to the direction and supervision of the General Partner" and that the

General Partner has "the exclusive right to do all things, which in its sole discretion are necessary to maintain and improve the Club, the football organization and their activities."

I realized when I hired you that you were young and inexperienced and that there would be a learning process for you. Your mistakes on player personnel and coaches were overlooked based on our patience with you. But I never dreamt that you would be untruthful in statements to the press as well as on so many other issues. Your actions are those of a coach looking to makes (sic) excuses for not winning, rather than a coach focused on winning.

For example, with the exception of Gibril Wilson, you were involved in recruiting all free agents and determining salaries for them and you were explicit about your desire to sign Javon Walker and DeAngelo Hall amongst others. All were a must to sign in your eyes, Hall, in particular, because he played for Greg Knapp in Atlanta and Knapp gave him high grades. Do not run from that now.

I do realize that you did not want us to draft JaMarcus Russell. He is a great player. Get over it and coach this team on the field, that is what you were hired to do. We can win with this team!

In regards to your recent fabrications about the defense, during the final cuts you made every cut on offense and every cut on defense except for (Fred) Wakefield on defense and (Seth) Wand on offense. Furthermore, during the game Monday night Rob (Ryan, defensive coordinator) played your Cover 2 defense and we got killed on an approximately 50-yard touchdown pass and an approximately 70-yard gain that led to a field goal.

You meet every week with the defensive coaches to go over both the past game and to get a general feel for what will happen during the week in practice. You have the ability and authority to provide your input during those meetings and the preparation of the game plan. I do not have weekly meetings with Rob — you do.

During the week, no one has ever told you what to do on either offense or defense. In addition, no one has ever told you during a game what to do on either offense or defense and you call every play on offense. During a game if you want to blitz more, all you have to do is let Rob know what blitz you want and he will do it.

Although you continue to use the media to express your dissat-
isfaction with others, no one has publicly pointed out to you that in
4 preseason games and one regular season game played this year,
your offense has scored one first half touchdown. That put tremen-
dous pressure on the defense.

I know that you wanted me to bring your father in to run the
defense and that Monte told me that he wanted to come here even
though he as (sic) under contract to Tampa. However, I did not
want to tamper with another team. In any event, that was over sev-
en months ago. Do not now also run from the defense and your
responsibilities.

This letter constitutes notice that if you further violate any term
of your contract, in any manner whatsoever, you will be terminated
for cause. I trust that this will not occur.

A.D. Football, Inc.
By: Al Davis

Since the departure of Jon Gruden after the 2002 season, Davis
had experimented with a variety of head coaches. He recycled veteran
coaches Norv Turner and Art Shell. He promoted assistant coaches Bill
Callahan and Tom Cable. He went all-in on Kiffin, whose prior NFL experience consisted of one year as an offensive quality control assistant with
the Jacksonville Jaguars. Callahan was the only coach during this period
of time who achieved a winning record, 11-5 in 2002.

Thirty miles away, in Palo Alto, a former Raiders assistant was
making a name for himself at Stanford University. The man Davis had in
mind for his next head coach was Jim Harbaugh, who had been successful
at every level of football as both a player and a coach.

Davis once again saw a similarity to Jon Gruden. Harbaugh and
Gruden were strong-willed individuals who possessed natural leadership
ability. Both were passionate about the game of football and willing to
devote all their energy to the game.

As a Raiders assistant, Harbaugh had sought out Davis and asked
his advice about a possible career move in 2004. During that meeting,
Harbaugh asked Davis whether it was in his best interests to leave the

Raiders for the head coaching job at the University of San Diego.

Davis counseled Harbaugh not to make the move. Harbaugh reminded Davis that he himself had taken a college job early in his coaching career.

"That was U-S-*C*," not U-S-*D*, Davis said in explaining the difference.

By 2010, Davis had followed Harbaugh's success at both the University of San Diego and Stanford University, and was ready to offer him the Raiders job. After two seasons with the Raiders, Harbaugh had ignored Davis' advice and accepted the head coaching position at the University of San Diego. He compiled a 29-6 record in three seasons at USD and parlayed that success into the head job at Stanford, where he resurrected a 1-11 team into a national power. Suddenly, he was on everyone's shortlist of coaching candidates.

"I knew Jim would become a hot item the first time I saw him run his practice at Stanford," Kingdon said. "Stanford was never an intense place and when they started practice, it was kind of sloppy. Harbaugh exploded."

"We're starting this fucking practice all over," Harbaugh yelled.

"The atmosphere on the field changed immediately and they had a very crisp and productive practice."

Prior to the 2010 season, Davis brought Harbaugh to the Raiders offices in Alameda to interview him and gauge his interest in being his head coach. The meeting went on for a long time, Kingdon recalled.

"Though I did not hear Al make Jim the offer to be the team's head coach," Kingdon said, "as I walked Jim back to his car, he told me that he had told Al that he felt he wasn't ready to be an NFL coach and needed another year as a college coach, but that he was really appreciative of the offer."

Once Harbaugh left, Kingdon returned to the building. At that point, Davis asked Kingdon what Harbaugh had to say.

"When I told him what he said, he then asked if I felt that it would do any good to call Jim again and make the offer again," Kingdon said. "I told Al that Jim seemed very decisive in his decision."

Harbaugh returned to Stanford for the 2010 season and then was prepared for a return to the NFL. By that time, not only the Raiders, but a number of other NFL teams were in hot pursuit of Harbaugh, who was ready to cash in on his stunning success at Stanford.

Stories swirled of Harbaugh being wooed by the San Francisco 49ers, Miami Dolphins and Denver Broncos, to name a few. Dolphins owner

Stephen Ross, general manager Jeff Ireland and former NFL executive Carl Peterson went so far as to fly to California for a meeting with Harbaugh.

Davis jumped into the fray. He had just fired Tom Cable as his head coach and had every reason to think that he had the inside track at landing Harbaugh.

After all, Harbaugh worked for Davis as the Raiders quarterbacks coach in 2002 and 2003, had sought advice from Davis in 2004 and the two sides had spoken the year before.

Davis, now in his 80s, viewed Harbaugh as the coach that could finally help him achieve his goal of winning another Super Bowl.

"When Stanford played in the Orange Bowl that year, Al told me to call Jim that week and set up a time that Al could talk with him," Kingdon said. "The call was arranged and they had their conversation.

"The next day, when Stanford was flying home, Al told me to get Jim on the phone as soon as he landed. I placed several calls to his cell phone and left messages for him to contact Al, though he never did."

Soon after Harbaugh's triumphant return from the Orange Bowl, the announcement was made that he would become the new head coach for the San Francisco 49ers.

Kingdon didn't speak with Harbaugh again until they crossed paths in 2012 during a memorial service for Davis in Las Vegas.

Kingdon asked Harbaugh whether he knew that Davis had been trying to contact him to offer him the Raiders head coaching job. Harbaugh said that he wasn't aware of Davis' efforts to contact him but that he would not have taken the call anyway.

"I was afraid that I couldn't tell Mr. Davis no," Harbaugh told Kingdon.

Brad Mangin

JaMarcus Russell displays the passing form that led to his being the first player selected in the 2007 NFL draft. Al Davis was enamored with Russell's size and arm strength and couldn't be talked into drafting wide receiver Calvin Johnson by head coach Lane Kiffin, which marked the beginning of their rift.

CHAPTER THIRTEEN

JaMarcus Russell: The Bust

After the disastrous 2006 season in which the Raiders posted a league-worst 2-14 record, Al Davis was committed to making sweeping changes. The first move came when he hired Lane Kiffin as the replacement for fired head coach Art Shell. Taking such a huge risk on an unproven 31-year-old Kiffin paled in comparison to what Davis did a little more than three months later.

Kiffin's hiring coincided with the Raiders having secured the first pick in the NFL draft for the first time in franchise history, thanks to a bit of good fortune and an unlikely outcome.

The Lions and Raiders entered the final day of the 2006 season tied for the league's worst record at 2-13. The Lions played the 9-6 Dallas Cowboys, while the Raiders visited the New York Jets.

The Cowboys had already clinched an NFC playoff berth, but they still had a chance to win the NFC East title if they won their regular-season finale. The Lions, on the other hand, couldn't wait for their season to end. Yet somehow the Lions upset the Cowboys 39-31 on December 31, 2006, while the Raiders lost to the Jets 23-3.

That parlay dropped the Lions out of the No. 1 spot and catapulted the Raiders into the premier position for the 2007 NFL draft.

Quarterback JaMarcus Russell and wide receiver Calvin Johnson were considered two of the top prospects, along with running back Adrian Peterson and offensive tackle Joe Thomas.

From the outset, Davis was resolute in his desire to select Russell with the first pick in the draft, even though Kiffin and his coaches, as well as the Raiders' scouts, favored Johnson.

"This probably started the conflict between Lane and Al," Bruce Kebric said, "because Lane was really strong against Russell. He did not want Russell. He wanted Calvin Johnson."

Contributing to Kiffin's opposition to Russell was the fact that his father, Monte Kiffin, who was the well-respected defensive coordinator of the Tampa Bay Buccaneers at the time, also was not a Russell fan.

At one point, Lane Kiffin told Kebric that, "My father said JaMarcus is the kind of quarterback that he would like to play against 16 times a year."

When Kebric relayed Kiffin's comment, Davis replied, "I don't think Monte can coach."

The one thing everyone agreed upon was that the Raiders needed an upgrade at quarterback. The spotty play of Andrew Walter and Aaron Brooks in 2006 solidified that belief. The question became whether to take a massive gamble on Louisiana State's Russell, who did not always display the pride or discipline needed to be successful, or to play it safe and go with Georgia Tech's Johnson at No. 1 and perhaps select a quarterback in the second or third round.

University of Oklahoma running back Adrian Peterson also was a high first-round consideration. The Raiders already had running backs LaMont Jordan and Justin Fargas under contract, so in Davis' mind, Peterson was out of the running.

Johnson remained in the spotlight, as the Raiders desperately needed a top receiver. Tim Brown and Jerry Rice had retired. Randy Moss had made it clear that he wanted out of town. Default No. 1 receiver Jerry Porter was fresh from a season in which injuries limited him to four games and one reception.

While Russell was burdened with a number of question marks, there was a groundswell for the Raiders to take Johnson. Davis remained unmoved.

"I don't even know what Al thought about Calvin Johnson," Kebric said. "He was set on JaMarcus Russell."

It wasn't for lack of effort on the part of Kebric and his fellow scouts, as well as the coaches.

"I thought that Al would get excited when I told him that Georgia Tech coach Chan Gailey said Johnson was the 'best receiver he had coached,'" Kebric related. "I assumed that Gailey's background as a former Dallas Cowboys head coach and as an assistant at Denver, Pittsburgh and Miami would carry some weight. I was wrong. Al was not impressed."

Davis did, however, want detailed information on both Johnson and Russell. Kiffin, offensive coordinator Greg Knapp, quarterbacks coach John DeFilippo and scouts Kebric and Angelo Coia attended Russell's pre-draft workout.

Russell threw pass after pass for the slew of evaluators in attendance. The session lasted for more than hour. He had everyone awed over his arm strength and accuracy. He stopped only because some of the coaches had planes to catch. Otherwise, he seemed content to throw until the last person left.

"It was an amazing workout," Kebric remembered. "He ran a 4.80-second 40 at 256 pounds prior to his throwing session and then displayed excellent arm strength, accuracy and stamina."

Russell's impressive performance at his workout did little to change Kiffin's mind. He had Knapp and DeFilippo, among others, on his side, too. Kiffin and Knapp were implementing the West Coast Offense, so they wanted a quarterback that could make quick, accurate reads. Davis, of course, was enamored with Russell because of his 6-foot-5 height and strong arm.

Coia attended the workout at Davis' insistence because he was the only Raiders scout who had witnessed Pittsburgh Steelers quarterback Ben Roethlisberger work out prior to the 2004 draft, and Davis viewed Russell's skillset as being comparable to that of Roethlisberger.

"I've only seen Russell in this workout," Coia said at the time, "but he's exceptional. He's better than Roethlisberger, as far as the workout goes."

Calvin Johnson worked out the following day at Georgia Tech. Kiffin, Kebric and Coia flew to Atlanta for that one, too. Johnson made the Raiders' decision even more difficult when he recorded a vertical leap of almost 43 inches, a standing broad jump of 11 feet, 7 inches, and shined with his catching ability. Earlier, at the scouting combine in Indianapolis, Johnson had weighed in at 239 pounds and had run a spectacular 4.40 time in the 40-yard dash.

Kebric had extensively researched Russell as both a player and a person. He had seen Russell in practice, at a game and on game tapes. He also had traveled to LSU in advance of Russell's workout so that he could speak with Russell's coaches and the football support personnel who had been around Russell for the previous four years.

In short, Kebric was told that Russell was a great teammate and gifted player. But Russell needed to be monitored round the clock. There also were weight-gain concerns and the LSU football team dietitian told Kebric that Russell needed to be given a weekly diet menu and with direction he would follow it faithfully. If not, "he would end up at IHOP."

Kebric passed along all the information to Davis, along with the recommendation that, if the Raiders drafted Russell, they should consider hiring the LSU dietitian.

Kebric also was told that Russell was abusing a liquid concoction called "purple drank," a mixture of Sprite, cough syrup and codeine. Purple drank, also known as "lean," "syzzurp" and other nicknames, is a popular narcotic cocktail in southern hip-hop circles.

"Al did not seem concerned," Kebric recalled.

Most of the top NFL draft prospects go to various training facilities to prepare for the NFL scouting combine. As it turned out, Russell was attending the Athletes Performance training facility in Tempe, Arizona, along with Notre Dame quarterback Brady Quinn and a number of other highly regarded, draft-eligible players.

Kebric did not live far from that facility, and he was told by an acquaintance who had access to the training site that Quinn worked out twice daily, while Russell showed up only for the afternoon session.

"He told me the dedicated ones come in the morning and then come back in the afternoon," Kebric said of his contact at the facility. "Ja-Marcus came in the afternoon only."

Kebric also was told that Russell and his father were regulars at the strip clubs in Scottsdale.

"I gave all this information to Al," Kebric said.

To no avail.

Davis also received the results from one of the psychological evaluations conducted on Russell. Such reports provide an overview of a player's physical and mental makeup and a summary of what to expect from that player.

This particular report said that Russell was tough, competitive, willing to play through pain and injuries, and determined to find ways to win games. At the same time, Russell was diagnosed as having issues with his learning, execution and focusing. It was unlikely that he would be able to master an offense more complex than the one he functioned in at LSU. His limitations, in turn, likely would lead to self-doubt.

Following a lunch break during the Raiders pre-draft meetings, the door to the draft room remained shut. Kiffin was pleading his case in a one-on-one discussion with Davis when Kingdon accidentally walked in on the meeting and quickly realized what was transpiring.

"As I walked in, I saw that Lane was making his personal case against taking JaMarcus," Kingdon recalled.

In the process of being informed by Davis that he wasn't going to get his way with the top pick, Kiffin also learned first-hand that his tenure as head coach of the Oakland Raiders wasn't going to play out as he expected.

"I'm sure that Lane had been told that he was going to make the draft picks," Kebric said.

With the Raiders on the verge of making a decision that had the potential either to spearhead the franchise's return to relevance or set it back for years, Kiffin was finding out what his predecessors had learned.

Kiffin didn't back down. Instead, he dug in and fought for what he believed, that Russell was not the answer to the Raiders' quarterback woes.

Davis had taken big-time gambles in the past, and oftentimes succeeded, but none of such magnitude as the Russell selection, in terms of money and the value of a No. 1 pick.

"I think what appealed to Al about JaMarcus, besides his talent, was that he was told by the scouts that, as talented as he was, you would have to be on top of him round the clock," Kingdon said. "Al saw that as a challenge. That, and trying to repeat history, when he was able to take talented players that others had given up on, brought them to the Raiders and by his dint of will, he was able to bring out their best."

That worked with the likes of Jim Plunkett, Lyle Alzado, John Matuszak and Burgess Owens, sure, but the times had changed.

"The difference was the money that JaMarcus would receive as soon as he signed his contract," Kingdon said. "That large sum of money, along with JaMarcus' pride in performance, was in stark contrast to the money and self-pride that brought the aforementioned players to the Raiders. The system had changed."

Russell received a six-year contract that guaranteed him $32 million. In return, the only guarantee the Raiders received was that Russell would show up for work. It remained to be seen whether he would come in on Tuesdays and other off days for players, as quarterback Rich Gannon had done from the time he arrived in 1999 until his career ended in 2004. During this time, Gannon was a major reason for the transformation of the Raiders into a Super Bowl team. On the other hand, all signs pointed toward Russell putting in only as much work as was necessary for him to get by. He was not known as a self-starter.

On one occasion, the coaches gave Russell a disc of an upcoming opponent and requested that he view the video at home. When Russell reported to work the next day, he was asked if he had watched the disc. His reply was, "Yes." A short time later, the Raiders video department discovered that they inadvertently had given Russell a blank disc. This unintentional act served to verify the coaches' suspicion that Russell had little interest in preparing himself once he left the Raiders facility each day.

For a brief period, there was a glimmer of hope. Russell had a handful of shining moments during a career in which he started only 25 games. At the tail end of the 2008 season, Russell guided the Raiders to impressive wins over the Houston Texans and Tampa Bay Buccaneers, teams that won eight and nine games, respectively, that year.

"He appeared on the verge of becoming something special," Kebric said. Russell had a 128.1 passer rating, along with two touchdown throws in the Raiders 27-16 win over Houston. In the season finale, he passed for two more scores in a 31-24 victory over Tampa Bay in Jon Gruden's final game as the Buccaneers head coach.

Not long thereafter, his two uncles, whom Kebric had been told were his closest male relatives, died within a month of each other.

"He went back home to Mobile, Alabama, for a spell and later returned to Oakland weighing more than 300 pounds," Kebric said.

Russell had cashed in before he ever played in an NFL game and never produced at a level commensurate with his projection as a franchise-type quarterback. He played three seasons for the Raiders before Davis released him in May of 2010. After he was released, he was arrested two months later for possession of codeine syrup, a controlled substance, at his house in Mobile, Alabama. He later claimed that he had codeine syrup as a means of helping him combat sleep apnea, which the Raiders had diagnosed in Russell's first season.

Ultimately, Russell is remembered more for being one of the biggest busts in NFL history and a major factor for a new collective bargaining agreement that included a wage scale for first-year players. Russell earned approximately $39 million from the Raiders during his three years.

In 2010, quarterback Sam Bradford signed a six-year contract that guaranteed him $50 million. In 2011, four years after Russell was drafted and during the first year of the revised CBA, quarterback Cam Newton, the No. 1 selection, received a four-year contract from the Carolina Panthers that guaranteed only $22 million.

After his release from the Raiders, Russell attempted a couple of NFL comeback efforts, none of which made it out of the starting blocks. In a 2016 interview with ESPN, he blamed the Raiders for his struggles:

Some of the neighbors revealed that Russell's house was the scene of what amounted to a non-stop party, while others said they had either canceled or were about to cancel their season tickets if Russell remained on the Raiders roster.

"I didn't know until later that Oakland didn't want to draft me. Like, how is that going to work? We'll just get him just because. Nobody reached out to see if I had a level head, if I was all right in the mind frame to play football."

Russell's personal behavior and lack of pride manifested itself in myriad ways and led to some of the dysfunction he suggested. On one stormy night, a fallen branch knocked down a wire fence that kept Russell's pit bulls on his property. The dogs got loose, roamed the neighborhood and, according to the neighbors, "scared the hell out of some of them." When the Raiders were notified, four front office members showed up in an effort to locate the dogs and restore order to the neighborhood. While two of the employees repaired the fence, the others had the opportunity to speak with Russell's neighbors, many of whom expressed annoyance at Russell's behavior. Some of the neighbors revealed that Russell's house was the scene of what amounted to a non-stop party, while others said they had either canceled or were about to cancel their season tickets if Russell remained on the Raiders roster.

In the past, Davis had kept players such as Russell longer than seemed logical, if only to put off admitting that he made a mistake. He had no choice but to act sooner in this case.

"Al was smart enough to know that it was hopeless," Kingdon said.

At various times, the Raiders had received calls from the Oakland Police Department informing the team about Russell's presence in a park south of the Oakland Coliseum, an area well known for drug dealing. As a result of these warnings, the Raiders hired former player and coach Donnie Martin to keep company with Russell. Martin's duties entailed making sure that Russell was on time for meetings, practices and team functions, as well as monitoring his personal habits.

"Before a game in Houston, I was sitting behind Donnie on one of the team buses," Kingdon remembered. "Donnie was studying the team's game plan and didn't hear the fuss concerning JaMarcus' absence. I alerted Donnie that Russell was missing. He ran off the bus and returned shortly with JaMarcus in hand."

That marked Martin's final game with the Raiders. He soon was replaced by former Raiders safety Eddie Anderson, who experienced similar problems in his role as Russell's caretaker.

Kingdon also recalled another incident, while walking with fellow scout George Karras through the players' parking lot at training camp in Napa.

"George pointed out a big white car to me and said that it was JaMarcus' Rolls Royce," Kingdon related. "I remarked that it was really a good-looking car."

"Look closer," Karras said. "See how dirty it is. Can you believe someone would have such an expensive car and not wash it?"

It hadn't been just the Raiders coaches and scouts that had opposed the selection of Russell over Johnson. It had even carried over to the public at large.

In 2015, while Kingdon was testifying at a trial which involved the Raiders, he was asked by an attorney to describe the drafting of Russell. Kingdon proceeded to fully explain the process that led to the selection of Russell over Calvin Johnson. During a break in the testimony, Alameda Superior Court Judge Stephen Kaus, obviously a Raiders fan, leaned over to Kingdon in the witness stand, and whispered: "Wow, we could have had 'Megatron?'" in reference to Calvin Johnson.

Many pro football experts, in hindsight, have stated that they never would have selected Russell with the first pick. Davis, however, was not alone in his affinity for Russell. Brian Billick, who led the Baltimore

Ravens to a Super Bowl title and was the Ravens head coach at the time of Russell's drafting, later said: "JaMarcus Russell was the highest-rated player I've ever seen on any of our boards. So we all missed on JaMarcus Russell. Make no mistake."

Ron Riesterer

Al Davis and Marcus Allen (32) in happier times. Allen, who was Davis' personal first-round selection in 1982, helped Davis win his third Super Bowl ring with a MVP performance against the Washington Redskins. Only a few years later, Allen was in the Davis "doghouse" and claimed that the Raiders owner was trying to "sabotage his NFL career." Despite the animosity, Allen was another Davis selection who was elected to the Pro Football Hall of Fame.

CHAPTER FOURTEEN

Saving Face

Imagine the Mount Rushmore a diehard NFL fan might construct in honor of his or her favorite NFL team. The Steelers zealot could opt for a monument bearing the visages of Chuck Noll, "Mean" Joe Greene, Terry Bradshaw and Lynn Swann. The 49ers faithful could counter with Bill Walsh, Joe Montana, Jerry Rice and Ronnie Lott.

There is no evidence that Raiders owner Al Davis ever envisioned such a tribute for his franchise. But if he had, based on the available evidence, it would have looked like this: Four faces of Al.

Davis loved unearthing undervalued talent. He had a soft spot for renegades and rejects. He was a sucker for fearless big-game players. He gravitated to the celebrated, unconventional, bejeweled, outsized, unnaturally swift and unthinkably strong.

He thrilled in assembling a roster that struck fear into the opposition. But heaven help the renegade who accumulated accolades and credit for the team's success to the extent it challenged Davis' standing as the unquestioned face of the Raiders. When that occurred, Davis reacted as if a traitor was in his midst.

"I once asked Al, in front of the other scouts, why the media guide cover never had a picture of a player or coach," Bruce Kebric said. "His answer was, 'No player or coach was bigger than the Raiders.'" The implication was clear: If Davis' picture wasn't going to be on the cover, no one else's would be, either.

Through the years, the Raiders had a number of players and coaches worthy of acclaim beyond the ordinary. Coach John Madden, quarterback Kenny Stabler, defensive lineman Howie Long, running back Marcus Allen, cornerback Willie Brown and numerous other standouts from the Raiders' illustrious teams during their dominance — enough for two or three Rushmores.

However, any time one of those figures attained a certain level of status and notoriety, as was the case with Stabler, Allen, Jon Gruden and perhaps Bruce Allen and Rich Gannon, Davis stanched their assault on his reign as the face of the Raiders organization as if adhering to the Japanese proverb: "The nail that sticks up will be hammered down."

Stabler was traded to the Houston Oilers after six seasons as the full-time starter in Oakland. During his time with the Raiders, he guided them to a 69-26-1 regular-season record and the first of their three Super Bowl titles. Stabler also had an outsized personality that resonated with fans and anyone who enjoyed a party any night of the week. In time, he came to embody Oakland's blue-collar ethic, and hard-working, hard-living Raiders fans. It was easy to appreciate a guy who performed at the top of his profession while thumbing his nose at the establishment and refusing to sacrifice the things he loved besides football — booze, women and good times.

"We knew if we did our job, Kenny would find a way to win," Raiders Hall of Fame offensive tackle Art Shell once said when Kebric asked him what made Stabler so successful.

"With Al, it was a team sport," said Terry Robiskie, who played with Stabler all three of his seasons with the Raiders, from 1977-79. "It wasn't about the individual. With the Raiders, they just had a bunch of great players, they didn't have a face. Nobody's face was going to be the face. If there was going to be a face, it was going to be Al Davis'. Al Davis was going to be the face of the franchise."

And yet, if he needed something extra to enhance his image, Davis did not refrain from asking a star player for a special favor. During a conversation with Bruce Macgowan, a Bay Area television station employee at the time, Stabler recalled a locker room encounter with Davis after the Raiders' 1977 Super Bowl win:

"You know, Al Davis and I had our problems, but when we won the Super Bowl, he came over and put his arm around me and said, 'Great game, Kenny.' I was feeling like the king of the world. We won the game, my best buddy (Fred Biletnikoff) was MVP. What could be better? Al then looked straight into my eyes and with a very straight, serious expression, said, 'Can you do it for me again next year?' That was Al Davis. 'Can you do it for me again next year?'"

Over the years, a handful of Raiders players broke from the herd and gave Davis a run for his money. It was Stabler in the 1970s, bolstered by an NFL MVP Award in 1974 and a cult-like following. Running back Marcus Allen became that guy in the 1980s, as he went from the Heisman

Trophy winner at Southern California in 1981, to the NFL Rookie of the Year in 1982, and then the Super Bowl MVP in 1983. He was the NFL MVP in 1985 and a perennial Pro Bowl player, playing before fans who had watched him in high school and college football before he starred for the Raiders.

Allen had the movie-star smile, the smooth grace and the unrivaled all-around game that captivated the masses. His face was plastered on billboards, splashed across the pages of newspapers and magazines, and he dominated highlight shows.

It wasn't long before Allen had become the most popular Raiders figure and every bit as recognizable, if not more so, than Davis.

"After we won the Super Bowl, Marcus Allen was to the Raiders what Magic Johnson was to the Lakers," said Robiskie, who began his coaching career with the Raiders the year Allen arrived. "Al felt like when we were in Los Angeles, too much of it was about Marcus Allen. It wasn't the Raiders. Marcus had just got the MVP and all that. All the press and the reportings, everything in Los Angeles was Marcus Allen, Marcus Allen, Marcus Allen. Al felt like, at that time, Marcus was just getting too big."

Ironically, it was Davis who once had overlooked Allen's perceived shortcoming and supported him as a prospective Raider. Davis was in Los Angeles when it came time for the Raiders to make their first-round pick in 1982. He was testifying in the retrial of a suit brought by the Raiders and the Los Angeles Memorial Coliseum against the NFL over its refusal to allow the Raiders to move from Oakland to Los Angeles. Davis stayed in constant contact by phone with the Raiders' draft room in Oakland.

> " ... *Marcus Allen was to the Raiders what Magic Johnson was to the Lakers ... everything in Los Angeles was Marcus Allen, Marcus Allen, Marcus Allen. Al felt ... Marcus was just getting too big.*"

Davis was required to be in court, but the Raiders needed his input just as badly. Scouts and coaches weren't able to reach a consensus on which player to select at No. 10. Personnel chief Ron Wolf and Kebric wanted Baylor University running back Walter Abercrombie. Running backs coach Ray Willsey preferred University of Richmond running back Barry Redden. Others in the draft room coveted Southern Cal standout Marcus Allen.

Ultimately, the pick came down to Allen or Abercrombie.

Allen had just won the Heisman Trophy as the best collegiate player, and he had the kind of appeal that would help the Raiders gain traction in a market dominated by the Los Angeles Rams since 1946.

"This was a real selling point for Al when we drafted Marcus," Kingdon said. "We were going to be moving to Los Angeles that season."

Additionally, Davis pointed out to his staff that Allen played his home games on a grass surface at the future home of the Raiders, while Abercrombie accomplished his feats on an AstroTurf field in Texas.

Even so, Davis still wanted a bit more information on Allen before giving his blessing for the Raiders to submit Allen's name to the NFL. Hence, Davis contacted Raiders administrative aide Jeff Birren, who had attended USC and worked in the football office at USC prior to being hired by the Raiders. Birren also had watched every one of Allen's games.

"Can Marcus Allen block?" Davis asked Birren, who later became a general counsel for Davis and the Raiders.

"Yes, he's the best blocking running back on the team," Birren assured Davis.

Davis received the answers he was looking for and informed those in the draft room that he wanted Allen.

No one had any doubts about Allen's talent and football prowess. However, there was real concern over Allen's lack of blazing speed, knowing Davis' penchant for dismissing players who didn't meet a certain standard in the 40-yard dash.

Allen had recorded a rather slow 4.75-second 40 time. By the time the scouting report reached Davis' desk, that time had been massaged to 4.65, which still didn't reach Davis' threshold, especially for a first-rounder. In this case, however, Davis was willing to overlook Allen's lack of desired speed because of Allen's obvious natural running skills and his appeal to the Southern California fan base.

Injuries and Bo Jackson's arrival in 1987 cut into Allen's playing time for a three-year period. It kept getting more difficult for Allen to receive extensive playing time. Davis signed veteran Greg Bell in 1990, signed veteran Roger Craig and drafted Nick Bell in 1991, then traded for aging superstar Eric Dickerson in 1992. He even tried to replace Allen with Vance Mueller. Allen had a combined 378 rushes from 1989-92, or two fewer than his total in 1985.

Allen played the good soldier and did what was asked of him by his coaches. He even moved to fullback, where he was asked to block for guys who weren't anywhere near as accomplished as Allen as a running back. Still, there was the holdout before the 1989 season and the antitrust suit against the NFL in 1991 that challenged the legality of the Raiders prohibiting Allen from playing for another team — free agency as we know it today hadn't been implemented.

By 1992, Jackson was gone as a result of a career-ending hip injury and Dickerson had arrived. Allen still was playing for $1.1 million, as he had the three previous seasons. He didn't play much and finally unloaded in an interview with Al Michaels that aired at halftime of a Monday Night Football game between the Raiders and the Miami Dolphins late in the season.

"What do you think of a guy who has attempted to ruin your career?" Allen asked Michaels. "When someone messes with your livelihood — this is what I've wanted to do since I was eight years old, and this very thing has been taken away from me and not, I don't think, for a business reason, but for a personal reason."

Michaels asked Allen if there was a personal vendetta.

"No question about it," Allen responded.

Allen said that in past talks with Davis, he was told that Davis "was going to get me, and he has. I don't know for what reason, but he told me he was going to get me. I think he has tried to ruin the latter part of my career, tried to devalue me and tried to stop me from going to the Hall of Fame. It has been an outright joke to sit on the sidelines and not get an opportunity to play."

Davis then called upon head coach Art Shell, who tried to deflect blame from Davis by saying it was his call to bench Allen. Few bought into that.

"The reason I made the choice was that Eric was here the whole training camp," Shell said. "So was Nick Bell. Marcus wasn't (here). ... You can't have a rotation of three backs. So, I tried to figure out a way for each of them to make a contribution to our football team."

Shell took umbrage with Allen saying his benching was solely Davis' decision.

"I'm taking it personal," Shell said. "I'm disappointed in (Allen). To say that I told him I was out of it and had no control over it is wrong. I dispute that.

"Look, Al Davis has a lot of input in our personnel decisions, and rightfully so, because he understands personnel. He doesn't always agree with me when I make a decision on who is going to play and who is not going to play. But, in the final analysis, I was hired to make the decisions and, if those decisions don't work out, then I'll be fired, because I am the head coach. I, one person, made the choice as to who would be the featured running back."

Robiskie played an integral role as a buffer between the players and Davis. Allen thanked Robiskie for his part during his Pro Football Hall of Fame induction speech in 2003.

"It's no secret I had some difficult times with the Raiders," Allen said, "but if it wasn't for Terry Robiskie, his humor and his friendship and a person who taught me more about football than just about anybody ... Thanks, Terry."

Robiskie said there was only so much he could do when it came to Davis wanting his way.

"I don't think Al ever looked at Marcus as a threat," Robiskie said. "Nobody was going to be a threat. He just wasn't going to have one guy be the face of his organization. It wasn't Kenny Stabler, it wasn't Jack Tatum, it wasn't Freddie Biletnikoff."

And it certainly wasn't Marcus Allen.

Allen's final season with the Raiders came in 1992. He signed with the Kansas City Chiefs and played five more seasons, including two games a year against the Raiders.

Allen retired after the 1997 season. Davis hired Gruden as his head coach less than a month later. The Raiders were fresh from the worst season, at least in terms of wins, in Davis' 35-year reign. Gruden doubled the Raiders' win total, from four to eight, his first season. The Raiders hosted the AFC Championship Game in Gruden's third season, having been transformed from an NFL afterthought for players into a desired destination.

Gruden, like Marcus Allen, became an instant fan and media favorite. His surfer-dude appearance, comical facial expressions, and unrivaled intensity made him must-see TV. He also delivered on the field, as his teams provided the kind of results that fans yearned for, and Davis expected.

By 2002, though, Davis had had enough. The Raiders were back to their winning ways, which he loved. But Gruden was getting too much of the credit and was supplanting Davis as the face of the organization, as evidenced by the billboards, signs, commercials, the face on the ads for the team's flagship radio station and glowing stories that spread from local to national like a wildfire.

Davis was bombarded with constant reminders of Gruden's burgeoning celebrity and omnipresence in the Bay Area. A particular irritant to the Raiders owner was a billboard featuring Gruden's mug which Davis couldn't help but notice each day he received a ride to the office.

"Who the fuck put those up?" Davis said one day, as he passed the billboard. "I'm the one who signs the players. I'm the one who pays the players."

Davis was confident the Raiders could keep up their winning ways, with or without Gruden. So, rather than give Gruden a contract extension, Davis traded Gruden to the Buccaneers after the 2001 season for four draft picks and $8 million.

Gruden was Davis' kind of coach, Kebric said, because of his passion, conviction and drive to win.

"But I never heard him say anything good about Jon after Jon left," Kebric said.

With Gruden on the opposing sideline, the Buccaneers blew out the Raiders in the 2003 Super Bowl. The Raiders had won 11 games in the regular season and manhandled the New York Jets and Tennessee Titans in the playoffs. As a result, The *Sporting News* named Raiders senior assistant Bruce Allen as the Executive of the Year, with Davis the runner-up.

During the playoffs, Kebric walked into Allen's office one day to recognize Allen for his achievement.

"Congratulations, and good-bye," Kebric said.

"What do you mean?" Allen responded.

Allen didn't need an answer. He knew. He had a front-row seat for the Gruden saga. Now it was his turn.

Kebric told Allen that if he had won the award he would have called *The Sporting News* before the public announcement and pleaded with them to give the award to the runner-up, Al Davis.

Sure enough, Davis was none too pleased by Allen's honor. He felt Allen was receiving undue credit for the Raiders' success. In fact, Davis summoned one of his front-office employees to undermine Allen through tailored quotes to the media that made it clear how Davis was the one who signed the players.

A year later, Kingdon bumped into Bruce Allen during an East-West Shrine Game practice at City College of San Francisco. Allen was on his cell phone and suddenly his face turned ashen.

"Is everything all right?" Kingdon asked.

Allen responded that, he had just "been fired" by the Raiders.

As shocked as Allen was, Kingdon tried to break the tension.

"Can I have your stereo?" Kingdon asked.

Allen initially gave Kingdon a perplexed look and then smiled, a sure sign that he comprehended Kingdon's joke.

A few days earlier, Allen had accepted the general manager position with the Tampa Bay Buccaneers where he would reunite with Gruden, but it had not been announced. He told Kebric that he had informed Davis that he would be leaving the Raiders and that he returned to Oakland to get things in order for his successor.

"But, as usual, Al had to have the last word," Kebric said.

Then, there was Rich Gannon, a journeyman quarterback who blossomed into an NFL star and league Most Valuable Player when teamed with Gruden in Oakland beginning in the 1999 season. Gannon, primarily a backup at earlier stops in Minnesota, Washington and Kansas City, helped rekindle national interest in both the Raiders and Al Davis during a three-year period when the Raiders compiled a 33-15 record and advanced to the Super Bowl on one occasion and to the AFC Championship game twice.

Despite his numerous achievements, Davis generally referred to Gannon as "the head coach's guy" since, like Stabler, Gannon did not possess the size and "big arm" that Davis so coveted in his quarterbacks. Davis also managed to place some blame on Gannon for the loss of three potential Super Bowl rings: Gannon suffered a game-ending injury in the 2000 AFC Championship Game loss to the Baltimore Ravens, when the Raiders were favored and playing at home; he misfired on a short pass late in the regular-season finale in 2001, which enabled the New York Jets to rally for a victory that cost the Raiders the No. 2 seed in the AFC Playoffs and forced the trip to New England for the "Tuck Game," and, finally, Gannon was intercepted five times in Oakland's Super Bowl loss to Tampa Bay after having only 11 passes picked off in the previous 18 games.

After a frustrating 2003 season in which he spent nine games on injured reserve with a shoulder injury, Gannon further annoyed Davis with his post-season comments. Among the statements attributed to Gannon were: That he knew the 2003 Raiders were in big trouble as far back as training camp due to confusing changes in the offensive playbook; that "the structure and integrity of what we do around here has really eroded" and that he thought the organization needed to start from scratch — "I wouldn't say I'd take a torch to the place, but it wouldn't be far from that."

Davis seethed in silence while making plans to move on from Gannon. He hired former Washington head coach Norv Turner, a known advocate of the vertical passing game, as his new head coach and then signed Kerry Collins, a big, strong-armed quarterback who had led the New York Giants to the Super Bowl in the 2000 season.

Gannon entered the 2004 season as the starter but the odds were it wouldn't be long before Collins assumed the starting signal-caller role. Three games into the season, Gannon collided with Tampa Bay linebacker Derrick Brooks, a player whom Davis tried to acquire in the 1995 draft, and who had a 44-yard touchdown return of a Gannon pass in the Raiders' Super Bowl loss. The collision with Brooks caused a neck injury that ended Gannon's career. The 6-foot-5, 240-pound Collins then moved into the starting role but the results were not as Davis had anticipated. The Raiders were victorious in only three of his eight starts. Collins managed to throw 21 touchdown passes that season, but had 20 of his passes intercepted.

Five years later, Gannon, employed as a CBS Sports announcer, remained in Davis' doghouse. Gannon was scheduled to provide the analysis for a 2009 Raiders game, when team spokesperson John Herrera announced, at the behest of Davis: "Rich Gannon is not welcome here, He's attacked us on a regular basis since becoming a member of the media. After affording him the opportunity to establish a career here, he has since gone on to attack us in a way that is totally unacceptable. He seems to be a guy who can't get over the fact that he played the worst Super Bowl game in the history of the game and he wants to blame everybody but him. I guess it's our fault he threw five interceptions."

Gannon, in reply, was quoted by Sam Farmer of the *Los Angeles Times*: "I've talked to several players and not one of them has any issue with anything I've ever said or done in reference to their team. But there's certainly someone who's not happy."

Ron Riesterer

Al Davis selected quarterback Eldridge Dickey in the first round of the 1968 draft. Personnel director Ron Wolf pushed for the selection of quarterback Ken Stabler (above) in the second round of the same draft, and Davis obliged in what turned out to be a stroke of good fortune. Dickey flamed out after playing only 18 games, while Stabler helped the Raiders win their first Super Bowl during a Hall of Fame career.

CHAPTER FIFTEEN

Draft Room Decisions

When the AFL-NFL merger became a formality, Al Davis lost his position as the AFL commissioner and returned to Oakland, this time as the Raiders' managing general partner. Davis, who played a major role in the merger, left New York with a bitter taste in his mouth. He felt that he, and not Pete Rozelle, the NFL commissioner, should have been chosen to head the new venture. For the next four decades, his sole goal was to create and sustain an organization that would dominate the world of professional sports.

One way to do that, he decided, was to navigate the draft like no one had ever done — with counterintuitive decisions that resulted in some spectacular success stories, as well as some abject failures.

The two football leagues maintained separate structures for three years (1967-69) after the merger was announced, which meant there were 16 NFL teams battling for the right to go to the Super Bowl compared to 10 in the AFL. The on-field merger was finalized prior to the 1970 season, with three former NFL teams (Baltimore, Cleveland and Pittsburgh) being compensated to join the AFL legacy teams in the AFC, and regular-season games were played for the first time.

The initial joint venture between the previously warring parties came in March, 1967 and was referred to as the 1967 AFL-NFL draft. By then, Davis was back in Oakland and ready to unleash his player personnel talents on the rest of the league.

With the 17th pick that year, Davis immediately surprised his NFL brethren with the selection of Gene Upshaw, an offensive lineman from the small college power Texas A&I (now known as Texas A&M-Kingsville). The Javelinas were N.A.I.A. (National Association of Intercollegiate Athletics) affiliated and the program was not highly regarded as a producer of NFL talent at the time.

Most of the other teams that year, in a draft that produced four

Hall of Famers in the first round and eight overall, opted to select players from the national collegiate powers. Michigan State contributed four of the first eight players selected, including defensive tackle Bubba Smith and running back Clinton Jones at Nos. 1 and 2.

Upshaw was one of two small-college performers picked in that first round, and Davis received immediate gratification as Upshaw quickly moved into the left guard position and anchored an offensive line that achieved a Super Bowl berth at the end of the season. Upshaw, in a 15-year NFL career, became the prototype pulling guard and achieved numerous honors, including being selected to the NFL's 75th Anniversary All-Time team and to the Pro Football Hall of Fame in 1987.

Upshaw, whom Davis referred to as "The Senator" at times, later had a distinguished career as the executive director of the National Football League Players Association.

Davis had hit a home run in his first draft. In year two, he went down swinging when he picked another small-college prospect in the first round. Quarterback Eldridge Dickey, from Tennessee State University, proved to be a bust, but Davis managed to escape a big blow to his reputation when he listened to Ron Wolf, Davis' personnel guru, and drafted another quarterback in the second round. Ken Stabler, from the University of Alabama, developed into an NFL star who helped deliver Davis his first Super Bowl victory in 1977. Dickey dropped out of the picture quickly but, fortunately for Davis, all the public remembered was his smart choice of Stabler.

Thus was established a home run-or-strikeout pattern, with a few singles sprinkled in along the way, for Davis over the next 43 years. His biggest string of success came in the early 1970s, when in the first round he hit on tight end Ray Chester, safety Jack Tatum, punter Ray Guy, offensive tackle Henry Lawrence and safety Neal Colzie, while missing only on wide receiver Mike Siani.

Davis' selection of Guy was his biggest surprise of that era. Guy not only was the first punter to be taken in the first round but, at the time of his selection, he was recovering from a broken leg suffered while playing safety for Southern Mississippi in his final collegiate game.

The late '70s saw the Raiders with no first-round picks during the four-year period from 1976-1979 as Davis, with his win-now philosophy, opted to trade the selections for proven veterans. He did acquire additional second-rounders during that period, but only one of the six, defensive back Mike Davis, fulfilled expectations. Davis' two second-rounders in 1976, defensive end Charles Philyaw and quarterback Jeb Blount, not only shocked the NFL but led to the resignation of personnel director Ken Herock after the draft.

Davis started the 1980s with his first-round choices intact and still as robust and healthy as ever. With the 15th pick in 1980, Davis thought he had selected his quarterback of the future in Marc Wilson of Brigham Young University. This marked the first draft that Bruce Kebric attended as a member of the Raiders' scouting staff.

"When it appeared as though Wilson was going to be the choice, I finally got the nerve to say something and uttered, 'Al, I don't think he is a first-rounder,'" said Kebric, who had scouted Wilson.

"When you have a chance to get a potentially great quarterback, you have to take him," Davis quickly replied.

"Then why have 14 teams passed on a potentially great quarterback?" Kebric replied.

Kebric also was puzzled by a comment on the questionnaire that Wilson had prepared for the Raiders.

One of the final questions on the questionnaire was, "Are You Interested in Playing Professional Football with the Oakland Raiders?" Wilson had answered "No."

"That's the only time I saw a negative response to this question in my 30-plus years with the organization," Kebric said.

Just prior to drafting Wilson, Davis asked assistant coach Steve Ortmayer to phone Wilson and ask him about his "No" answer on the questionnaire. Wilson, who at that point had to be despondent since he was slated to go much higher, told Ortmayer that the reason for the "No" response was because he thought the Raiders were set for the future at quarterback. Kebric speculated that Wilson, a high character, clean-cut, Mormon Church member, wanted no part of the Raiders' "bad boy" image of that era.

Another interesting scenario at the 1980 draft occurred in the second round. Davis sought to trade up for North Carolina linebacker Buddy Curry. Davis called close friend Bill Walsh, the 49ers' head coach, and offered Walsh linebacker Rod Martin as an incentive to trade positions in that round.

"I had Martin last year in training camp and cut him," Walsh replied.

"Oh, I forgot," Davis said, in an embarrassed tone.

This turned out to be a case of the best trade being the one you don't make. Martin remained on the Raiders roster and blossomed into a star linebacker whose NFL resume included two Super Bowl wins and a like number of Pro Bowl and All-Pro selections.

Before Davis could recover, Curry was taken by Atlanta. Davis then opted for Matt Millen, a Penn State nose tackle who Davis projected as a middle linebacker. Millen lived up to Davis' expectations, quickly made the transition to the new position and was a major factor in two Raiders Super Bowl wins.

As the 1980s evolved, Davis was spending more of his time sitting in court rooms and less time in his draft room.

In 1982, he was battling the NFL over his threat to move to Los Angeles and had little time for draft preparation. The Raiders' first-round choice that year was between two running backs, Walter Abercrombie of Baylor University and Marcus Allen of the University of Southern California.

Davis opted for Allen and hit the jackpot, as Allen excelled and one year later was the most valuable player of the Raiders' Super Bowl victory over the Washington Redskins.

Allen became one of four Hall of Fame choices that Davis had selected in the first round.

The next year Davis picked another USC player in the first round, Don Mosebar, whom he converted from a college tackle to a star NFL center.

Davis' "golden touch," however, failed him for most of the remainder of the decade, with first-round selections such as wide receiver Jessie Hester, defensive end Bob Buczkowski and offensive tackle John Clay.

The Clay pick might have turned out well, as the Raiders later traded Clay and running back Napoleon McCallum to the San Diego Chargers for All-Pro offensive tackle Jim Lachey.

Lachey, however, played just one game for the Raiders before being traded, along with a third-round pick, to Washington for quarterback Jay Schroeder. This move temporarily satisfied Davis' continual lust for a strong-armed quarterback. Lachey went on to play in a Super Bowl for the Redskins, was selected to three Pro Bowls and earned All-Pro honors three times, as well as being named one of the top 70 Redskins all-time players. Schroeder, on the other hand, had a largely forgettable five seasons with the Raiders. He did play in one AFC Championship Game while with the Raiders, throwing five interceptions as the Raiders lost to the Buffalo Bills 51-3.

"You finally beat Al," Kebric said to Redskins general manager Bobby Beathard a few years after the Lachey-for-Schroeder trade.

Davis had prevailed over Beathard and the Redskins in the teams' 1983 Super Bowl clash, as well as trades that netted a second-round draft pick for wide receiver Malcolm Barnwell — a seventh-round draft pick of the Raiders in 1980 — and a third-rounder for receiver Calvin Muhammad, a Raiders 12th-round pick in the 1980 draft.

"Yeah," Beathard replied. "After the first two trades, (owner) Jack Kent Cooke told me, 'No more trades with the Raiders.' Fortunately, the Lachey deal worked out."

Davis' final first-rounder of the 1980s was Notre Dame wide receiver Tim Brown, who rewarded Davis with a Hall of Fame career. Davis also traded for two other first-round picks in that 1988 draft and selected cornerback Terry McDaniel and defensive end Scott Davis.

The Raiders' first-round selections from the early 1990s featured many players encumbered with off-field problems that Davis was willing to overlook due to their physical attributes. Selections such as defensive end Anthony Smith, quarterback Todd Marinovich, safety Patrick Bates and defensive tackles Chester McGlockton and Darrell Russell were tremendously talented players but, in the end, those players became victims of their personal makeup and self-destructive preferences.

Russell was twice an All-NFL selection and played in a like number of Pro Bowls during his five seasons as a Raider. McGlockton, who spent six years as a Raider, was an All-NFL pick on three occasions and played in four Pro Bowls. Sadly, both Russell and McGlockton died at a young age. Russell was only 29 when he was killed in a car accident, while McGlockton, who at the time was coaching at Stanford University, died at the age of 42 from a left ventricular hypertrophy.

In 1998, Jon Gruden's first draft with the Raiders, the team possessed the fourth overall selection. It was anticipated that the two highly-rated quarterbacks, Peyton Manning and Ryan Leaf, would be gone by that time, so the coaches and scouts turned their focus to Heisman Trophy winner Charles Woodson of Michigan and Florida State defensive lineman Andre Wadsworth. Davis was so sure that Leaf was going to the San Diego Chargers with the second pick that he sent Raiders defensive coordinator Willie Shaw to Leaf's Washington State workout.

When asked by Bruce Kebric why he scheduled Shaw to attend the workout of an offensive player, Davis replied, "The Chargers are going to draft him, and we will play him twice a year. I want Willie to get an early look at him."

Three Raiders scouts — Kebric, Mickey Marvin and Ken Herock — were sent by Davis to Tallahassee, Florida, for Wadsworth's workout, which also included massive offensive tackle Tra Thomas (6-foot-8, 349 pounds). Unfortunately, Wadsworth pulled his hamstring prior to completing the 40-yard dash, which brought an abrupt ending to his workout. Though he had excellent 10- and 20-yard times, a player without a confirmed 40 time was unlikely to be drafted by Davis.

The Arizona Cardinals, however, solved Davis' quandary by selecting Wadsworth with the third pick of the draft. Kent McCloughan and Herock, who represented the Raiders at Woodson's workout, returned with glowing reports on the Heisman Trophy winner. At 6-foot-1 and 200 pounds, and with a 4.45 40-yard dash time, it was assumed that Davis would not bypass Woodson should he be available when the Raiders drafted.

But Davis, at least fleetingly, thought about going in a different direction. Tebucky Jones, a safety from Syracuse, Davis' alma mater, was bigger and faster than Woodson, and soon became Davis' target. Even Davis knew that Jones was not a top-10 selection, so he tried to convince the coaches and scouts that the Raiders should go another route — trade down for two first-round selections and then take Florida State offensive tackle Tra Thomas first and Jones later on. Thomas was rated as the draft's top offensive lineman, but Davis surmised that he might fall due to a positive drug test at Florida State.

The potential did exist for Davis to engineer his trade. The Jacksonville Jaguars and New England Patriots each owned the rights to two picks in the first round that year.

"Would you guys be interested in doing this?" Davis asked his coaches and scouts. "I'll trade our pick for the ninth pick and a pick in the middle of the first round. How about Tra Thomas at nine and Tebucky Jones with the second first-round pick?"

The scouting staff told Davis that they liked Manning, Leaf, Woodson and Wadsworth, and that all four were more talented than Thomas and Jones.

Manning, Leaf and Wadsworth had been drafted by the time the Raiders were scheduled to pick. Davis had left the draft room. He had moved to an adjacent room, in which he had stationed a few Raiders employees to place and field telephone calls from other NFL teams during the draft. The room also had a television set which was always tuned to ESPN for the draft.

It marked the first time since 1982, when Davis was in a courtroom battling the NFL over his move to Los Angeles, that Davis wasn't in the draft room when the Raiders made their first-round pick.

Executive assistant Al LoCasale sat at the back of draft room, manning a phone hookup to the Raiders' representative at the draft headquarters in New York.

"We got five minutes left," LoCasale announced to the coaches and scouts. Each team had a maximum of 15 minutes in the first round at that time.

"I'll go ask Al what he wants to do," Herock volunteered.

When Herock returned, Gruden asked: "What did he say?"

"Do whatever you guys want to do," Davis had told Herock.

"Well, do we want Woodson?" Gruden asked.

"Yeah, we want Woodson," was the unanimous verdict from the room.

Gruden instructed LoCasale to tell the Raiders' New York contact to deliver the name Charles Woodson, University of Michigan, to the podium.

"I can't do that," LoCasale said. "Al's not here to make the pick."

"You just heard what Ken Herock said," Gruden said. "Al said to pick who we want to pick. Put the guy's name in."

Davis had the TV on in the adjacent room, so he learned of the Woodson selection soon after it happened. A few minutes later, Davis walked back into the draft room and sat down.

"Well, you got your guy, huh?" Davis said to Gruden.

"Al had the attitude that anyone can draft Charles Woodson, but 'I'm going to show I am smarter than everyone else and I'll take Tebucky Jones and an offensive lineman named Tra Thomas,'" Kingdon said.

One week later at a mini-camp, Woodson was paired against wide receiver James Jett, whose world class speed he was not prepared for. When Jett streaked past Woodson for a long catch, Davis' belief that he had made a mistake in picking Woodson was fortified. Woodson, however, recovered quickly and was named the 1998 NFL Defensive Rookie of the Year. An 18-year career also included nine Pro Bowl berths, his selection as the 2009 NFL Defensive Player of the Year and a spot on the NFL All-Decade Team of the 2000s.

With the Woodson saga resolved, Davis still wanted Jones. Another development caught Gruden's attention, though. Marshall University wide receiver Randy Moss was falling into the latter half of the first round.

"Well, you know Moss is still on the board," Gruden said to Davis.

"Oh, fuck, Moss is still on the board," Davis said. "That's great. We'll make a trade with Tampa and we'll get one of two guys. We'll get Moss or Jones."

The Raiders traded two second-round picks to the Tampa Bay Buccaneers for the 23rd pick in the first round. Fate did not favor Davis that day, as Moss went to the Minnesota Vikings at No. 21 and Jones to the Patriots at No. 22. The Raiders settled for University of Florida offensive lineman Mo Collins at No. 23.

Gruden's posture led to the selection of Woodson, the Raiders' best first-round pick since Allen in 1982. The following year, Gruden promoted another first-rounder who did not turn out so well. Gruden was a strong advocate for University of Georgia offensive tackle Matt Stinchcomb. While the scouts graded the injury-prone Stinchcomb no higher than a third-round prospect, Gruden was so steadfast in his approach that Davis suddenly was calling Stinchcomb another Jim Lachey, the tackle Davis had reluctantly traded to Washington years before in exchange for quarterback Jay Schroeder. Not long after the Raiders selected Stinchcomb at No. 18, offensive line coach Bill Callahan and Kebric were working out in the Raiders weight room. Kebric asked Callahan why he had spoken in favor of Stinchcomb, given that Stinchcomb's body structure was much different than what Callahan had described to the scouts as to what he wanted an offensive lineman to look like.

"I did what Jon told to me to do," Callahan said.

Stinchcomb was with the Raiders for five injury-plagued seasons and never quite panned out at tackle, guard or center. He sat out his rookie season due to a shoulder injury that required surgery, and finished his NFL career with Gruden in Tampa Bay.

Gruden finally lost a draft battle in 2001, when he fought hard for Arizona State tight end Todd Heap, who enjoyed a superb 11-year career with the Baltimore Ravens that yielded two Pro Bowl selections and a Super Bowl ring.

"By this time, Al might have grown tired of Gruden's strong personality, national attention and on-field success," Kebric said.

Heap was the unanimous choice among scouts and coaches for the Raiders, who held the 28th pick. However, with the only vote that really counted, Davis selected Derrick Gibson, a safety from Florida State.

Gibson was a late entry into the Raiders draft discussions since Davis missed most of the draft preparation while testifying in a Los Angeles trial, where he claimed that he had not given up the rights to that city by relocating the Raiders to Oakland.

"One afternoon Al called me from Los Angeles and asked about Derrick Gibson," Kebric related. "I told him that four scouts, including myself, had written reports and the highest grade was the third round."

Davis asked about Gibson's workout.

"I told him that I had been there and actually moved Gibson from the fourth to third round based on the workout and his 4.53-second 40 at 214 pounds," Kebric said

"I think you are wrong," Davis said.

Gruden and everyone else wanted a game-changing tight end. Rickey Dudley and Jeremy Brigham combined for 42 receptions for 457 yards and six touchdowns in 2000 for the Raiders. Heap was viewed as the missing piece to an already-potent offense. Davis wanted Gibson so that he had the kind of safety he thought could match up with Kansas City Chiefs tight end Tony Gonzalez, who had tormented the Raiders since arriving in the NFL in 1997.

Kebric on draft day made a last-ditch attempt at convincing Davis that he should select Heap. He reminded Davis of a promise Davis had made to him a month earlier, when he asked Kebric to sign a player.

Davis wanted to sign Roland Williams, a free agent tight end who had played for the St. Louis Rams.

"He told me that he had heard that Williams was going to sign with Tennessee and asked me to call his agent, Harold Lewis, and work out a deal with the Raiders instead," Kebric said. "At the time, I asked if the signing of Williams would affect the drafting of Heap."

"No," Davis replied.

Kebric quickly negotiated a deal with Lewis, and Davis was excited that Williams, a Syracuse graduate, was a member of the Raiders.

"On draft day, I mentioned this conversation to Al," Kebric said.

"Heap will only confuse things," Davis responded.

"I assumed that this meant that he had decided that Williams and his size-speed project, Mondriel Fulcher, were the team's tight ends, and he didn't want competition from Heap," Kebric said.

Once Davis fixated on a player, it was almost impossible to change his mind. Time and again, the scouting department ran into this obstacle.

In 1999, Davis became enamored with Florida State defensive end Tony Bryant. Davis was convinced that Bryant was worthy of an early-round pick and that other teams were hot after him as well.

"Al, the guy will be there in the third round," Kebric said. "He might be there in the fourth round."

"Oh, no, I see something in Bryant," Davis said.

Davis didn't back down.

"Al, I'll bet you $10,000 that he is there in the third round," Kebric said.

"OK, you've got a bet," Davis said.

Davis kept pestering Kebric as to whether Bryant would make it to the third round.

"Can you guarantee me that Bryant will be there in the third round?" Davis said to Kebric, in a strident tone, when the second round started.

"If I could make that type of guarantee, I would be in Las Vegas," Kebric said.

Without the complete assurance, Davis, in a panicked tone, ordered senior assistant Bruce Allen to engineer a trade so that the Raiders could move up from the middle of the second round to early in the second.

Allen traded Oakland's second-rounder (No. 48 overall), third-rounder (No. 78) and a fourth-rounder (No. 111) to Chicago for the Bears' second-rounder (No. 40) and fourth-rounder (No. 102).

Davis used the 40th selection on Bryant, and then he turned toward Kebric.

"You owe me $10,000," Davis said.

Davis then requested the reports on Bryant.

Davis read the reports, then slammed down the book.

"Oh, fuck, what's going on?" Davis said. "You guys have a 4.84 down here for Bryant. I was told he ran a 4.4."

"I don't know who told you that he ran a 4.4," Kebric said. "We went to his workout, and he ran a 4.84."

"Oh, God damn it!" Davis yelled, and then he stormed out of the room.

Two years before Bryant, another defensive lineman mesmerized Davis and ended up being drafted higher than projected.

In 1997, at a time when there were few sleepers in the draft, the scouts came up with someone who was flying under the radar — Grady Jackson. Jackson, who had played at Hinds Community College and ended up at Knoxville College, did not get a lot of exposure.

The Grady Jackson narrative began in the fall of 1995.

Kebric was attending a Jackson State practice in Mississippi, when he ran into Rick Cleveland, the sports editor of the *Jackson Clarion-Ledger* newspaper.

"What are you doing here?" Cleveland asked.

"Scouting Jackson State," Kebric replied.

"Bruce, you should be at Hinds Community College," Cleveland said. "They have two University of Alabama signees who didn't qualify: Michael Myers, the Mississippi High School Defensive Player of the Year; and Grady Jackson, the Alabama High School Defensive Player of the Year. And, by the way, Hinds is playing tonight in Raymond, which is just down the road."

Kebric attended the first half of the game that night and made a mental note to try to keep tabs on these two dominating players.

After Hinds, Myers played one season at Alabama and later was drafted in the fourth round by the Dallas Cowboys. Jackson, however, continued to struggle with his academics and moved from Hinds, where he was named National Junior College Player of the Year, to Carson-Newman College in Tennessee, where he failed to gain eligibility, and finally to Knoxville College.

Raiders scout Mickey Marvin diligently tracked Jackson's trail through the South and had graded him as a seventh-rounder during Jackson's final season at Knoxville College. Marvin spoke highly of Jackson's potential but was concerned about his problems maintaining a proper football weight.

Yet, a few months later, all it took was one look at Jackson's huge hands for Davis to say, "We're going to draft him."

Since Jackson was not invited to the scouting combine, he was brought to Oakland for a physical examination and to meet the coaches, scouts and staff. Prior to his meeting with Davis, Jackson was spotted by the Raiders owner.

"Who's the big guy in the hall?" Davis asked the scouts. "He has the biggest fucking hands."

"That's Grady Jackson," Kebric said.

"Where are we going to draft him?" Davis asked.

Before Kebric had a chance to respond, George Karras burst into the room and said, "I got Grady's measurements — 6-foot-2, 320 pounds ... and you're not going to believe his hand size, 11 and one-half inches!'"

"Why do I need you guys?" Davis said to the scouts. "Where are we going to draft him?"

"We were thinking free agent, Al," Kebric replied. "We brought him in for a physical and a visit to sort of recruit him."

"Free agent? No way," Davis said. "We're going to draft him."

From that point, the challenge was keeping Davis from drafting Jackson too high. Everyone was in agreement when Davis took Jackson in the sixth round.

A few days after the draft, Kebric was visiting with Baltimore Ravens scout Terry McDonough.

"How did you guys know about Grady Jackson?" McDonough asked, in a disturbed manner. "He was my sleeper. I thought we would have no problem signing him as a free agent."

Kebric breathed a sigh of relief when he heard what McDonough had to say.

"Al never would have let us forget if we had allowed Grady 'Big Hands' Jackson to slip away," Kebric said.

Jackson developed into the type of player that Davis imagined, a big run-stuffer who could penetrate and pressure the quarterback. During his 13 years in the NFL, five with the Raiders, Jackson recorded 35.5 sacks and led the league in tackles for loss during the 2006 season.

While preparing for the 1995 draft, Davis had been enamored with Florida State linebacker Derrick Brooks and Florida A&M offensive tackle Jamie Brown. He missed out on Brooks when he wasn't able to secure an extra first-round pick. Davis had used his own first-round pick on running back Napoleon Kaufman. Losing Brooks to the Buccaneers sent Davis into a "total funk," Kebric said.

Eventually, Davis emerged from seclusion and asked, "What about Jamie Brown?"

"The fourth round, fifth round, yeah, but we can't take him in the second round." Kebric and other scouts replied about Brown, a 6-foot-8, 340-pounder.

"Who do you guys want to take?" Davis asked.

"Barret Robbins," Kebric replied. Everyone else in the room was in favor of Robbins, especially offensive line coach Joe Bugel.

Davis signed off on the selection of Robbins, a center out of Texas Christian. He then retreated to a private room once again, where he solicited feedback from friends around the league.

"He was really upset," Kebric said. "He went back in his room and we didn't see him for a while. All of a sudden he came out and he was happy."

"Guess what, guys?" Davis asked in an excited tone. "I just got a call from Mike Lombardi (then the Cleveland Browns player personnel director), and he said that they have Barret Robbins as their best center. Mike really thinks he's going to be a top player."

"So many times, Al would select a player and then leave the room in a total funk, like he had buyer's remorse," Kebric recalled. "Then an NFL coach or colleague might call and say that Al had made a good pick. He would return to us in a euphoric state of mind. He also was always anxious to know what ESPN and Mel Kiper, Jr. had to say about his picks."

In a bizarre twist to that day's draft proceedings, both Robbins and Brooks played pivotal roles in Super Bowl XXXVII. Brooks returned an interception for a touchdown that sealed the Tampa Bay win, while Robbins, a Pro Bowl selection who spearheaded the Raiders blocking attack, was suspended for the game when he mysteriously departed the team hotel on Friday night and did not return until nearly 24 hours later.

In an effort to mollify Davis, the scouts suggested taking Jamie Brown in the third round.

"Where are you guys?" Davis asked as the Raiders neared their third-round selection.

"If you like Jamie Brown that much, let's go ahead and take him," Kebric said.

"Why would I want to take him here?" Davis asked.

The scouts and coaches looked around the room at each other in disbelief.

"Al, you wanted to take him in the second round," Kebric said.

"You don't understand. You take a guy like this in the second round, not the third round," Davis said.

This logic was a source of humor for years to come, Kingdon said. Ultimately, Davis selected Central Oklahoma running back Joe Aska in the third round. Brown went to the Denver Broncos in the fourth round. Naturally, Aska was the fastest player on the Raiders' draft board at the time.

Aska, 5-10 and 230, had an excellent combination of size and speed — he ran a 4.4 40 — though his vision was limited to one eye. The highlight of his three-year NFL career came in 1996, when he rushed for 136 yards and a touchdown in a game against the New York Jets. Later, the Jets offered Davis a second-round pick for Aska.

"Al turned it down," Kingdon said. "If there was the slightest chance one of his picks could develop, he would ride that horse to the end."

As he had in 1973 with the selection of punter Ray Guy, Davis once again bucked convention by using a first-round pick on a kicker in 2000. Sebastian Janikowski of Florida State became only the third kicker in NFL history to be selected that early. Davis also intended to double down by taking Texas A&M punter Shane Lechler in the same draft, though later on in the proceedings.

No one was quite sure how long Lechler would last. He was regarded as one of the best-ever punter prospects.

"We intended to draft Shane Lechler in the fourth round," Kingdon said.

However, Davis also wanted Arizona State defensive tackle Junior Ioane, who showed promise as an underclassman but suffered a serious knee injury his senior season. Kebric graded Ioane as a third-rounder, but he was concerned about Ioane's recovery from the knee injury.

"He was talented, but he didn't rehab the knee really well," Kebric said of Ioane.

When Kebric raised the possibility of taking Lechler in the fourth round, Davis balked.

"I couldn't sleep all night because Junior was still up on the board," Davis said.

Fortunately for Davis, Ioane was still available when the Raiders picked in the fourth round.

Lechler, on the other hand, was "the best punter I had seen since Ray Guy," Kebric said, referring to Davis' first round pick in the 1973 draft who ended up in the Pro Football Hall of Fame.

As the Raiders turn to pick in the fifth round neared, Davis put some names to consider up on the draft board.

"Lechler's name was prominent by its absence," Kingdon said.

Kingdon got up, walked behind Davis and talked so only Davis could hear.

"Did you forget to put Lechler's name on the board?" Kingdon asked, just in case Davis had overlooked Lechler.

"No, I didn't forget to put his name up there," Davis said in an explosive tone.

Davis quickly caught himself once he realized that he was the only one who heard Kingdon's question. He regained his composure and in a muffled tone said, "No, I didn't forget his name. I don't want it up on the board."

Davis had developed a superstition about posting names of players the Raiders were interested in taking that particular round. Many times in previous drafts, the players Davis had put up on the board were snatched by another team just ahead of the Raiders choice.

Hence, Davis wasn't about to put Lechler's name on the draft board.

"Fortunately, Lechler was there when we drafted in the fifth round," Kingdon said, "since I'm sure I would have been blamed had he been taken because I had dared to mention his name."

Davis had many idiosyncrasies as it pertained to the draft. Over time, Kingdon came to know how Davis operated. Hence, whenever the Raiders hired a new coach, he pulled aside that coach and briefed him on the best way to proceed.

"I would tell them that if they agreed with Al in whatever he was suggesting, they should by all means agree with him," Kingdon said. "However, if they didn't agree with Al, they should make it clear that they did not go along with his opinion."

Kingdon explained to coaches that, if they didn't agree with Davis but went along with his opinion on a subject, and that move panned out, Davis would take all the credit. If the move didn't work out, they would get blamed by Davis.

"As much emphasis as he put on winning, he placed more emphasis on proving that he knew more than the rest of the world knew," Kebric said. "The thing that he did, he always had an out."

In 2009, Davis became enamored with Oregon State defensive end Slade Norris, who was projected as a linebacker in the NFL. He asked what others thought about Norris.

"Bruce and I both scouted him, and we gave him a sixth-round grade," Kingdon said.

Kingdon added that Norris played defensive end in college, so Norris was even more of a projection at linebacker.

Davis asked about taking Norris in the fourth round.

Kingdon countered.

"That's too high," Kingdon said. "If you really want to push him up, you might take him in the fifth round. But this is too early to take him."

"I want to take him here," Davis said.

First, he needed someone to back him.

"He wanted one person to support him," Kebric said. "He searched the room for one person to support him."

"Is this a good spot to take Norris?" Davis asked linebackers coach Mike Haluchak.

"Yes, I really like him here," Haluchak said.

The Raiders selected Norris in the fourth round. He played in four games his rookie season and then he was released before the 2010 season. Whenever Norris' name came up after his Raiders career ended, Davis' response was the same: "That's the guy that Mike Haluchak talked me into taking."

In the 2004 draft, the Raiders had the rights to the No. 2 pick. The San Diego Chargers selected Ole Miss quarterback Eli Manning with the first pick and promptly traded him to the New York Giants.

The Raiders were in the midst of a roster overhaul, one year removed from a Super Bowl appearance. Their needs were many.

Some scouts and coaches wanted wide receiver Larry Fitzgerald, some favored safety Sean Taylor, and others had no problem with the likes of tight end Kellen Winslow II and receiver Roy Williams.

Ultimately, the Raiders drafted Iowa offensive tackle Robert Gallery. He was the least sexy of the first 11 picks or so, given the position he played. However, the consensus among most draft analysts was that Gallery was the safest pick in the draft. Some said Gallery had the potential to be the best left offensive tackle since Tony Boselli, who starred for the Jacksonville Jaguars from 1995-2001 and was selected to five Pro Bowls and three All-Pro teams.

Even so, it was suggested to Davis that he consider trading down — the Raiders had offers from the Cleveland Browns for the fifth pick and the Detroit Lions at No. 7.

Sure, the Raiders likely would miss out on Gallery if they traded down, but they still could get a top-flight prospect, in addition to another draft pick or two for their effort.

Kent McCloughan, who had scouted Gallery, pointed out that, for all of his impressive talents, Gallery's 32 1/4-inch arm length and 9 ¼-inch-hand size posed a real concern for a player at the left tackle position.

Davis was interested in making the trade so that he could take Roy Williams, a wide receiver out of the University of Texas. However, Davis was concerned about what he would do if Williams was gone before the Raiders picked.

With Kebric out of the room, Davis asked Kingdon who he would draft if Williams wasn't available at No. 7.

"Steven Jackson," Kingdon said, without hesitation, of the highly rated Oregon State running back.

Soon thereafter, Kebric returned to the room. Davis posed the same question.

"Steven Jackson," Kebric said, not missing a beat. "Steven Jackson would be a good alternative, since we have him rated ahead of Roy Williams."

Afterward, Davis told Kebric and Kingdon that he was glad he didn't listen to them and go with Jackson, who went to the St. Louis Rams at No. 24.

"I couldn't take Jackson that high," Davis said.

"Why?" Kebric asked.

"Because Kiper didn't even have him in his top 10," Davis said, when explaining his rationale.

Jackson amassed 15,121 yards and 78 touchdowns rushing and receiving combined during his 12-year career, including an eight-season stretch in which he rushed for at least 1,000 yards.

Gallery fell well short of the kind of career that Boselli cobbled together. In fact, as McCloughan had stated in discussing his shortcomings, Gallery did not pan out as a left offensive tackle. He spent most of his eight-year career at left guard and battling injuries.

It's likely Davis was one of the few NFL player personnel experts who concerned themselves with what a draft analyst like Kiper, Jr. thought about prospects. After all, NFL scouts spend hundreds of hours breaking down prospects and provide detailed analyses for the decision makers to draw upon when it comes time to selecting players in the draft. But Davis wasn't like anyone else in the league.

For instance, Davis tended to place a lot of emphasis on college all-star games when he formed his opinions. Oftentimes, he became enamored with a player based upon one play. In one particular instance, that paid huge dividends.

In 1981, Davis selected a talented, but questionable, prospect out of Villanova University named Howie Long.

But Davis saw something from Long in an all-star game in 1980 that caught his eye. In particular, Davis liked that Long had blocked a punt in the Blue-Gray All-Star Game.

Long developed into a Hall of Famer, but there were some early doubts about his ability. By the time he entered the NFL, he was accustomed to being doubted. While working at Sid Gillman's coaching camp in 1983, Long told Kebric that he was among a group of local college players invited to a workout with the Philadelphia Eagles. Coach Dick Vermeil called the players into his office after the workout and dished out some feedback.

"Howie, you're a great guy, you're well respected, but we don't think you can play for the Eagles," Vermeil told Long, according to Kebric. "So, I just want you to know that we're not going to draft you."

Davis used a second-round draft pick on Long, who started no games his rookie season and didn't record any sacks. He showed some promise in his second season but not enough to quiet the doubters, even on his own team.

The Raiders discussed moving Long to the offensive line, at the suggestion of Joe Madro. When Madro had coached offensive linemen, he preferred converted defensive linemen because he felt that they were superior athletes and tougher than the usual offensive lineman type. Madro had been successful with a number of these transitions during a lengthy and distinguished career as an offensive line coach. Madro became even more excited about the change when he learned that Long also had boxed at Villanova.

Defensive line coach Earl Leggett saw enough potential in Long to fend off those who questioned Long's ability to flourish in the NFL on the defensive side of the ball. "Let me have one more year with him," Leggett said. In year three, Long developed into an elite player who ultimately was selected to eight Pro Bowls.

Long was so appreciative of what Leggett had done for him that he asked Leggett to be his presenter at his 2000 Pro Football Hall of Fame induction.

Five years after Davis found a gem in Long, he thought he had uncovered another one in University of Pittsburgh defensive end Bob Buczkowski. Davis' evaluation once again was based upon what he witnessed at an All-Star game, this time the East-West Shrine Game.

Buczkowski was playing right defensive end that game when he executed what Davis termed a hump move to gain an advantage on an offensive lineman. In this instance, Buczkowski used his left hand as the primary source of lifting the offensive tackle off his feet.

"That was all that Al had to see," Kingdon said. "He prided himself on being able to determine whether someone was a player just by looking at him."

Davis often told people that he saw running back Mark van Eeghen work out in a gym at Foothill College in Los Altos Hills one day during the week of the East-West Shrine Game and declared that van Eeghen was destined to be a productive NFL player.

Indeed, van Eeghen enjoyed great success during a 10-year pro career in which he recorded three straight seasons with more than 1,000 yards rushing for the Raiders. Davis selected van Eeghen in the third round of the 1974 NFL draft.

Buczkowski, 6-foot-5 and 265 pounds, joined the Raiders as a first-round pick in the '86 draft. He was an average player at the University of Pittsburgh, but was blessed with an impressive combination of size and speed. However, no one projected Buczkowski as a first-round draft pick.

Davis wanted another running back in this draft, even though the Raiders already had Marcus Allen, who had rushed for 1,759 yards and 11 touchdowns and caught 67 passes for 555 yards and three touchdowns the previous season. Neal Anderson of the University of Florida was the one the scouts recommended.

First, though, Davis wanted Buczkowski. Special teams coach Steve Ortmayer came into the draft room and said that the Raiders could get a seventh-round pick if they moved back a few spots.

"Fuck it," Davis said. "Let's just take Buczkowski."

The Raiders nabbed Buczkowski with the 24th pick. The Chicago Bears pounced on Anderson three picks later.

"Nothing made Al happier than selecting a player that no one else wanted and seeing the player develop into a top player," Kingdon said. "In his mind, anyone could select the top player in the draft but to show you he was smarter than everyone else was a true motivation in his persona."

Anderson totaled 8,929 yards and 71 touchdowns rushing and receiving combined during an eight-year career.

Buczkowski first hurt his back in a mini-camp his rookie season when he attempted a spin move on a pass rush. He awoke the next day barely able to move. He had three surgeries before he ever played a down in a regular-season game for the Raiders. He was diagnosed with hepatitis before his second season and missed the first three games.

"Al still tried to sell Buczkowski," Kingdon said.

One day, Davis asked Kingdon if he had seen Buczkowski of late. Kingdon said that he had and that he wasn't impressed.

"He looks like an Adonis," Davis said.

"Yeah, Adrian Adonis," Kingdon said, in reference to an overweight, out-of-shape professional wrestler.

"Yeah, he does look good," Davis responded.

"I knew that Al had never heard of Adrian Adonis and that was my little inside joke," Kingdon said.

Buczkowski played in only two games before he was released by the Raiders in 1988 during the exhibition season.

Davis bypassed Anderson in favor of Buczkowski without pause because he had another running back in mind.

Occidental College's Vance Mueller is the running back Davis wanted all along, not Anderson. Anyone could spot Anderson's talent. He averaged 5.1 yards rushing for a major college. It required a keen eye to find a productive player from an obscure college such as Occidental, a tiny liberal arts college in Los Angeles.

Mueller, in particular, caught Davis' attention because of his speed. He had posted a 4.6-second 40-yard dash in the spring before his senior season. Kingdon gave Mueller a late-round grade, at a time when the NFL draft was 12 rounds. He went to Occidental to work out Mueller, but it rained that day. Mueller, who also ran track at Occidental, didn't want to run on a wet surface and risk pulling a muscle. As a courtesy, Kingdon invited Mueller to the Raiders' facility in El Segundo so that he could work out at his convenience.

Mueller accepted the invite and ran a 4.32-second 40 on an Astro-Turf field. The Raiders adjusted times run on the more favorable AstroTurf by .08, which dropped Mueller to a 4.40.

"That still was a great time for Mueller," Kingdon said.

Some of Kingdon's co-workers wanted to know why Kingdon graded Mueller so low. Raiders running backs coaches Ray Willsey and Terry Robiskie traveled to Occidental the next day so that they could watch film of Mueller. After having done so, they informed Kingdon that they agreed with his assessment.

During the draft meetings, Davis came across Mueller's 40 time and asked for more information.

The Raiders requested film on Mueller from Occidental's football staff. There was only one copy of the college's games, and it was cut up into highlight tapes for the seniors. It was so impressive that Davis, at one point, considered taking Mueller in the second round.

Ultimately, the Raiders drafted Mueller in the fourth round.

"Al promised that Mueller would be good for 10 touchdowns a year," Kingdon said.

Soon after drafting Mueller, Davis sought validation. Who better to consult than long-time friend Bill Walsh, who was coaching the 49ers and presiding over his team's draft. So Davis exited the Raiders draft room and phoned Walsh.

According to Kingdon, here's how the one-sided conversation unfolded.

"Bill, how are you doing?" Davis said. "What did you think of our pick in the fourth round?"

Pause.

"Mueller," Davis said.

Pause.

"Vance Mueller," Davis said.

Pause.

"He's a running back," Davis offered.

Pause.

"From Occidental," Davis added.

Pause.

"Bill, I tell you, he's going to be a player," Davis said.

Mueller started only five of the 73 games he played in for the Raiders during his five seasons. He rushed for 469 yards and scored three touchdowns, in addition to catching 40 passes for 452 yards and two touchdowns.

"Mueller was never what Al thought he would be," Kingdon said.

"Once Al got a good 40 time on a player, that was what Al believed he could run, regardless of whether he had played 10 years in the league."

During a mini-camp prior to the 1991 season, the scouts were timing the rookies in the 40. Mueller jumped in line, even though as a veteran he wasn't required to run. Mueller posted a 4.83 time. All of the player times eventually made their way to Davis.

"Who told Mueller to run?" Davis asked Kingdon by phone.

"No one," Kingdon said. "Vance just jumped in on his own and, before I could stop him, he ran the 40."

Davis needed some time to accept that Mueller no longer was a running back with 4.40 speed and reluctantly cut him in training camp, which ended Mueller's NFL career.

Ron Riesterer

Willie Brown (left) carved out a Hall of Fame career as a cornerback for the Raiders. He joined the team's coaching staff upon his retirement and remained loyal to owner Al Davis. Hence, when Brown (pictured with head coach Tom Flores and former Raiders safety Jack Tatum, in 1979) called Mike Mitchell "another Jack Tatum" before the 2009 draft, it piqued Davis' interest in the little-known player from Ohio University.

CHAPTER SIXTEEN

More Draft Intrigue

Al Davis' idiosyncratic approach to the NFL draft left him open to skepticism whenever he made unconventional draft selections, and to withering criticism whenever one of those picks struggled or underperformed.

The criticism reached a fever pitch in 2009 when Davis drafted wide receiver Darrius Heyward-Bey in the first round and safety Mike Mitchell in the second.

That draft class was regarded as the year of the wide receiver, with Texas Tech's Michael Crabtree considered a can't-miss prospect and the likes of Percy Harvin and Jeremy Maclin not far behind. Heyward-Bey, a University of Maryland product, wasn't considered a first-round prospect until he ran the fastest 40-yard dash at the NFL scouting combine.

Though Crabtree was the consensus No. 1 receiver prospect, he was not an option for Davis because he hadn't run a 40-yard dash prior to the draft. Crabtree had suffered a stress fracture in his left foot and opted for surgery. Davis ruled out players who hadn't posted a reliable 40 time.

Still, the Raiders needed a receiver in the worst way. Johnnie Lee Higgins had led the team's wide receivers in receptions (22), receiving yards (366) and touchdowns (4) the previous season, all inconceivably paltry figures for a 16-game season.

The scouts had Crabtree, Harvin and Maclin rated ahead of Heyward-Bey. In the end, Davis did what he had done so many times in his career: he ignored the scouts and went with the fastest option, Heyward-Bey.

A few hours later, Davis gave analysts, media and fans even more fodder for mockery when he selected Mitchell, a little-known safety from Ohio University.

It was customary for Davis to meet with his coaches and scouts for endless hours in advance of the draft, going over both the draft-eligible offensive and defensive players. Davis wanted everyone in the same room with him for the viewing of tapes and to thoroughly discuss all the prospects.

During one of these meetings, defensive backs coaches Lionel Washington and Willie Brown surprised the scouts by bringing up Mike Mitchell and speaking of him in the most glowing terms. Brown, a Hall of Famer, in addition to being a long-time defensive backs coach, said he felt that Mitchell should be an early selection by the Raiders. The room was further taken aback when Brown called Mitchell "another Jack Tatum." Washington quickly compared Mitchell to former Raiders cornerback Charles Woodson. Defensive coordinator John Marshall chimed in and compared Mitchell to Hall of Fame safety Ronnie Lott, who Marshall had coached at San Francisco.

Angelo Coia was the area scout and had given Mitchell a fifth-round grade.

Mitchell had not been invited to the National Scouting Combine in Indianapolis and had not been selected to participate in any of the post-season all-star games. Moreover, the Raiders had not traveled to Athens, Ohio, for Mitchell's pre-draft workout.

Mitchell's stock soared in the eyes of the coaches, in large part, as a result of his strong performance against Ohio State, a game in which he made five tackles and broke up one pass.

Washington and Brown got the ball rolling. Support for Mitchell picked up steam in a hurry, with head coach Tom Cable jumping on the Mitchell bandwagon.

Cable told Davis that he wanted either Mitchell or University of Oregon safety Patrick Chung in one of the early rounds, adding a hard-hitting, play-making safety to the suspect Raiders defense.

One by one, the defensive coaches took turns extolling the virtues of Mitchell. He was fast, strong, hard-hitting and cut an imposing figure. In other words, he was everything Davis liked in a player.

For good measure, assistant coach Randy Hanson assembled several videos of Mitchell. Typically, such videos are supposed to portray a prospect in a representative manner, displaying both positive and negative plays.

"It was like a tidal wave," Kingdon added. "Mitchell could not be stopped. We must have watched four 'profile' tapes on Mitchell, and each one was better than the other."

Kingdon decided to put together a videotape that he felt would be more representative of Mitchell's play. This way, he believed, Davis would at least get a better feel for Mitchell's all-around game. It was easy to fall in love with Mitchell because of his penchant for delivering huge hits on receivers and ball carriers.

"The video I made showed Mitchell making some big hits, but it also showed some hip tightness that would pose a problem for him in coverage and in breaking down to make a tackle in the open field," Kingdon said.

Kingdon contacted Davis and informed him that he had put together a "more accurate" video of Mitchell and that it would be prudent for Davis to watch. Davis told Kingdon that he already had seen all the videos on Mitchell. Kingdon clarified for Davis that he had just made his own video that morning.

"Put it down, I'll watch it later," Davis said.

"He never did," Kingdon said.

The Raiders used one of their 30 allocated pre-draft visits on Mitchell, who was flown to the Raiders facility to meet with Davis and Raiders staff members.

As the draft neared, Davis became a little nervous and phoned Kingdon, in a panic:

"Mike Mitchell is not in the books. There are not reports on him."

"That couldn't be," Kingdon said. "I just reviewed the written reports on Mitchell earlier that day. I assured Davis that Mitchell's reports, indeed, were in the books."

"Not our books! Kiper's book," Davis said.

In an attempt to glean more information on Mitchell, Davis had turned to draft analyst Mel Kiper, Jr.'s Blue Book.

Kingdon saw that Kiper, Jr. had Mitchell as his 73rd-ranked safety and told Davis that Mitchell was ranked low by Kiper, Jr. because Mitchell wasn't as good as the Raiders coaches made him out to be.

"Now you bring it up," Davis said. "Did a cat have your tongue?"

Davis was aware that, if the Raiders picked Mitchell in the second round, Davis and the Raiders would get destroyed in the press.

Knowing this, Davis felt comfortable in trading his high second-round pick to the New England Patriots for the third of the Patriots' four second-round picks — seven spots lower than the Raiders' original selection — and a fourth- and sixth-rounder in the same draft. Coincidentally, the Patriots selected Chung with the first of their second-round picks.

The Pittsburgh Steelers then called the Raiders and offered their second-round and third-round pick in exchange for the second-round pick the Raiders had acquired from the Patriots.

Given that Chung had been drafted, Cable told Davis that the Raiders "can't take the risk of losing Mitchell." Davis picked Mitchell in the middle of the second round.

After Mitchell had been drafted, former Raiders coach Jon Gruden, by then an ESPN analyst, came to Davis' defense and said Davis didn't care what people said about his draft picks. Gruden's defense was drowned out by a sea of criticism from coast to coast.

Kingdon pulled up on his laptop a YouTube video of Mitchell's college highlights and showed it to Davis.

"He got all excited again," Kingdon said. "Whenever he talked to someone about the draft, he made it a point to tell them to look at Mitchell on YouTube."

As it turned out, Mitchell pulled a hamstring in a mini-camp soon after he was drafted and played sparingly his rookie season. He still had done little to validate the Raiders' faith in him by the time his second season rolled around.

Mitchell had competition his second year from Stevie Brown, a player the Raiders had taken in the seventh round of the 2010 draft. Brown, a linebacker at the University of Michigan whom the scouts had projected as an NFL safety, ended up outplaying Mitchell and the other safety on the roster, Hiram Eugene, from the first day of camp.

Davis realized how well Brown had performed and that he deserved a spot on the 53-man roster. However, he already had committed to Eugene and Mitchell.

Davis presided over the roster cuts. He had the final say. In his mind, Brown was the 54th player on the roster. He gave a copy of the final roster to Kingdon. Brown's name wasn't on the list.

"I suggested cutting Mitchell," Kingdon said. "I told Al that, not only was Stevie Brown a better player, he would certainly cost a lot less than Mitchell."

"Now you're worried about our finances?" Davis said.

"In his own way, Al agreed with what I was saying but declined to cut Mitchell," Kingdon said.

"Do you know how embarrassing that would be?" Davis said.

"Yeah, but no more embarrassing than when you drafted him," Kingdon replied.

"Now listen, you," Davis responded. He then stopped himself and said he would watch more video on Mitchell before he made a final decision.

The night before the final cut, John Otten, who worked in information technology for the Raiders, shared with friend Andy Slater that Davis intended to cut Brown, even though the coaches and scouts wanted to keep him on the roster instead of Mitchell. Slater wrote about the conversation and put it out on the internet.

It wasn't long before Davis learned of Slater's post.

"He exploded," Kingdon said of Davis.

"Who is this Andy Slater?" Davis asked. "How does he know what's going on?"

Davis eventually discovered that Slater had worked in the video department, and he blamed Otten for the leak. He asked Kingdon if he should fire Otten.

"That would be a major mistake," Kingdon replied.

Davis heeded Kingdon's advice. However, he fined Otten a substantial amount of money for his disclosure of confidential information.

With deadline day having arrived, Davis still couldn't bring himself to make a decision. Typically, the cuts are made before practice. Brown and Mitchell were on the practice field, along with 52 other players. Davis cut Brown after practice.

Brown cleared waivers, and the Raiders re-signed him. But only after his agent, Harold Lewis, had intervened and reminded Brown that it was obvious the Raiders liked him as a player and that he would eventually be added to the 53-man roster.

Sure enough, Brown ended up on the 53-man roster soon thereafter. He played in 15 games, with one start, and made an immediate impact on special teams.

During their stay with the Raiders, neither Mitchell nor Brown made much of an impact. Both, however, went on to start for other NFL teams. Mitchell was let go after the 2012 season and joined Carolina as a starting safety for one season before moving on to Pittsburgh in 2014, where he became an integral starter in the Steelers secondary. Brown was released by Oakland prior to the 2011 season, signed with Indianapolis for one year and then moved into a starting safety position with the New York Giants in 2012. During the course of that season, Brown twice was named NFL Defensive Player of the Week as he intercepted eight passes and set a franchise season record with 307 interception return yards. A serious knee injury ended his career the following year.

Davis spent considerable time each day talking to people. He valued feedback, even if he seldom factored in what others thought. He simply wanted to hear what they had to say before he made a decision. His decision. It became commonplace for Davis to interview a long list of candidates for a coaching vacancy. He particularly enjoyed talking with people who worked for other teams, especially division rivals Kansas City, Denver and San Diego. This afforded Davis an opportunity to gain some insight into what rival coaches felt about things such as a defensive scheme, a player, whatever. More times than not, Davis asked questions and listened. He volunteered little in return.

Ultimately, Davis did what he thought best, even if it bucked convention or went against the advice of those who worked for him. Bill Parcells counted as one of the few who had the ability to sway Davis' thinking.

One such instance occurred in 2010, when the Raiders were contemplating which player to select with the eighth pick of the NFL draft.

During a pre-draft meeting, the name of Alabama's Rolando Mc-Clain was mentioned during a discussion about linebackers.

"Bill Parcells says McClain is the next Ray Lewis," Davis interjected.

Parcells was with the Miami Dolphins at the time, as their executive vice president of football operations. Before that, he had coached 19 seasons for the New York Giants, New England Patriots, New York Jets and Dallas Cowboys. His teams won two Super Bowl titles.

"I scouted Ray Lewis, too, and the only thing McClain has over Ray Lewis is size," Kebric said. "McClain is a big guy, but he's not a banger."

Lewis, a 13-time Pro Bowler, was 6-foot-1 and 245 pounds during his standout career as a middle linebacker with the Baltimore Ravens from 1996-2012. McClain was 6-3 and 254.

"That's not what the coaches at Alabama say," Davis said.

"Well, I don't know who you're talking to at Alabama, but I've worked with some of the coaches there and have some excellent contacts,"

Kebric said. "They like Rolando, but think Dont'a Hightower is the better player."

Former NFL linebacker William Thomas was scouting for the Raiders in 2010, when the debate over McClain was raging. He had played for Davis and the Raiders in 2000-01. Thomas spoke up about McClain:

"Al, the secondary coach at Alabama, who I played with at Texas A&M, told me the same thing that Bruce said."

Coincidentally, the Raiders had shown interest in Lewis in 1996.

"We all liked Ray Lewis," Kebric related, "so I suggested to Jon Kingdon that he ask Mike White if we could send linebackers coach Fred Whittingham to Ray's workout. I guess I should have asked Al myself, since Jon took the burden when Al found out that Fred was in Miami."

As it turned out, Davis called for a meeting with the coaches on the day Whittingham was in Miami for Lewis' workout.

"Al asked where Fred was and he was told he was at the University of Miami for Ray Lewis' workout," Kingdon recalled. "Al got really mad and asked Mike White if he knew that Fred was sent out on this assignment."

White, of course, knew where his defensive coordinator was that day, but he pleaded ignorance.

Davis called Kingdon into his office and asked him why Whittingham had been sent to Lewis' workout. Kingdon explained the reasoning.

"Al got really mad and, for the first time, he mentioned money to me, how expensive it was to send Fred across country," Kingdon said.

Kingdon told Davis that the scouts really liked Lewis and felt that the Raiders should send a coach to Lewis' workout in Miami.

"He said we already had Greg Biekert and that it was a waste of money," Kingdon said.

As Kingdon was leaving Davis' office, Davis said, "Mike White said he did not know that Fred was out on a scouting trip."

"He said that?" Kingdon asked, with incredulity.

"Yeah," Davis confirmed.

"Well, he's a fucking liar," Kingdon said, with a sharp tone.

Davis said, "OK," and resumed what he had been doing.

Upon Whittingham's return, he came into Kingdon's office.

"I heard what Mike White did," Whittingham said in his deep, gravelly voice. "You give me the word, and I'll kick his ass."

"I knew that Fred did not make empty threats," Kingdon said. "So I said, 'Let's give him another chance and if he pulls something like this again, we'll both kick his ass.'"

While in the midst of draft preparations, the Raiders received word that McClain didn't want to play for the team. The information was immediately passed along to Davis.

Davis dispatched scout Zack Crockett to Tuscaloosa, Alabama, to meet with McClain and his agent, Pat Dye, Jr. Crockett returned and gave Davis the assurance that neither McClain nor Dye, Jr. had made such a statement.

When the discussion returned to McClain, Kebric reiterated that McClain was not the player as described by Parcells. "He's a space-and-chase guy," Kebric said. "He has real problems taking on and getting off blocks."

"Well, he weighs 260 pounds," Davis said.

"I don't care what he weighs," Kebric said. "McClain can play with leverage, and he moves well in space, but he is not very physical."

None of that mattered. Parcells raved about McClain, and that carried far more weight with Davis than the advice of his scouts. Parcells had pushed the right button.

"Al always liked comparisons," Kingdon said. "He was big on comparisons. He wanted to be able to visualize the player."

"Who was he like? What was he like?" Davis would ask. Or, he might say, "Well, you coached this guy. How does he compare to that guy?"

The scouts realized that Davis was dead set on taking a linebacker in 2010. They tried to persuade Davis to trade down to get extra picks, and then draft Sean Lee, a promising prospect out of Penn State whom the scouts felt was better than McClain. Davis thought Lee was an excellent player, too, but was concerned that he was coming off a knee injury. Davis wanted to draft someone he felt could contribute immediately.

Davis selected McClain, and he was so convinced that McClain was going to have the kind of impact that Lewis had for the Ravens, that he traded incumbent middle linebacker Kirk Morrison the next day.

Davis finally got the last word on Morrison, a player he never wanted to draft in the first place. Morrison started 79 of 80 possible games during his five seasons with the Raiders, but he wasn't what Davis had in mind at that position. Nothing Morrison did was going to change that, even though Davis conceded that Morrison turned into a solid player. To his credit, Davis called Morrison soon after he had been traded to the Buffalo Bills so he could deliver the news and thank Morrison for how well he had played and wished him the best of luck in the future.

Cable anointed McClain the starter from the outset. McClain started 15 games his rookie season, but he looked nothing like the dominant force he had been for the University of Alabama.

"McClain pretty much lived down to expectations," Kingdon said. "His inability to take on and get off blocks became readily evident. It was suggested that, rather than force him to do something that was not his forte, it would make sense to move him outside and take advantage of his athletic ability. He did not have a terrible rookie season, but it was nowhere near where Al had hoped he would be."

Early that season, Davis called Kingdon to discuss the previous week's game. At some point, the discussion turned to McClain's inability to take on and get off blocks.

"I was hoping you guys were wrong about Rolando," Davis sighed, with resignation.

"That was as close to a mea culpa as you could get from Al," Kingdon said.

McClain played in 41 games during his three seasons with the Raiders. His time with the team was marked by an arrest in Decatur, Alabama, for assault, reckless endangerment, menacing and wrongful discharge of a firearm. He had been allowed to return home for his grandfather's funeral by coach Hue Jackson. The arrest came after McClain's role in a fight that quickly escalated.

"The victim told officers that following the fight, he crawled to his car," the police statement said. "He said that when he reached his car, Rolando McClain produced a pistol and aimed it at him. He said that while he was still on the ground, McClain walked over to him and put the gun to his head."

The victim also told police that, "He begged McClain not to shoot him and that McClain took the gun away from his head, held it next to his ear and fired it."

McClain was suspended for two games by coach Dennis Allen in

2012 for conduct detrimental to the team. The Raiders released McClain in April 2013. He later signed with the Baltimore Ravens, and then retired at the age of 23, shortly after he had been arrested for the third time in a little more than 16 months. McClain eventually reconsidered and joined the Dallas Cowboys where he played well at times and started to establish himself as a solid NFL player. More off-field problems hindered his progress, and he was suspended for the first 10 games of the 2016 season when he tested positive for performance-enhancing drugs. He was suspended indefinitely later that year when he once again violated the league's substance-abuse policy.

Parcells also had Davis in a frenzy over another player in the 2010 draft — University of Mississippi guard John Jerry.

"Bill Parcells loves John Jerry," Davis told his scouts.

Again, Parcells had spoken, and Davis listened. The onus was upon Davis' scouts to wage an uphill battle.

The scouts and offensive line coach Jim Michalczik touted Jared Veldheer, a big offensive tackle out of Hillsdale (Michigan) College.

Calvin Branch had scouted Veldheer and felt he was a legitimate prospect, even though Veldheer was coming out of a small college whose most famous football graduate had been Chester Marcol, a kicker drafted in the second round by the Green Bay Packers in 1972.

Davis questioned Veldheer's strength. Michalczik vouched for Veldheer. He had worked out Veldheer in a private session and assured Davis that strength was not an issue for the 6-foot-8, 325-pound offensive tackle. Cable supported Veldheer as well.

Davis was unable to find anyone within his own organization to back him on Jerry, so he relented and took Veldheer. Parcells drafted Jerry four picks later.

Davis also respected and consulted with New England Patriots coach Bill Belichick. Their relationship reached the point where Davis interviewed Belichick for Oakland's head coaching vacancy in 1998. Ultimately, Davis hired Jon Gruden. Numerous times, Davis and Belichick worked out trades. The most lopsided of those trades favored the Patriots. It would have been even more one-sided if Davis hadn't intervened.

After two seasons with the Raiders, mercurial wide receiver Randy Moss made it known that he had no interest in returning for a third. Davis agreed it was time for a parting of ways. The only question that remained was, could Davis save face and recoup some of the high cost from trading for Moss in 2005?

The Raiders had traded the rights to their first-round pick, No. 7 overall, starting middle linebacker Napoleon Harris, a 2002 first-round draftee, and a seventh-round draft pick to the Minnesota Vikings in exchange for Moss.

Moss caught 60 passes for 1,005 yards and eight touchdowns in his first season with the Raiders, well below what he averaged in seven seasons with the Vikings. But Moss still was a welcome figure for a Raiders team transitioning from a time when they enjoyed the receiving riches of Tim Brown, Andre Rison, Jerry Rice and Jerry Porter.

In reality, though, Moss had flamed out after his first four games, in which he caught 19 passes for 446 yards and two touchdowns. He suffered a groin injury in Oakland's fifth game in 2005 and wasn't a factor again until he caught seven passes for 117 yards and two touchdowns in a season-ending loss against the New York Giants.

Moss played in 13 games during the 2006 season, sitting out the final three with an ankle injury. He finished with a career-low 42 receptions for 553 yards and three touchdowns.

Davis changed coaches after the 2006 season, firing Art Shell and replacing him with Lane Kiffin. One of Kiffin's first tasks was to trade Moss, and Kiffin's personal assistant Mark Jackson was charged with the task of making a deal.

Jackson had worked with Kiffin at the University of Southern California, and he had some prior NFL experience with the New England Patriots. He soon found himself on the phone with Belichick, someone regarded as one of the most savvy football minds of all time.

Jackson and Belichick finally agreed upon a sixth-round draft pick for Moss.

"Al was aghast," Kingdon said.

Davis phoned Belichick from the Raiders meeting room and accused him of taking advantage of Jackson, who had no experience in this area.

"Bill replied that that was what was asked for," Kingdon said, "and he had agreed to it. Al said that it just wasn't right. So Bill asked him what he wanted. Al said a fourth-round pick, and Bill agreed to it."

When Moss suddenly rejuvenated himself in New England, catching an NFL record 23 touchdown receptions in 2009, Davis tried to justify why he gave up the future Hall of Famer for such a low draft choice.

"You know how many teams turned him down?" Davis said. "That guy in Green Bay thought he couldn't run anymore. Even Denver, where they'll take anybody, turned him down."

> *Davis immediately pushed aside his walker, took a step and prepared to show Kebric how he could improve Schilens' form on his release. Fortunately, Pearson was carefully watching and grabbed Davis just before he face-planted on the floor.*

Davis last coached an NFL game in 1965, but he always fancied himself a coach and teacher for life. After the final day of the 2008 rookie mini-camp, Kebric was working out in the Raiders' weight room when Davis entered, assisted by both a walker and Chris Pearson, the team's assistant strength and conditioning coach. Davis immediately waved Kebric over.

"The coaches don't like Chaz," Davis said of the Raiders seventh-round draft pick, wide receiver Chaz Schilens. "Lane and (James) Lofton (wide receivers coach) don't think he can play."

Kebric offered a thumbnail scouting report from what he had seen in practice:

"He is more of a wind-up guy and has some problems with his release."

In response to that comment, Davis immediately pushed aside his walker, took a step and prepared to show Kebric how he could improve Schilens' form on his release. Fortunately, Pearson was carefully watching and grabbed Davis just before he face-planted on the floor.

"Despite his physical limitations, Al was not about to give up coaching his guys," Kebric said.

Schilens was the prototypical Davis receiver, standing 6-foot-4, weighing 204 pounds and running a 4.4-second 40-yard dash. Even better, by Davis' standards, he was considered a bona-fide sleeper who had not been invited to the Indianapolis scouting combine. Schilens had suffered a foot injury as a senior and received little recognition that season, though prior to his injury he set the record for longest reception in San Diego State history with a 97-yard touchdown against Texas Christian University.

"He had an excellent pro day and since he had not gone to the combine, we brought him in for a physical and he checked out healthy," Kingdon said. "The knocks on Schilens were that he was a bit tight in his overall movements and he had more wind-up speed than initial burst. He used his height well and showed excellent hands."

Therefore, Kingdon said, the seventh round seemed like a legitimate spot to take a player such as Schilens.

Davis landed Schilens despite the wait, but his excitement wasn't shared by Kiffin and Lofton.

"Kiffin and Lofton were adamantly opposed to the pick," Kingdon said. "Lofton thought that Schilens was just a workout wonder. But Al really liked the potential he saw in Schilens."

Kingdon paid particular attention to Schilens during that first mini-camp, given he had lobbied for Schilens. As it turned out, all five draftees — Darren McFadden, Tyvon Branch, Arman Shields, Trevor Scott and Schilens — impressed.

Kingdon was at home, feeling good about the draftees, when the phone rang. It was Davis.

Kingdon imagined that it was going to be a congratulatory call once Davis asked how Kingdon was doing.

"Fine," Kingdon said.

"Lane Kiffin hates Schilens," Davis continued. "He said he can't play, that we should cut him immediately."

Kingdon was caught off guard. In fact, he thought that Schilens looked better than he had expected.

"Did you watch the tape?" Kingdon asked.

"Yes," Davis replied.

"What did you think of Schilens?" Kingdon asked.

"I liked him," Davis replied.

"Then the hell with them," Kingdon concluded.

Schilens caught everything thrown him the next day, too, and ended up having a decent rookie season, with 15 receptions for an average of 15.1 yards per catch. Injuries dogged him throughout his career, though, and he never realized his potential. Davis, however, was ready to coach Schilens, even while hanging on to a walker.

Kebric learned early on that he should be prepared for anything with the Raiders.

Four days before the 1988 draft, Ron Wolf summoned Kebric to his office and related that the Raiders had just traded with San Francisco for the 49ers' first-round pick. This meant the Raiders would have three first-round selections in the draft. Wolf assigned Kebric to travel to Champaign, Illinois, on a Saturday afternoon, and work out a player named Scott Davis and be back in Los Angeles in time for the Monday morning draft meeting.

Upon his arrival in Champaign, Kebric, as instructed, called the phone number he had been given for Davis. The number was for a fraternity house, and the person who answered told Kebric that he could not locate Davis but would leave a message for him to return the call. After an hour of sitting by the phone, waiting for Davis' response, Kebric decided he would walk to the fraternity in search of Davis.

"Upon arrival, I immediately encountered a friendly fellow and told him that I was with the Los Angeles Raiders and wanted to see Scott Davis," Kebric said. "He checked with other fraternity members but no one seemed to know where Davis might be, so I left another message for him to call me as soon as possible."

Kebric still hadn't heard from Davis by 7 a.m. the next morning. With a 1 p.m. flight looming, Kebric called Davis' agent, Randy Vataha, and asked him about his client's whereabouts. Vataha said he would contact Davis, and 15 minutes later Davis phoned Kebric and said to meet him at the local IHOP restaurant at 9 a.m.

Kebric arrived at the restaurant and patiently awaited Davis' arrival. Just before 9 a.m., a motorcycle roared into the IHOP parking lot. Off jumped a 6-foot-7, 270-pound man, a blond mane flowing down his back when he removed his helmet.

"This must be Scott," Kebric said to himself. "Looks like a Raider to me. Davis not only got my attention, but everyone else in the restaurant was staring out the window at this impressive figure. I think many of the surprised guests thought the Hells Angels had arrived for breakfast."

Kebric greeted Davis and they then sat down for breakfast. He asked

Davis if he would run a 40-yard dash so that the Raiders had an updated time. Davis told Kebric that he had worked out at the scouting combine and had told all the NFL teams that had inquired, including Raiders defensive line coach Earl Leggett, that he was not going to run or work out again. The two had a cordial meeting, lasting an hour or so, during which Davis related his personal and football backgrounds, his future plans and, much to the dismay of Kebric, that basketball, not football, was his favorite sport.

Two days later, the Raiders selected wide receiver Tim Brown with the first of their three first-round picks, cornerback Terry McDaniel with the second and Davis with the third. Shortly after the Raiders had selected Davis, Wolf received a call from a person who told him that their most recent draft pick had spent the past Saturday night in jail for an incident in which he was accused of molesting a woman in a bar. Wolf immediately asked Kebric for an explanation, and Kebric for the first time realized why he was not able to track down Davis until Sunday morning.

Armed with this new information, Kebric raced to the phone, thankful he had retained Davis' number. This time, Davis actually answered.

"Hey, Scott, congratulations," Kebric said, when he reached Davis at his fraternity house. "We drafted you. What about Saturday night? Were you in jail?"

"Yeah," Davis said.

"Why didn't you tell me that you had been in jail?" Kebric asked.

"You didn't ask me," Davis said.

Davis told Kebric that he had, indeed, spent Saturday night in jail, had called Kebric after his Sunday morning release and journeyed straight from the jailhouse to the IHOP.

Scott Davis did have some bright moments during his five-year career with the Raiders, including a 10-sack season in 1990. He also blocked field goals in games during the '90 and '91 seasons that preserved Raiders wins.

Though talented and productive for the Raiders, Davis never displayed a real passion for football, as he had indicated in his initial conversation with Kebric, and he retired after the 1991 season. Al Davis was so determined to get Scott Davis back in uniform for the 1994 season that he offered him a $1 million signing bonus. Davis appeared in all 14 games that season but suffered a career-ending injury in the regular-season finale.

In 2009, Al Davis once again surprised the draft room when he announced that he planned to select Missouri defensive end Stryker Sulak with the first of the Raiders' two sixth-round picks. Head coach Tom Cable and the scouts previously had expressed support for Iowa tight end Brandon Myers and Harvard defensive lineman Desmond Bryant with the Raiders' final two picks that year.

Davis was reading through the scouting reports when he inquired about Sulak. Davis was told that Sulak was a decent college player but a bit of a tweener — not big enough for defensive end, nor athletic enough for linebacker — and that his best position would be as a stand-up end in a 3-4 defense, a defense the Raiders didn't employ at the time.

"Al made the selection over the objections of the room," Kingdon said.

When Sulak showed up at the team's first mini-camp, it became readily apparent that there wasn't a position for him on the team.

Davis called Kingdon a few days after the camp.

"I was just told I did not have to sign Sulak," Davis said in an excited tone. "We don't have to give him any signing bonus."

Kingdon didn't share Davis' excitement.

"I told him that I was embarrassed for the team that we would draft a player and not even sign him," Kingdon said. "I then added that this was not going to sit well with all of the agents around the league."

Davis replied, "I don't care."

Sulak became the third player in NFL history who was drafted and then cut prior to being signed. He eventually was signed as a free agent by the Green Bay Packers and was released soon thereafter.

Late one afternoon in the spring of 2011, the scouting staff was watching a video of a draft-eligible player, when Davis unexpectedly entered the room. Kingdon immediately turned off the projector and asked Davis what he needed from the scouts.

"Just continue what you are doing," Davis said.

After a few minutes watching the video, Davis said to the group, "We need to do well in the later rounds this year."

The scouts knew what he meant since he had traded away the Raiders' first- and third-round picks.

Davis turned to Kebric, who was sitting nearby.

"Bruce, name some of our good late-round picks."

Kebric thought for a second and then reeled off the names of Cliff Branch, Lester Hayes, Mickey Marvin (who was sitting in the room) and Shane Lechler. He then paused and added Stryker Sulak.

Two of the Raiders scouts later told Kebric that they expected an explosive response from Davis to Kebric's inclusion of Sulak in the group. Quite to the contrary, Davis merely turned toward Kebric and said, "That one's on me."

Ron Riesterer

Quarterback Rich Gannon (12) is protected by Barret Robbins (63) during the Raiders' last Super Bowl season. Robbins' disappearance from team headquarters two nights prior to the 2003 Super Bowl upset the game plan and foiled Davis' last shot for a fourth Super Bowl win.

CHAPTER SEVENTEEN

The Last Act

During an eight-year span, the Raiders won three Super Bowl titles. When the Raiders beat the Washington Redskins in the Super Bowl at the conclusion of the 1983 season, only the Pittsburgh Steelers owned more Super Bowl trophies. Al Davis had achieved his goal of building a dominant franchise. But he wanted more. He wasn't satisfied with three Super Bowl rings. The quest for a fourth title consumed him, and the flames of desire burned even hotter in the ensuing years as the San Francisco 49ers, Dallas Cowboys, Washington Redskins and Green Bay Packers matched or surpassed the Raiders in Super Bowl victories.

Davis never imagined it would take the Raiders 19 years just to get back to the big game, let alone win another one. Twice after the 1983 season, the Raiders reached the AFC Championship Game. Both times they endured resounding losses. Finally, in 2002, the Raiders broke through and reached the Super Bowl, where they were favored to beat the Tampa Bay Buccaneers.

The game against the Buccaneers offered Davis a shot at a return to glory, a chance to bolster his claim that the Raiders still were "The Team of the Decades."

"Winning that game was extremely important to him," Bruce Kebric said. "It would have validated that the game had not passed him by, that he still had it."

After the 2002 AFC Championship game, Kebric entered the Raiders' victorious locker room and spotted a lone figure at the back of the room carefully watching his players and coaches celebrate the team's 41-24 win over the Tennessee Titans.

Kebric walked across the room to congratulate Davis on his first AFC Championship in nearly two decades.

"As I moved toward him and extended my hand to say 'congratulations,' he backed away," Kebric said.

"Not now, wait till next week," Davis stated.

Next week. Davis' big game, Super Bowl XXXVII in San Diego. It had been a long wait but now he finally was back to where he wanted to be.

"We used to think it was easy," Kebric said, in reference to Davis' past Super Bowl successes.

"It is easy," Davis said, "if you have the right people."

Davis' comment led Kebric to believe that he was pleased with his decision to trade coach Jon Gruden and replace him with Bill Callahan after the 2001 season.

In 2003, there was only one week between the conference championship games and the Super Bowl. Fortunately, for the Raiders, it was merely a one-hour flight to the site of the game. For Tampa Bay, however, the travel logistics were much more difficult; a late-night departure from Philadelphia, the site of the NFC Championship Game, and then a next-day departure on the cross-country journey to San Diego.

Tampa Bay sported a 12-4 regular-season record compared to the Raiders' 11-5 mark, but the Raiders had won nine of their final 10 games, including the playoffs, and had outscored their two playoff opponents by a combined 37 points. The Super Bowl provided Davis two big opportunities—the chance to notch a fourth Super Bowl title, and the ability to silence those critics who claimed he had made a huge mistake in trading his former head coach, Jon Gruden, to Tampa Bay. A victory also would vindicate his decision-making on and off the field as well as silence those who felt that he long ago had abdicated his "genius" stature.

Davis' dream ended with a nightmarish performance against the Buccaneers, a 48-21 loss.

"He took this one to his grave," Kebric said. "For a number of years after that loss, he was just miserable."

Kebric could only imagine Davis' inner turmoil as he saw Jon Gruden holding the Super Bowl trophy, with a "Chucky-like" grin on his face. Gruden, the coach who Davis had bypassed on two occasions because he thought Gruden looked like an 18-year-old, whom he finally signed and then later traded away, now was etched in Super Bowl lore as the youngest Super Bowl-winning coach ever. Gruden later said about that day, "It was the greatest game I ever coached in. You're playing against your former team and you're playing for a world title."

Despite his extreme disappointment in the outcome of that game, Davis continued to focus on his return to the limelight. His want was still there. His will was still there. As late as 2008, Davis believed in his ability to get back on top. "I just want to win two more" Super Bowls, he said.

It wasn't to be. On January 26, 2003, the "Team of the Decades" entered a period of futility, the likes of which the NFL had seldom seen. During the next nine years, constant obstacles, many of them created by Davis, impeded the path of the Raiders. Davis faced extensive health problems, impatience with his coaches (six head coaching changes in a nine-year period) and players, and ineptitude on the field (39 wins in 131 games prior to his death in October, 2011). Additional lawsuits and grievances filed by two of his head coaching selections added to the mounting problems.

The harbinger for the most unproductive period of Davis' life might be traced to a Friday night, less than 48 hours prior to the Super Bowl, when All-Pro center Barret Robbins appeared for an 11 p.m. room check, then proceeded to go AWOL for nearly 24 hours. Upon his return the next evening, Robbins, who was living with bipolar disorder and who experienced depression when not faithfully taking his prescribed medication, was immediately suspended by Callahan, much to the chagrin of Davis.

> *Davis continued to focus on his return to the limelight. His want was still there. His will was still there. As late as 2008, Davis believed in his ability to get back on top. "I just want to win two more" Super Bowls, he said. It wasn't to be.*

Wide receiver Tim Brown said in a radio interview a decade later that Callahan changed the game plan from a run-heavy attack to a pass-happy approach on Friday, before Robbins disappeared. Brown said Callahan "blew this thing up" and wanted to "throw the ball 60 times."

"Barret Robbins begged coach Callahan, 'Do not do this to me. I don't have time to make my calls, to get my calls ready. You can't do this to me on Friday. We haven't practiced full speed, we can't get this done,'" Brown said.

Robbins hadn't been heard from or located by the time Callahan gathered his players and coaches for a team meeting on the eve of the Super Bowl. A pregame meeting of this type certainly was not unusual but for this one, Callahan, according to senior executive John Herrera, had placed the team on "lockdown" and that no one, other than the coaches and players, was to attend the meeting.

By the time the meeting was called, Callahan had decided that Robbins wasn't going to play in the game. The head coach wanted the time to go over a new game plan, which now included long-snapper Adam Treu as the starting center.

Davis, however, felt that the strong blocking skills of Robbins were a key to running the football against Tampa Bay's stout defense, which ranked number one in the NFL during the regular season. Davis also had been told by his team doctors, upon Robbins' return Saturday night, that the doctors and training staff could get Robbins ready to play the next day. Callahan, however, did not give in to Davis' insistence that Robbins start at center, which created a schism between the coach and the owner that was never resolved. Less than one year after Callahan made the decision not to play Robbins, he received his walking papers from Davis. The Raiders had dropped from the AFC's best record in 2002 to a tie with the San Diego Chargers for a conference-worst, 4-12 mark in 2003.

Callahan had tinkered with the offense prior to the Super Bowl game. During the offseason, he set about changing an offense that had topped the NFL in 2002, with quarterback Rich Gannon throwing for a Raiders record 4,689 yards. In the minds of many in the organization, especially offensive players, Callahan was determined to fix something that was not broken, but merely the consequence of one bad game (the Super Bowl).

From the outset, Gannon appeared to be uncomfortable in the new scheme and his frustration was on display early in training camp. At one afternoon practice, Gannon had words with offensive coordinator Marc Trestman, then proceeded to line up under center, drop five steps and hurl the football out of the Napa training camp site and on to the roof of a nearby intermediate school. A few weeks later, in the season's third game, a 31-10 loss in Denver, Gannon was seen yelling at both Callahan and Trestman during the course of the contest.

One month later, the Raiders record stood at 2-5 and Gannon was sidelined for the remainder of the season with a shoulder injury. After Gannon's departure, the Raiders managed only two more wins and ended the season with the team's worst record since 1997.

One day prior to Callahan's termination by Davis, veteran defensive back Terrance Shaw aptly summed up the 2003 season, when he told *New York Times* writer Damon Hack: "That one year, we loved playing for coach Callahan. We ran through the wall for that guy. But once this season started, guys felt like they were jilted without explanation."

Callahan's departure led to the most unstable period of the Davis regime.

The Gruden-Callahan combination had provided five-plus years of stability, with Callahan going it alone beyond the 2001 season.

Davis then moved from the West Coast-oriented offense of the Gruden-Callahan era to his favored vertical passing game with the hiring of former Washington Redskins head coach Norv Turner. After nine wins over a two-year period, Turner was gone. Davis' next coaching move brought Art Shell, who previously led the Raiders from 1989 through 1994, back "into the fold," in Davis' words.

"This was Al's opportunity to have a coach that would follow his every direction," Kingdon said. "He also brought back Tom Walsh, who would reinstitute the 'Sid Gillman offense.' Rather than forward looking, Al was trying to resurrect the past."

Hall of Fame defensive tackle Warren Sapp had another name for Walsh's offensive attack.

"Some players called it the Bed-and-Breakfast Offense," said Sapp, referring to the fact that Walsh was operating a bed and breakfast when summoned by the Raiders to be Shell's offensive coordinator. "I called it the Smörgåsbord Offense. Do you want interceptions, fumbles or stupid play-calling? Just dial it up, and he's got it for you."

The Raiders finished last in the league in offense, points scored and turnovers committed under Walsh and successor John Shoop.

It wasn't difficult to understand why, Sapp said, based upon an exchange he heard between Shell and Walsh one day.

"I shit you not, I was going behind Tom Walsh and Art Shell one day to get some water and they were looking at each other," Sapp said. "And neither one of them got any kind of look that says, I'm a bright person.

They look at each other and then they look back at LaMont Jordan, then they look back at each other again and say, 'Run that play we used to run with Bo Jackson.' I almost fell the hell over.

"I walked over to them, looked at them both and whispered, 'Fellas, that's LaMont Jordan. It's not Bo Jackson. I know he got a number 34 jersey over him, but I can outrun his ass.' Are you shitting me? That's LaMont Jordan. It was unbelievable."

The problems extended beyond offense. The Shell hire proved to be a total failure. He was fired after only one season and a 2-14 record.

Then it was on to Lane Kiffin, a youthful coach with no head coaching and limited professional experience, for 20 games in 2007 and the first part of 2008. Many felt this was an attempt by Davis to discover another Gruden. In the end, Davis not only fired Kiffin but called him "a liar" and refused to pay the balance of his contract. Kiffin complained about his treatment, but the NFL favored Davis in an arbitration ruling.

Kiffin's arrival also coincided with Davis experiencing some cash-flow problems. The first manifestation of Davis' money woes occurred with the holdout of 2007 No. 1 draft pick JaMarcus Russell. Davis had a well-earned reputation for getting his players signed prior to the start of training camp. There were occasional exceptions, but none rivaled Russell's situation, where contract negotiations dragged on for months. Russell, whom Davis viewed as the answer to the franchise's on-field woes, missed all of the 2007 training camp, the four preseason games and the regular-season opener. He finally began to grasp the Raiders offense late in the season and started the final two games.

Davis soon solved the monetary problems that hampered the Russell signing. Later that same year, he sold a 20 percent stake in the Raiders for $150 million. The deal permitted him to retain controlling interest in the team, while bringing in much-needed cash flow. In 2008, he was able to sign first-round selection Darren McFadden just a few days after McFadden was drafted.

"Once he sold the interest in the team, he started spending like money was going out of style," Kingdon said.

Davis sent shockwaves across the NFL by awarding big contracts to non-elite players such as Javon Walker, DeAngelo Hall, Gibril Wilson, Tommy Kelly, Stanford Routt and Kwame Harris.

Tom Cable, the Raiders offensive line coach, took over when Davis fired Kiffin four games into the 2008 season. On the day of Cable's promotion, Davis told Kingdon that the deciding factor in the elevation was, "Tom had promised him that he would be throwing the deep ball a lot more than Kiffin did."

In his two-plus seasons as head coach, Cable was able to bring some respectability to the Raiders and led them to an eight-win season in 2010, halting an NFL-record seven consecutive seasons in which the Raiders lost at least 11 games. But once again, Davis became embroiled in personal matters with his head coach. When two lawsuits were filed against Cable, one by a former assistant coach and the other by a former girlfriend, Davis had had enough. During a news conference, Davis told the media that he had withheld $120,000 from Cable's last six checks because of the "strain on the organization" from the lawsuits. "Tom had been told earlier in his career that he could have been fired without pay for the wrath he brought on the Raiders organization," Davis said.

It wasn't so much that the game had passed him by as it was Davis' unwillingness to embrace change. He simply refused to adapt.

"He felt as if his way worked and always would work because it worked well at one time," Jon Kingdon said. "He made his share of mistakes and bad moves early in his career, it's just that the Raiders were talented enough to overcome those gaffes and the system then would allow you to bury your mistakes."

Additionally, there wasn't free agency, as we know it today, the salary cap and other present-day limitations to hamstring Davis earlier in his career. Davis believed that coaches and players could come and go, and that the Raiders would still be successful.

It had become common for people to accuse Davis of having fallen behind the times. Criticism such as this never appeared to bother him.

On one occasion, he said, "Don't worry about mistakes. Just win." In another response to his detractors, Davis said: "Very few organizations have a tradition and identity that the Raiders have … Image is not always substance, but the history of man is that a return to time-woven traditions and methods of doing things is best for the community in the long run. Usually, what worked will work."

Hence, Davis, with methods many now deemed unconventional,

sought a return to his early years, when the wins came in bunches, his team struck fear in the opposition and he was revered by many. In the new era of West Coast passing offenses and mobile quarterbacks, Davis continued to yearn for the big, rugged signal-caller with the strongest arm on the block. His 1960s passing philosophy, which he had learned early on in his pro coaching career, continued to dominate Davis' offensive thinking. As others evolved over the years, Davis was reluctant to stray from his roots.

All-Pro defensive back Albert Lewis played for the Raiders when the game was changing rapidly, and Davis' reliance upon certain characteristics no longer was enough to be successful, let alone dominant.

"He was too loyal," Lewis said. "The game passed him by because he didn't have the players to execute. He was a man intrigued by speed and toughness. He got exactly what he was looking for at that time, but the game had evolved to the point where that just didn't work in today's game."

There were few highlights during the final 10 years of Davis' life, as his mobility and retention skills slowly decreased. One of the biggest and most rewarding events of this period was his 75th birthday party in Las Vegas, one of his favorite haunts. Nearly 150 invited guests gathered to pay tribute to this aging legend. "Loyalty, Passion, Friends" was the theme Davis promulgated for his birthday celebration, his last occasion to cross paths with many of the players, coaches and friends who had contributed to his legacy and remained loyal to him over the years.

Thirteen of those on hand, including Davis, are enshrined in the Pro Football Hall of Fame, making Davis' birthday party probably the largest gathering of elite performers outside of the annual induction weekend in Canton, Ohio. Fred Biletnikoff, George Blanda, Willie Brown, Dave Casper, Mike Haynes, Ted Hendricks, John Madden, Ron Mix, Jim Otto, Art Shell, Gene Upshaw and Ron Wolf were among those in attendance whose busts line the passages of the Professional Football Hall of Fame. "Once a Raider, always a Raider," a favorite Davis homily, was evident at this lavish affair.

The pace slowed, the patience waned, the mind fumbled at times but the determination never wavered. In his later years, Davis always was excited when "his scouts," as he called them, came to town for the draft meetings. He would enter the room each morning with the aid of a walker, in his final years, determined to get to his seat with minimum assistance.

As he struggled to sit down, he sometimes would softly mutter, "Don't get old." After a sip of ice water, he would regain his composure and then announce to the group, "Let's get to work and make the Raiders great again."

Though Davis struggled frequently by this time, one had to admire his certainty that "success was not far away." His unwillingness to never concede or admit to his failings, brought to mind the scene from the Broadway musical *Cats*, where Grizabella, the aging, former star sings ...

> *Memory*
> *All alone in the moonlight*
> *I can smile at the old days*
> *I was beautiful then*
> *I remember*
> *The time I knew what happiness was*
> *Let the memory live again.*

Davis, however, preferred his mottos to lyrics, using as inspirational guideposts such well-worn slogans "The Commitment to Excellence," "The Greatness of the Raiders," "The Team of the Decades." They never faded from Davis' mind. For him, time just ran out.

Arthur Allen "Al" Davis was born July 4, 1929 in Brockton, Massachusetts. He passed away October 8, 2011 in Oakland. The death certificate issued by the County of Alameda listed three primary causes:

1. Ventricular fibrillation, which is "the most serious cardiac rhythm disturbance," according to the American Heart Association. "The lower chambers quiver and the heart can't pump any blood, causing cardiac arrest."

2. Congestive heart failure, which is defined by the AHA as, "When the heart does not circulate blood normally, the kidneys receive less blood and filter less fluid out of the circulation into the urine. The extra fluid in the circulation builds up in the lungs, the liver, around the eyes, and sometimes in the legs. This is called fluid 'congestion' and for this reason doctors call this 'congestive heart failure.'"

3. Cardiomyopathy, the AHA says, "Refers to diseases of the heart muscle. These diseases have many causes, signs and symptoms, and treatments. In cardiomyopathy, the heart muscle becomes enlarged, thick or rigid. In rare cases, the muscle tissue in the heart is replaced with scar tissue. As cardiomyopathy worsens, the heart becomes weaker. It's less able to pump blood through the body and maintain a normal electrical rhythm. This can lead to heart failure or irregular heartbeats called arrhythmias. In turn, heart failure can cause fluid to build up in the lungs, ankles, feet, legs, or abdomen."

He died at 2:45 a.m., according to the death certificate, at the Oakland Hilton Airport Hotel. He had been diagnosed with cardiomyopathy five years prior to his death. He suffered a ventricular fibrillation 15 minutes before he died. Dysphagia, or difficulty swallowing, also was cited as a contributing factor. He underwent throat surgery three days prior to his death.

The document also revealed that Davis, who loved sitting out in the sun bare chested, had suffered from Merkel cell carcinoma, an aggressive form of skin cancer related to extended exposure to the sun on the head, neck and face, and that he had had heart surgery in 1996 to repair a damaged mitral valve.